Final Report of the Fortieth Antarctic Treaty Consultative Meeting

ANTARCTIC TREATY
CONSULTATIVE MEETING

Final Report
of the Fortieth
Antarctic Treaty
Consultative Meeting

Beijing, China
22 May - 1 June 2017

Volume I

Secretariat of the Antarctic Treaty
Buenos Aires
2017

Published by:

Secretariat of the Antarctic Treaty
Secrétariat du Traité sur l' Antarctique
Секретариат Договора об Антарктике
Secretaría del Tratado Antártico

Maipú 757, Piso 4
C1006ACI Ciudad Autónoma
Buenos Aires - Argentina
Tel: +54 11 4320 4260
Fax: +54 11 4320 4253

This book is also available from: *www.ats.aq* (digital version)
and online-purchased copies.

ISSN 2346-9897
ISBN (vol. I): 978-987-4024-43-5
ISBN (complete work): 978-987-4024-42-8

Contents

VOLUME I

VOLUME II

Acronyms and Abbreviations

PART II. MEASURES, DECISIONS AND RESOLUTIONS (Cont.)

4. Management Plans

PART III. OPENING AND CLOSING ADDRESSES AND REPORTS

1. Opening and Closing Addresses

2. Reports by Depositaries and Observers

3. Reports by Experts

PART IV. ADDITIONAL DOCUMENTS FROM XL ATCM

1. Additional Documents
Abstract of SCAR Lecture

2. List of Documents
Working Papers
Information Papers
Background Papers
Secretariat Papers

3. List of Participants
Consultative Parties
Non-consultative Parties
Observers, Experts and Guests
Host Country Secretariat
Antarctic Treaty Secretariat

Acronyms and Abbreviations

ACAP	Agreement on the Conservation of Albatrosses and Petrels
ACBR	Antarctic Conservation Biogeographic Region
ASMA	Antarctic Specially Managed Area
ASOC	Antarctic and Southern Ocean Coalition
ASPA	Antarctic Specially Protected Area
ATS	Antarctic Treaty System or Antarctic Treaty Secretariat
ATCM	Antarctic Treaty Consultative Meeting
ATME	Antarctic Treaty Meeting of Experts
BP	Background Paper
CCAMLR	Convention on the Conservation of Antarctic Marine Living Resources and/or Commission for the Conservation of Antarctic Marine Living Resources
CCAS	Convention for the Conservation of Antarctic Seals
CCRWP	Climate Change Response Work Programme
CEE	Comprehensive Environmental Evaluation
CEP	Committee for Environmental Protection
COMNAP	Council of Managers of National Antarctic Programs
EIA	Environmental Impact Assessment
EIES	Electronic Information Exchange System
HSM	Historic Site and Monument
IAATO	International Association of Antarctica Tour Operators
IBA	Important Bird Area
ICAO	International Civil Aviation Organization
ICG	Intersessional Contact Group
IEE	Initial Environmental Evaluation
IGP&I Clubs	International Group of Protection and Indemnity Clubs
IHO	International Hydrographic Organization
IMO	International Maritime Organization
IOC	Intergovernmental Oceanographic Commission
IOPC Funds	International Oil Pollution Compensation Funds
IP	Information Paper
IPCC	Intergovernmental Panel on Climate Change
IUCN	International Union for Conservation of Nature

MARPOL	International Convention for the Prevention of Pollution from Ships
MPA	Marine Protected Area
RCC	Rescue Coordination Centre
SAR	Search and Rescue
SCAR	Scientific Committee on Antarctic Research
SC-CAMLR	Scientific Committee of CCAMLR
SGCCR	Subsidiary Group on Climate Change Response
SGMP	Subsidiary Group on Management Plans
SOLAS	International Convention for the Safety of Life at Sea
SOOS	Southern Ocean Observing System
SP	Secretariat Paper
UAV/RPAS	Unmanned Aerial Vehicle / Remotely Piloted Aircraft System
UNEP	United Nations Environment Programme
UNFCCC	United Nations Framework Convention on Climate Change
WMO	World Meteorological Organization
WP	Working Paper
WTO	World Tourism Organization

PART I
Final Report

1. Final Report

Final Report of the Fortieth Antarctic Treaty Consultative Meeting

Beijing, China, May 23 - June 1, 2017

(1)   Pursuant to Article IX of the Antarctic Treaty, Representatives of the Consultative Parties Argentina, Australia, Belgium, Brazil, Bulgaria, Chile, China, the Czech Republic, Ecuador, Finland, France, Germany, India, Italy, Japan, the Republic of Korea, the Netherlands, New Zealand, Norway, Peru, Poland, the Russian Federation, South Africa, Spain, Sweden, Ukraine, the United Kingdom of Great Britain and Northern Ireland, the United States of America, and Uruguay met in Beijing from 23 May to 1 June 2017, for the purpose of exchanging information, holding consultations, and considering and recommending to their Governments measures in furtherance of the principles and objectives of the Treaty.

(2)   The Meeting was also attended by delegations from the following Contracting Parties to the Antarctic Treaty which were not Consultative Parties: Belarus, Canada, Colombia, Denmark, Kazakhstan, the Democratic People's Republic of Korea, Iceland, Malaysia, Monaco, Pakistan, Portugal, Romania, Switzerland, the Slovak Republic, Turkey, and Venezuela.

(3)   In accordance with Rules 2 and 31 of the Rules of Procedure, Observers from the Commission for the Conservation of Antarctic Marine Living Resources (CCAMLR), the Scientific Committee on Antarctic Research (SCAR), and the Council of Managers of National Antarctic Programs (COMNAP) attended the Meeting.

(4)   Experts from the following international organisations and non-governmental organisations attended the Meeting: the Antarctic and Southern Ocean Coalition (ASOC), the International Association of Antarctica Tour Operators (IAATO), the International Group of Protection and Indemnity Clubs (IGP&I Clubs), the International Hydrographic Organization (IHO), the International Oil Pollution Compensation Funds (IOPC Funds), the

15

International Maritime Organization (IMO), and the World Meteorological Organization (WMO).

(5)   The Host Country China fulfilled its information requirements towards the Contracting Parties, Observers and Experts through the Secretariat Circulars, letters and a dedicated website.

Item 1: Opening of the Meeting

(6)   The Meeting was officially opened on 23 May 2017. On behalf of the Host Government, in accordance with Rules 5 and 6 of the Rules of Procedure, the Head of the Host Government Secretariat, Mrs Guo Xiaomei, called the Meeting to order and proposed the candidacy of Mr Liu Zhenmin, Vice Minister of Foreign Affairs, as Chair of ATCM XL. The proposal was accepted.

(7)   The Chair warmly welcomed all Parties, Observers and Experts to China. The Chair highlighted China's contribution to Antarctic affairs over the past three decades and noted that the meeting was the first time China had acted as the host of the ATCM and CEP. The Chair wished the delegates well in their future deliberations.

(8)   Delegates observed a minute of silence in honour of the passing of Dr Gordon Hamilton, Captain William Cranfield, Mr Malcom MacFarlane, and Major Alistair McColl. Professor Hamilton, a United States citizen, was a prominent glaciologist, a professor at the University of Maine and a researcher for their Climate Change Institute.

(9)   His Excellency Mr Zhang Gaoli, Vice Premier of the State Council of the People's Republic of China, joined the meeting. Vice Premier Zhang warmly welcomed delegates, noting that this was the first time China had hosted the meeting. He highlighted the unique geographical nature and ecological environment of Antarctica and its importance for global climate change and human survival and development. He praised the role of the Antarctic Treaty System in maintaining peace, stability and cooperation in Antarctica. Noting the fruitful results that countries had produced in a cooperative manner under the guidance of the Antarctic Treaty System, he called for all Parties to carry forward the spirit of the Antarctic Treaty and make unremitting efforts to create a better future for Antarctica and the world at large. He elaborated China's role and contributions in building of a peaceful, stable and green Antarctic order in three aspects, namely China

was: an important participant in Antarctic governance, a strong contributor to scientific investigation of Antarctica, and an active force for Antarctic environmental protection. He declared that since its accession to the Treaty in 1983, China had been committed to the purposes and principles of the Treaty and the overall interests of the international community, actively fulfilling its rights and obligations under the Treaty, steadily promoting the cause of Antarctica and contributing wisdom and strength to the understanding, protection and utilisation of Antarctica by mankind.

(10)   Highlighting Antarctic cooperation as a means of promoting world peace and prosperity, Vice Premier Zhang proposed that the ATCM consider the following five points. First, he stressed that peace and stability of Antarctica were the fundamental prerequisites for all human activities in the region. He encouraged Parties to further enhance mutual trust and assume a stronger sense of shared responsibility, stepping up dialogue and consultation, and promoting joint plans and solutions to tackle challenges in the region. Second, given the success of the Antarctic Treaty System, Parties should continue to advance governance of Antarctica within the existing framework, and the principle of consensus should be upheld. Third, Vice Premier Zhang urged Parties to expand the area and scope of effective cooperative governance by enhancing equal footing consultation and mutual cooperation. Fourth, he supported upholding and promoting the freedom of scientific investigation in Antarctica, and suggested that research on the impacts of global climate and environmental change should be prioritised. Fifth, he highlighted the need to protect Antarctica's natural environment and ensure maintenance of the ecological balance and sustainable development in the region. Finally, he wished Parties a fruitful meeting and encouraged them to keep working towards the protection of Antarctica. The full text of Vice Premier Zhang's remarks can be found in Volume II Part III.1.

Item 2: Election of Officers and Creation of Working Groups

(11)   Ambassador Mauricio Efrain Baus Palacios, Head of Delegation of Ecuador, Host Country of ATCM XLI, was elected Vice Chair. In accordance with Rule 7 of the Rules of Procedure, Dr Manfred Reinke, Executive Secretary of the Antarctic Treaty Secretariat, acted as Secretary to the Meeting. Mrs Xiaomei Guo, head of the Host Country Secretariat, acted as Deputy Secretary. Mr Ewan McIvor of Australia continued to act as Chair of the Committee for Environmental Protection.

(12) Two Working Groups were established:

- Working Group 1: Policy, Legal and Institutional Issues;
- Working Group 2: Operations, Science and Tourism.

(13) The following Chairs of the Working Groups were elected:

- Working Group 1: Ms Therese Johansen from Norway;
- Working Group 2: Mr Máximo Gowland from Argentina and Ms Jane Francis from the United Kingdom.

Item 3: Adoption of the Agenda and Allocation of Items

(14) The following Agenda was adopted:

1. Opening of the Meeting
2. Election of Officers and Creation of Working Groups
3. Adoption of the Agenda, Allocation of Items to Working Groups and Consideration of the Multi-year Strategic Work Plan
4. Operation of the Antarctic Treaty System: Reports by Parties, Observers and Experts
5. Report of the Committee on Environmental Protection
6. Operation of the Antarctic Treaty System: General Matters
7. Operation of the Antarctic Treaty System: Matters related to the Secretariat
8. Liability
9. Biological Prospecting in Antarctica
10. Exchange of Information
11. Education Issues
12. Multi-year Strategic Work Plan
13. Safety and Operations in Antarctica
14. Inspections under the Antarctic Treaty and the Environment Protocol
15. Science Issues, Scientific Cooperation and Facilitation
16. Future Antarctic Science Challenges
17. Implications of Climate Change for Management of the Antarctic Treaty Area
18. Tourism and Non-Governmental Activities in the Antarctic Treaty Area, including Competent Authorities Issues

19. Appointment of the Executive Secretary

20. Preparation of the XLI Meeting

21. Any other Business

22. Adoption of the Final Report

23. Close of the Meeting

(15)   The Meeting adopted the following allocation of agenda items:
- Plenary: Items 1, 2, 3, 4, 5, 18, 19, 20, 21, 22.
- Working Group 1: Items 6, 7, 8, 9, 10, 11, 12.
- Working Group 2: Items 13, 14, 15, 16, 17.

(16)   The Meeting also decided to allocate draft instruments arising out of the work of the CEP and the Working Groups to a legal drafting group for consideration of their legal and institutional aspects.

Item 4: Operation of the Antarctic Treaty System: Reports by Parties, Observers and Experts

(17)   Pursuant to Recommendation XIII-2, the Meeting received reports from depositary governments and secretariats.

(18)   The United States, in its capacity as Depositary Government of the Antarctic Treaty and its Environment Protocol, reported on the status of the Antarctic Treaty and the Protocol on Environmental Protection to the Antarctic Treaty (IP 158 rev 2). In the past year, there had been no accessions to the Treaty. There was one accession to the Protocol in the past year: Malaysia deposited its instrument of accession to the Protocol on August 15, 2016. Switzerland advised that it would accede by June 1 2017. The United States noted that there were currently 53 Parties to the Treaty and 39 Parties to the Protocol as of June 1 2017.

(19)   Australia, in its capacity as Depositary for the Convention on the Conservation of Antarctic Marine Living Resources (CCAMLR), reported that there had been no new accessions to the Convention since ATCM XXXIX. It noted that there were currently 36 Parties to the Convention (IP 32).

(20)   The United Kingdom, in its capacity as Depositary of the Convention for the Conservation of Antarctic Seals (CCAS), reported that it had not received any requests to accede to the Convention, or any instruments of accession since ATCM XXXIX (IP 1 rev. 1). The United Kingdom thanked all Parties

who had completed reporting for this year and encouraged all Contracting Parties to CCAS to submit their reports on time.

(21) Australia, in its capacity as Depositary for the Agreement on the Conservation of Albatrosses and Petrels (ACAP), reported that there had been no new accessions to the Agreement since ATCM XXXIX, and that there were 13 Parties to the Agreement (IP 31). Australia highlighted that ACAP shared the conservation objectives of other instruments of the Antarctic Treaty System and encouraged all Parties which were not members of ACAP to consider joining the Agreement.

(22) CCAMLR presented a summary of outcomes of the Thirty-fifth Annual Meeting of CCAMLR which was held in Hobart, Australia, 17-28 October 2016 (IP 11). It was chaired by Mr Vasily Titushkin (Russian Federation). Twenty-four Members, two Acceding States, one State Observer and eleven Observers from non-government organisations participated. Key outcomes of interest to the ATCM had included current endeavours to renew the arrangement for the release of CCAMLR vessel monitoring system (VMS) data to support search and rescue (SAR) efforts in the CAMLR Convention Area – an initiative started at a SAR workshop held in association with ATCM-XXXVI. Noting that the outcomes of the CCAMLR Scientific Committee from 2016 were presented to CEP XX, he reported on the harvest of toothfish and krill under CCAMLR-regulated fisheries in the 2015/16 season, continuing work in relation to marine protected areas (MPA), particularly the adoption of the Ross Sea region MPA and the adoption of a measure to establish special areas for scientific study in newly exposed marine areas following ice-shelf collapse, climate change, and capacity building initiatives for early career scientists. He also noted that a second Performance Review of CCAMLR had been approved, the outcomes of which would be reported to CCAMLR-XXXVI in October 2017.

(23) SCAR presented IP 35 *The Scientific Committee on Antarctic Research Annual Report 2016 - 2017 to the Antarctic Treaty Consultative Meeting XL*. SCAR drew Parties' attention to the new format of their report, and their general focus on plain language reporting for the meeting across the range of their contributions. SCAR informed the Meeting that it had welcomed four new Associate members: Austria, Colombia, Thailand and Turkey, and initiated a new partnership with the Asian Forum for Polar Sciences. SCAR highlighted several examples of its activities including a high level of participations at the XXXIV SCAR Meetings and Open Science Conference (Kuala Lumpur, Malaysia August 20-30 2016) and major education and

outreach efforts including a "wikibomb" to upload detailed biographies of 110 female Antarctic scientists to Wikipedia. SCAR acknowledged Dr Robert Dunbar (USA), Dr Heinrich Miller (Germany) and Dr Francisco Herve (Chile) who received major awards at the SCAR Delegates Meeting and Open Science Conference. SCAR directed the Meeting's attention to their webpage (*http://www.scar.org/*) for more details of current activities.

(24)   COMNAP introduced IP 9 *The Annual Report for 2016/17 of the Council of Managers of National Antarctic Programs*, and noted the recent acceptance of the Malaysian National Antarctic Programme as an Observer, bringing the total membership to thirty members and four observer organisations. Intersessionally, COMNAP convened two workshops, on Search and Rescue (IP 10) and on "Winter-over Challenges", whose proceedings are published and are freely available. IP 9 highlighted two projects: the COMNAP database and the COMNAP Station Catalogue. COMNAP noted the COMNAP database (IP 64) is a comprehensive information system including National Antarctic Programme facility, vessel, and contact information, and pointed out that the database informs a range of COMNAP products, including the newly revised Antarctic Flight Information Manual. COMNAP noted that much of the data is made publicly available by the interactive on-line geographic information system (GIS) on the COMNAP website and through the COMNAP Station Catalogue (IP 12).

(25)   In relation to Article III-2 of the Antarctic Treaty, the Meeting received reports from other international organisations.

(26)   The IHO presented IP 4 *Report by International Hydrographic Organization (IHO) and a Proposal for a Seminar on the Importance of Hydrography in the Antarctic Region*. The paper focused on the limitations of hydrographic knowledge in Antarctica and the consequent risks to scientific and maritime operations. The IHO expressed its view that scientific investigations and conclusions are compromised by the lack of sea floor topography and depth data, which was also an inherent risk to safety. The IHO reiterated that it considered the measurement, recording, and rendering of depth data as a routine environmental observing activity that should be undertaken at all times when vessels are at sea and where no restrictions apply. The IHO invited the ATCM to include a seminar to examine in detail the impact of the current state of hydrographic knowledge in the Antarctic, particularly in relation to safety, operations, environmental protection, climate change, oceanographic modelling and research in the region to be delivered by the IHO as part of the programme for ATCM XLI in Ecuador in 2018.

It expressed the desire to work collaboratively with SCAR, COMNAP, CCAMLR, and IAATO to help address the data deficiencies. It also urged Parties to include in their relevant policy, and/or regulations covering all ship operations, an encouragement that the measurement, recording and rendering of depth data should be undertaken at sea at all times as a routine environmental observing activity, unless particular restrictions apply.

(27)   IMO presented IP 139 rev.1 *An overview of the International Code for Ships Operating in Polar Waters*. Recalling a previous submission from 2009, the IMO stated that the paper had been prepared to update the Meeting on IMO work. It provided an overview of the requirements of the International Code for Ships Operating in Polar Waters, known as the "Polar Code", with regards to maritime safety and marine environment protection. It also addressed the Polar Code's place in the existing global framework regulating international shipping. IMO highlighted the associated training and certification requirements for officers and crew serving on ships operating in polar waters, as included in the International Convention on Standards of Training, Certification and Watchkeeping for Seafarers (STCW). It further examined what more could be done to ensure the safety of polar shipping for all vessels, taking into account on-going discussions at IMO.

(28)   WMO presented IP 112 WMO *Annual Report 2016-2017*, which described its activities during the period since ATCM XXXIX. It explained how the WMO Polar and High Mountain regions priority activity of the WMO Strategic Plan 2016-2019 promotes and coordinates relevant observations, research and services that are carried out in the Antarctic, Arctic and high mountain regions by nations and by groups of nations. WMO noted that the Year of Polar Prediction (YOPP) covers the period 2017-2019 and that a special Observing Period is planned in Antarctica from 16 Nov 2018 to 15 Feb 2019 (IP 116). It also referenced the WMO Integrated Global Observing Systems: the Antarctic Observing Network (AntON) (IP 117); WMO's Polar Space Task Group (IP 114); the Global Cryosphere Watch (IP 113); the World Climate Research Programme (WCRP) (IP 115); and the development of an Antarctic Polar Regional Climate Centre (PRCC) Network (IP 118). It further noted that the WMO is committed to a positive, mutually beneficial engagement with Parties in Antarctic weather and climate observation, services and research.

(29)   The IOPC Funds presented IP 88 *The International Oil Pollution Compensation Funds*, which provided an overview of the functioning of the IOPC Funds in order to facilitate a comparison with the mechanism envisaged under Annex VI to the Protocol on Environmental Protection to

the Antarctic Treaty. The IOPC Funds reminded the Meeting of its purpose, to provide financial compensation for oil pollution damage that occurs in its Member States resulting from spills of persistent oil from tankers. It noted that as at 22 April 2017, the 1992 Fund had 114 Member States and the Supplementary Fund had 31 Member States, and reiterated that the Director and Secretariat of the IOPC Funds would be happy to share their experience and provide further assistance to the ATCM with regards to the establishment of the Fund referred to in Article 12.

(30) The IGP&I Clubs presented IP 87 *Liability Annex: Financial Security*, and informed the Meeting that the 13 principal underwriting associations comprising the IGP&I Clubs provide third party liability insurance cover for approximately 90% of the world's ocean going tonnage. The IGP&I Clubs stated that the insurance cover provided by the Clubs is extensive, including most of the liabilities a ship owner is likely to encounter in the operation of his ship. It noted that Pollution liability includes oil pollution damage as one of the covered liabilities. The IGP&I Clubs was pleased to be invited to attend the ATCM, and provide any relevant advice.

(31) ASOC presented IP 146 *Report of the Antarctic and Southern Ocean Coalition*, which briefly described ASOC's work over the past year, and outlined some key issues for this ATCM. It noted that during the last year ASOC and its member groups' representatives had participated actively in intersessional discussions in the ATCM and CEP fora, as well as in other international meetings. ASOC introduced its three major priorities for the ATCM: protected areas, precautionary management of human activities, and climate change. ASOC recommended actions that the Antarctic Treaty Parties could take that would advance these priorities: initiate systematic conservation planning to expand the ASPA network; pursue precautionary management of tourism and other activities and specifically to support Phase 2 of the Polar Code; and develop an ATCM response to climate change. ASOC had engaged with many organisations in the Antarctic Treaty System, including IAATO, SCAR, the Coalition of Legal Toothfish Operators (COLTO), and the Antarctic Wildlife Research Fund (AWR) over the past year, to try and identify strengths and weaknesses in the Antarctic Treaty System procedures and practices, and suggest solutions to any gaps. Finally, ASOC encouraged the ATCM to be proactive on issues that influence significant Antarctic values, and to move from discussion to active decision-making.

(32) IAATO presented IP 162 *IAATO Report of the International Association of Antarctica Tour Operators 2016-17*. IAATO reaffirmed its mission to

advocate and promote environmentally safe and responsible visitation to the Antarctic Treaty area, and welcomed opportunities for collaboration with other organisations. It noted that since 2010, IAATO has represented almost all passenger vessels operating in Antarctic waters under the International Convention for the Safety of Life at Sea (SOLAS). In the 2016-17 season, it noted one exception: the Japanese operated cruise-only vessel *Ocean Dream* in 2016-17. IAATO reported that the 2016-17 season saw a total of 44,367 visitors, representing an increase of 15% compared to the previous season. IAATO reported that the 39,000 recorded visitor landings for 2016/17 represented the highest number of landings recorded in any season. It also drew the attention of the Meeting to work conducted with SCAR to develop a systematic conservation planning initiative; to work relating to the Polar Code; and to their Antarctic Ambassadors programme. Finally, IAATO introduced its recently appointed next Executive Director, Dr Damon Stanwell-Smith.

Item 5: Report of the Committee for Environmental Protection

(33)   Mr Ewan McIvor, Chair of the Committee for Environmental Protection, introduced the report of CEP XX. The CEP had considered 30 Working Papers and 67 Information Papers. In addition, 5 Secretariat Papers and 6 Background Papers had been submitted under CEP agenda items. The Chair of the CEP highlighted the items on which the CEP had agreed specific advice to the ATCM, but encouraged Parties to review all parts of the CEP Report.

Opening of the Meeting (CEP Agenda Item 1)

(34)   The Chair of CEP advised that the CEP had welcomed Malaysia as a new Member and looked forward to welcoming Switzerland and Turkey as Members in the near future. He also highlighted that the CEP had acknowledged the work of the many current and past representatives of CEP Members and Observers over the past 20 years, and had given special recognition to representatives attending CEP XX who had maintained a close association with the Committee since its first meeting in Tromsø, Norway, in 1998.

Strategic Discussions on the Future Work of the CEP (CEP Agenda Item 3)

(35)   The Chair of the CEP noted that the Committee had updated its Five-year Work Plan to incorporate actions that arose during the meeting.

Operation of the CEP (CEP Agenda Item 4)

(36)   The Chair of the CEP reported that the Committee had discussed a paper by the CEP Chair about ways to ensure the Committee remained well-placed to support the Parties' efforts to comprehensively protect the Antarctic environment.

(37)   The Committee had agreed to advise the ATCM that a list of science needs would help with promoting and supporting science to better understand and address the environmental challenges facing Antarctica, which would be useful for the Committee's work as well as the ATCM's discussions on Antarctic science priorities. The Committee would review the list of CEP science needs contained in WP 34 from CEP XXI. The Committee had also acknowledged the need for additional mechanisms to help the CEP address its increasing workload, and had agreed that its work could be strengthened by access to modest financial support. With respect to financial support, the Committee had welcomed the offer by the CEP Chair to undertake further work during the intersessional period, in consultation with the Secretariat and interested Members, to consider options for obtaining and managing possible CEP funding.

(38)   With regards to the CEP's development of a list of science needs, Parties agreed that this was a useful initiative and would serve as a valuable tool both for CEP and ATCM discussions, noting that this item aligned with ATCM discussions on future Antarctic science challenges and priorities. The Meeting also looked forward to further advice from the CEP regarding its consideration of options for modest financial support for CEP work. Parties expressed the view that any requests to the ATCM for funding should be specific and targeted.

(39)   The Chair of the CEP advised that the Committee had also considered a paper by Australia, Japan, New Zealand, Norway, SCAR, and the United States, which provided an update on the operation of the Antarctic Environments Portal. The Committee had supported the decision taken by the 2016 SCAR Delegates Meeting to explore cost-neutral options for SCAR to take over operational management of the Portal after 2018 and had agreed to consider further opportunities to support SCAR's management of the Portal. The Committee had welcomed France's translation of Portal content into French and an offer made by the Netherlands during the meeting to provide financial support in the future. The Committee had also expressed general support for the Portal Content Management Plan.

(40) The Meeting thanked the co-authors of this paper and acknowledged the value of the Portal as an easy-to-access source of up-to-date scientific information for the CEP and ATCM, as well as for public education and outreach. The Meeting agreed that the Portal should remain an apolitical source of scientific information based on peer-reviewed science, and highlighted the role of the editorial panel in ensuring independence in all articles produced. The Meeting welcomed SCAR's in-principle agreement to take on management of the Portal after 2018, as well as the ongoing support provided by France and the offer by the Netherlands to provide financial support. While encouraging policy-makers and decision-makers to use the Portal to its full potential, Norway also expressed that it would explore options for contributing future financial support to the on-going operation of the Portal.

Cooperation with other Organisations (CEP Agenda Item 5)

(41) The Chair of CEP advised that the Committee had recalled its advice to ATCM XXXIX that it endorsed the recommendations arising from the Joint CEP / SC-CAMLR Workshop on Climate Change and Monitoring held in Punta Arenas, Chile, in May 2016, and recognised the importance of monitoring progress on implementation of these recommendations. Noting that the ATCM Multi-year Strategic Work Plan included an action for ATCM XL to consider the outcomes of the joint workshop, the Committee had agreed to advise the ATCM that: SC-CAMLR had also welcomed the workshop report and endorsed the recommendations arising; actions by the CEP to advance the workshop recommendations were largely being addressed in conjunction with its on-going work to implement the CCRWP; and, with reference to workshop Recommendation 16, the Committee had agreed to update its Five-year Work Plan to include an action on planning for a future joint workshop, including a review of the implementation of the recommendations from the 2016 workshop.

(42) The Meeting welcomed the Committee's advice on its work to address the recommendations from the joint workshop, and also welcomed increased interaction between CEP and SC-CAMLR as an important contribution to enhancing coherence between Antarctic Treaty System bodies. The Meeting noted that the CEP Chair would be representing the CEP in the panel established to undertake a second CCAMLR Performance Review, and that this would provide a further opportunity to strengthen the two committees' working relationship.

Repair and Remediation of Environmental Damage (CEP Agenda Item 6)

(43) The Chair of the CEP noted the Committee had agreed to establish an ICG to review the Antarctic Clean-Up Manual appended to Resolution 2 (2013).

Climate Change Implications for the Environment: Strategic approach (CEP Agenda Item 7)

Implementation and Review of the Climate Change Response Work Programme

(44) The Chair of the CEP reported that the Committee had considered a report on intersessional work led by New Zealand on implementation of the Climate Change Response Work Programme (CCRWP) and a paper outlining SCAR-affiliated research of relevance to the CCRWP.

(45) Noting the ATCM's request in Resolution 4 (2015) to receive annual updates from the CEP on implementation of the CCRWP, the Committee had requested the ATCM to: approve the establishment of a Subsidiary Group on Climate Change Response (SGCCR) in accordance with Rule 10 of the CEP Rules of Procedure to support the implementation of the CCRWP, as outlined in Appendix 2 to the CEP XX Final Report; and request Secretariat support for translation of key texts and technical support for coordinating and communicating updates to support good participation and efficient handling of work.

(46) The CEP had further requested the ATCM to: note that it had welcomed a comprehensive report from SCAR on the work of its subsidiary and affiliated groups relevant to the issues and needs identified in the CCRWP, which clearly indicated that SCAR groups were well placed to contribute; and it had welcomed an offer from the WMO to provide a report to CEP XXI on its activities relevant to the CCRWP.

(47) The Chair of the CEP advised that the Committee had also considered the recommendations from the 2010 ATME on Climate Change and Implications for Antarctic Management and Governance and had agreed that: the recommendations related to the work of the CEP had been incorporated into the CCRWP, other than Recommendations 18 and 29, which it had recorded as future work for the proposed SGCCR; CCAMLR Conservation Measure CM 24-04, on establishing time-limited special areas for scientific study in newly exposed marine areas following ice shelf retreat or collapse in the Antarctic Peninsula region, had been a positive contribution towards the delivery of ATME Recommendation 26; and further updates from the

Secretariat on actions taken on the ATME recommendations were not required by the CEP, while noting that the ATCM may still wish to be updated on progress against recommendations, particularly recommendations 1-17.

(48) The Meeting commended the CEP on its longstanding work on the environmental implications of climate change. It noted that the SGCCR would serve as a valuable mechanism for the CEP to support the implementation of the CCRWP. The Meeting also thanked SCAR and the WMO for their useful input on climate change research and effects, and encouraged them to continue updating the CEP and ATCM in this regard.

(49) Norway recalled that it had been ten years since the initial focused discussions on climate change in the CEP and ATCM, which had led to the 2010 ATME on climate change implications for governance jointly hosted by the United Kingdom and Norway. It recalled that the recommendations from the ATME included the proposal to develop a CCRWP. It welcomed the recent adoption by the CEP and ATCM of the CCRWP and its ongoing implementation by the CEP, and noted the important role the SGCCR would play in this context. The United Kingdom endorsed the comments made by Norway. Argentina encouraged broad participation in the SGCCR, and reiterated the importance of the translation of relevant documents into the four official Treaty languages, as this is an issue with likely policy implications.

(50) The Meeting approved the establishment of the SGCCR, in accordance with the terms of reference presented in Appendix 2 of the CEP XX Final Report, and looked forward to regular updates from the CEP on its progress in the future. The Meeting adopted the Decision 1 (2017) *Subsidiary Group of the Committee for Environmental Protection on Climate Change Response (SGCCR)*.

Environmental Impact Assessment (EIA) (CEP Agenda Item 8)

Other EIA Matters

(51) The Chair of the CEP reported that the Committee had considered a report on intersessional discussions led by the United Kingdom to examine the broader policy issues identified during its earlier intersessional work to review the *Guidelines for Environmental Impact Assessment in Antarctica* (the EIA Guidelines). The Committee had agreed to update the *Procedures for intersessional CEP consideration of draft CEEs* adopted at CEP XVIII to include an additional standard term of reference on 'Whether the CEE: i) has identified all the environmental impacts of the proposed activity;

and ii) suggested appropriate methods of mitigating (reducing or avoiding) those impacts'. It had also agreed to add several actions on EIA matters to its Five-year Work Plan.

(52) The CEP Chair advised that, noting the ATCM Multi-year Strategic Work Plan included an action for ATCM XL to "consider advice of the CEP and discuss the policy considerations of the review of Environmental Impact Assessment (EIA) Guidelines", the Committee had agreed to advise the ATCM that it recommended that all Parties provide the information requested in Resolution 1 (2005) in an appropriate and timely manner. The Committee had also requested advice from the ATCM on the extent to which the CEP should begin work on: creating an appropriate and effective method within the Antarctic Treaty System of preventing an environmentally-damaging project proceeding; potential application for Antarctica of 'screening and scoping' processes commonly applied as part of the EIA process for large projects in other parts of the world; and processes for regular independent review of CEE-level activities (including the assessment of compliance with any Permit Condition imposed by the Competent Authority).

(53) The Meeting emphasised the importance of the EIA process as a fundamental tool of the Environment Protocol, and of considering ways to keep the process up to date to reflect best practice. The Meeting also reaffirmed the importance of Parties' adherence to Resolution 1 (2005).

(54) Parties made a range of points regarding the matters raised in the CEP's requests for ATCM advice, including noting that: the Parties had at their disposal a range of valuable tools for ensuring that activities in Antarctica were being carried out in accordance with Annex I; the CEP and ATCM had continued to review and update its guidelines on EIA processes; some caution may need to be applied to consideration of a mechanism for preventing activities; the ATCM should draw Parties attention to the need to expedite implementation of the Environmental Protocol and its EIA provisions in their domestic legislation; Antarctic EIA processes should set a "gold standard"; reviews of CEEs by external organisations may not be desirable; and there may be utility in establishing clearly defined threshold values for environmental impact.

(55) Reiterating the need for robust and practical EIA procedures and the need to follow best practice processes to protect the environment, the Meeting welcomed the Committee's offer to continue its work in relation to EIAs, including incorporating further related work into its Five-year Work Plan and, looked forward to further discussions on this matter.

Area Protection and Management Plans (CEP Agenda Item 9)

9a Management Plans

(56) The CEP Chair reported that the Committee considered seven revised management plans for Antarctic Specially Protected Areas (ASPAs) and one revised management plan for an Antarctic Specially Managed Areas (ASMA), and had agreed to forward each of the revised management plans to the ATCM for approval by means of a Measure.

(57) Accepting the CEP's advice, the Meeting adopted the following Measures on ASPAs and ASMAs:

- Measure 1 (2017) *Antarctic Specially Protected Area ASPA No. 109 (Moe Island, South Orkney Islands): Revised Management Plan.*

- Measure 2 (2017) *Antarctic Specially Protected Area ASPA No. 110 (Lynch Island, South Orkney Islands): Revised Management Plan.*

- Measure 3 (2017) *Antarctic Specially Protected Area ASPA No. 111 (Southern Powell Island and adjacent islands, South Orkney Islands): Revised Management Plan.*

- Measure 4 (2017) *Antarctic Specially Protected Area ASPA No. 115 (Lagotellerie Island, Marguerite Bay, Graham Land): Revised Management Plan.*

- Measure 5 (2017) *Antarctic Specially Protected Area ASPA No. 129 (Rothera Point, Adelaide Island): Revised Management Plan.*

- Measure 6 (2017) *Antarctic Specially Protected Area ASPA No. 140 (Parts of Deception Island, South Shetland Islands): Revised Management Plan.*

- Measure 7 (2017) *Antarctic Specially Protected Area ASPA No. 165 (Edmonson Point, Wood Bay, Ross Sea): Revised Management Plan.*

- Measure 8 (2017) *Antarctic Specially Managed Area ASMA No. 5 (Amundsen-Scott South Pole Station, South Pole): Revised Management Plan.*

(58) The Chair of the CEP also noted that the Committee had considered a report on informal intersessional discussions about management options to protect the scientific and environmental values of the Dome A area, and had welcomed China's offer to draft a Code of Conduct for Dome A and to lead intersessional discussions based on that draft.

9b Historic Sites and Monuments

(59)   The CEP Chair reported that the Committee had welcomed a progress report by Norway and the United Kingdom on the ICG established at CEP XIX to develop guidance for conservation approaches for the management of Antarctic heritage objects, and agreed that the ICG would continue, with a view to producing guidance material for consideration at CEP XXI.

(60)   Parties welcomed the CEP's advice that the ICG would continue its work and produce further guidance material for consideration at CEP XXI. Argentina commented that some concepts related to heritage were not clearly defined in the Antarctic Treaty System e.g. universality which may have consequences on the national histories of the individual Parties. Therefore, it stressed that participants in the continuing CEP discussions should draw on relevant national experts.

9c Site Guidelines

(61)   Regarding the Committee's work on Site Guidelines, the United Kingdom noted that good progress had been made to develop guidelines for the most visited sites, but that continuing consideration should be given to keeping Site Guidelines under review and as appropriate developing new Site Guidelines.

9d Marine Spatial Protection and Management

(62)   The Meeting welcomed the CEP's agreement that it might be useful in the future for the Committee to consider and discuss means and opportunities to look at the connectivity between ocean and land, and to consider if and how complementary Measures within the framework of the Environment Protocol, in particular Annex V, could support and strengthen marine protection initiatives. It was noted that protected area designations should be based on sound science and that any decisions by CCAMLR should not automatically require complementary actions on the part of the Parties, but that the need for such actions would need to be considered on a case-by-case basis. Norway noted that it would be logical that the ATCM in such cases ask the CEP to consider and provide advice as to whether existing Measures on land in an area associated with an MPA are comprehensive. It was further noted that there is no formal geographic demarcation between the areas of interest and responsibility of the component parts of the Antarctic Treaty System.

9e Other Annex V Matters

(63) The Chair of the CEP noted that the Committee had considered the results of work by the Subsidiary Group on Management Plans (SGMP) to develop guidance materials for Antarctic Specially Managed Areas, and agreed to advise the ATCM it had endorsed the *Guidance for assessing an area for a potential Antarctic Specially Managed Area designation* and the *Guidelines for the preparation of Antarctic Specially Managed Area management plans*, and agreed to forward to the ATCM for approval a draft Resolution encouraging their dissemination and use.

(64) Accepting the CEP's advice, the Meeting adopted Resolution 1 (2017) *Guidance Material for Antarctic Specially Managed Area (ASMA) designations*.

(65) The CEP Chair noted that the Committee had considered papers presenting SCAR's *Code of Conduct for the Exploration and Research of Subglacial Aquatic Environments* and SCAR's *Environmental Code of Conduct for Terrestrial Scientific Field Research in Antarctica*. These papers were submitted following the Committee's agreement at CEP XIX to encourage the dissemination and use of further SCAR Codes of Conduct through a Resolution of the ATCM. The Committee had welcomed SCAR's willingness to undertake further consultations on the *Environmental Code of Conduct for Terrestrial Scientific Field Research in Antarctica*, with a view to presenting a new revision for consideration at CEP XXI. The Committee had endorsed SCAR's *Code of Conduct for the Exploration and Research of Subglacial Aquatic Environments*, and had agreed to forward it to the ATCM for approval by a draft Resolution on encouraging its dissemination and use.

(66) Accepting the CEP's advice, the Meeting adopted Resolution 2 (2017) *Code of Conduct for the Exploration and Research of Subglacial Aquatic Environments*.

(67) The Committee considered the results of intersessional work led by the United Kingdom and Norway to prepare a revised template for summarising the prior assessment of a proposed ASPA, consistent with the *Guidelines: A prior assessment process for the designation of ASPAs and ASMAs* adopted at CEP XVIII. The Committee had agreed to advise the ATCM that it had updated the *Guidelines: A prior assessment process for the designation of ASPAs and ASMAs* adopted at CEP XVIII, to include a non-mandatory ASPA prior assessment template to facilitate the provision of information consistent with the Guidelines. This new version of the Guidelines replaces the version that had been appended to the CEP XVIII report in 2015.

(68)　The Chair of the CEP noted that the Committee had considered a paper by Australia, New Zealand and SCAR that summarised a recent revision of the Antarctic Conservation Biogeographic Regions (ACBRs) adopted under Resolution 6 (2012). The revision reflected updates in underlying spatial layers, including the most current representation of Antarctica's ice-free areas, and included an additional (16th) biologically distinct area. To ensure that the work of the CEP and Parties is based on the most up-to-date understanding of the spatial distribution of Antarctic terrestrial biodiversity, the Committee had agreed to recommend that the ATCM adopts the revised Antarctic Conservation Biogeographic Regions (ACBRs Version 2) and had forwarded a draft Resolution to the ATCM for adoption to replace Resolution 6 (2012).

(69)　Accepting the CEP's advice, the Meeting adopted Resolution 3 (2017) *Antarctic Conservation Biogeographic Regions (ACBRs Version 2)*.

(70)　The CEP Chair also noted that the Committee had recalled Resolution 5 (2015) on Important Bird Areas (IBAs) in Antarctica and had supported a proposal by the United Kingdom, Australia, New Zealand, Norway and Spain to undertake intersessional work to develop criteria for assessing the suitability of bird colonies for ASPA designation, and to recommend to the Committee IBAs that meet those criteria.

Conservation of Antarctic Flora and Fauna (CEP Agenda Item 10)

10a. Quarantine and Non-native Species

(71)　The CEP Chair reported that the Committee had agreed on a process for updating the CEP Non-native Species Manual, and requested the Secretariat to update the online version as appropriate to incorporate SCAR's *Code of Conduct for the Exploration and Research of Subglacial Aquatic Environments*, the revised ACBRs, and a manual prepared by Argentina for preventing the introduction of non-native species through its National Antarctic Programme activities.

10c. Other Annex II Matters

(72)　The CEP Chair noted that the Committee had considered several papers containing information relevant to understanding and managing the environmental aspects of the use of unmanned aerial vehicles (UAVs)/remotely piloted aircraft systems (RPAS) in Antarctica, including a comprehensive report by SCAR on the state of knowledge of wildlife responses.

(73) Noting the ATCM Multi-year Strategic Work Plan included an action to consider advice from the Committee on UAVs/RPAS, the Committee had agreed to advise the ATCM that it had: encouraged the dissemination and use of the precautionary best-practice guidelines for UAVs/RPAS use in the vicinity of wildlife in Antarctica as presented in WP 20; agreed that future studies on wildlife response to UAVS/RPAS in the Antarctic should consider the matters identified by the same paper; and had agreed to establish an ICG to develop guidelines for the environmental aspects of the use of UAVs/RPAS in Antarctica for consideration for CEP XXI.

(74) The Meeting welcomed the Committee's agreement to develop guidance for the environmental aspects of UAVs/RPAS, and thanked Germany for agreeing to lead the ICG. It was noted that there should be a precautionary approach to the use of UAVs/RPAS, and that these approaches should be site and species specific. Bulgaria suggested that the ATCM consider combining the COMNAP guidelines on operational and safety matters with the guidance to be developed by the CEP on environmental matters, so operators would have a single set of rules.

(75) The CEP Chair reported that the Committee had considered a paper by Argentina proposing the evaluation of different protection mechanisms for the Snow Hill Island emperor penguin colony, in the current context of climate change and anthropogenic pressures. It supported further work by Argentina and other interested Members and Observers to consider and develop protection mechanisms for the colony. The Committee advised the ATCM it had welcomed the paper by Argentina and had agreed to recommend the application of *The Guidelines for Behaviour Near the Snow Hill Island Emperor Penguin Colony* as an interim measure until the need to develop more restrictive mechanisms of protection had been evaluated.

(76) Argentina referred to the Committee's discussion about a paper by SCAR, Monaco and Belgium, that summarized the outcomes of the meeting held in June 2015 to assess Antarctic and Southern Ocean biodiversity and its conservation status in the context of the Strategic Plan for Biodiversity 2011-2020 of the Convention for Biological Diversity and its Aichi Targets (WP 13). Argentina expressed some concerns about assessments of biodiversity on the basis of goals and parameters developed in United Nations forums. Whilst it was appreciated that Antarctic biodiversity would need to be reflected in any global overview prepared, Argentina wished to draw attention to two problems:

a) From a technical viewpoint, the goals and targets adopted in multilateral forums, such as the Aichi Biodiversity Targets, might not be adequate for the Antarctic Treaty area and the CCAMLR area, including due to the fact that neither of these areas were taken into account in the development of those goals and targets. Their application might therefore lead to distorted conclusions in WP 13.

b) From a legal-political aspect, even though the Antarctic Treaty promotes cooperation with the specialized agencies of the UN, it is clear that the regulatory framework for the Antarctic Treaty area is the Antarctic Treaty. Therefore, a careful approach is required for those cases which start from a regulatory approach with different goals, targets, measures and indicators.

(77) Argentina stressed the need to bring the findings of workshops to the CEP and of the Committee to consider this issue broadly.

(78) In noting the importance of cooperating and engaging with international organisations and global agreements, some Parties emphasised that the development of an Antarctic Treaty System-led biodiversity strategy to contribute to the global assessment presented an opportunity for leadership to be shown by Parties in the area of biodiversity of Antarctica and the Southern Ocean.

(79) In recalling that revisions to Annex II had come into force during the intersessional period, the United Kingdom noted that the amendments included coverage of species occurring in the Antarctic Treaty area naturally through migrations, and the need to develop procedures and criteria for designating specially protecting species. As such, the United Kingdom considered that it would be important to ensure that those changes are reflected in the tools used by Parties in the conservation of Antarctic fauna and flora.

Environmental Monitoring and Reporting (CEP Agenda Item 11)

(80) The CEP Chair reported that the Committee had noted that ongoing work outlined in a paper by Australia, New Zealand, Norway and the United States, to develop a methodology to assess the sensitivity of sites used by visitors, would contribute to advancing both Recommendation 3 and Recommendation 7 from the 2012 CEP Tourism Study. Recalling that ATCM XXXIX had requested the CEP to develop a series of 'best estimate' trigger levels to assist in guiding monitoring efforts, as outlined in Recommendation 7 of the Tourism Study, the Committee advised the ATCM that it had considered a report on ongoing work in accordance with Recommendation 3, to develop a methodology for assessing the sensitivity of sites to tourist visitation, and noted that this work would also be relevant to address Recommendation 7.

Inspection Reports (CEP Agenda Item 12)

(81) The CEP Chair reported that, under this agenda item, the Committee had considered papers reporting on inspections conducted by Argentina and Chile during January and February 2017, and separate inspections conducted by Australia in December 2016. The Committee had welcomed the general findings that the three inspected stations were in compliance with the Environment Protocol, and that the inspected ASMA was effective in achieving the management objectives for which it was designated.

General Matters (CEP Agenda Item 13)

(82) The CEP Chair advised that the Committee had considered a paper by China and several co-authors that introduced the "Green Expedition" concept, which referred to the promotion of environmentally friendly activities in the Antarctic by those planning and undertaking activities, including by implementing the methods and guidance detailed in current Resolutions and CEP/ATCM discussions, and any new methods developed as a result of recent advances in modern management and technology.

(83) The CEP had agreed to forward a draft Resolution to the ATCM for adoption, encouraging and promoting the concept of "Green Expeditions".

(84) China thanked the co-authors of the paper for their participation, and thanked the Committee for agreeing to forward the new concept to the ATCM for consideration.

(85) Accepting the CEP's advice, the Meeting adopted Resolution 4 (2017) *Green Expedition in the Antarctic.*

Election of Officers (CEP Agenda Item 14)

(86) The CEP Chair noted that the Committee had warmly thanked Dr Polly Penhale from the United States for her excellent work and significant contributions as CEP Vice-Chair. The Committee had also elected Dr Kevin Hughes from the United Kingdom as Vice-chair for a two-year term.

(87) The Meeting warmly thanked Dr Polly Penhale for her involvement and outstanding work as CEP Vice-chair and congratulated Dr Kevin Hughes on his appointment.

Preparation for Next Meeting (CEP Agenda Item 15)

(88) The Chair of the CEP noted that the Committee had adopted a Preliminary Agenda for CEP XXI, reflecting the agenda for CEP XX.

(89) The Meeting expressed its appreciation to the CEP, noting the significance of the Committee's advice and recommendations to the Parties in connection with the implementation and operation of the Environment Protocol. Parties acknowledged the importance of ensuring adequate time was allocated during the ATCM consideration of the CEP's advice, including through the scheduling of CEP and ATCM sessions.

(90) The Meeting thanked Mr McIvor for his comprehensive report on the work of the CEP, and for his leadership of the CEP.

Item 6: Operation of the Antarctic Treaty System: General Matters

(91) Uruguay introduced WP 3 *Report of the Intersessional Contact Group (ICG) on Criteria for Consultative Status*, prepared jointly with Chile and New Zealand. It outlined some of the main points raised during ICG consultations.

(92) The Meeting noted that a set of clear guidelines for Consultative status would benefit both prospective Consultative Parties and also those assessing applications for Consultative status. It was noted that the proposed guidelines did not attempt to generate new requirements for Treaty Party requesting Consultative Status, but were aimed at assisting them and the ATCM in clarifying what kind of information was desired for this decision-making process.

(93) After discussion, the Meeting adopted Decision 2 (2017) *Guidelines on the procedure to be followed with respect to Consultative Party status.*

(94) The Executive Secretary presented SP 3 *List of Measures with status "not yet effective"*. He reported that, according to the information in the ATS database, there were several Measures that were not yet effective. The United Kingdom said it would be useful for a similar list to be produced and presented annually by the Secretariat. Noting that some of the Measures listed in SP 3 had been withdrawn or superseded by other Measures, the Meeting adopted Decision 3 (2017) *Measures withdrawn.*

(95) The United States introduced WP 6 *Approval of Observers to the CEP*, which proposed two new rules for the ATCM Rules of Procedure to allow

the ATCM to approve scientific, environmental, and technical organisations as CEP observers. It noted that the current ATCM Rules of Procedure did not clearly allow for the ATCM to approve of Observers to the CEP who were not "international organisations," despite the fact that Article 11 (4) of the Protocol and the CEP Rules of Procedure opened observer status to all "relevant scientific, environmental and technical organisations".

(96) The Meeting thanked the United States for its paper and for bringing attention to the possible need for greater clarity in the ATCM Rules of Procedure with respect to the approval of CEP Observers. Noting that this matter would benefit from further consultations, as well as input from the CEP, the United States agreed to lead further informal intersessional consultations and to report back to ATCM XLI.

(97) Australia introduced WP 27 *Appointment of ATCM Working Group Chairs*, jointly prepared with Argentina, Norway and the United Kingdom. It recalled that ATCM XXXIX agreed to develop procedures for the election of chairs and co-chairs for the Working Groups of the ATCM. Australia commented that the suggested process for appointing ATCM Working Group Chairs outlined in the paper drew on practices for election of officers in the CEP, and aimed to ensure greater transparency, efficiency and effectiveness in the operation of the ATCM. Following a brief discussion, the Meeting adopted Decision 4 (2017) *Procedure for Appointing Antarctic Treaty Consultative Meeting Working Group Chairs*.

(98) New Zealand introduced WP 32 *Establishment of the CCAMLR Ross Sea Region Marine Protected Area*, prepared jointly with the United States, Argentina, Chile and France. The paper noted that CCAMLR adopted its first large-scale marine protected area (MPA) – the Ross Sea Region Marine Protected Area (RSRMPA) – during the 35th CCAMLR Meeting in October 2016. At 1.55 million square kilometres (598,200 square miles), the RSRMPA was the world's largest MPA.

(99) New Zealand said that the new MPA, designed to achieve a range of conservation and scientific objectives, was a significant step toward achieving CCAMLR's goal to create a representative system of MPAs in the Southern Ocean. It was also an important milestone for the Antarctic Treaty System, reinforcing the science-based marine conservation decision-making that was the hallmark of the CCAMLR Convention.

(100) Some Parties considered that the ATCM and CEP should consider taking further action to complement and encourage CCAMLR's conservation

efforts. It was suggested that the ATCM could seek advice from CEP on the connectivity between ocean and land in Antarctica, and whether complementary Measures could support marine protection initiatives through the application of Annex V.

(101) Many Parties thanked the proponents of the draft resolution on the Ross Sea Region MPA, and encouraged CCAMLR to continue its work in developing a representative system of MPAs in the Southern Ocean. The importance of this work was stressed by Sweden. ASOC expressed its support for the adoption of the resolution and agreed that the ATCM should undertake further work to complement CCAMLR's efforts.

(102) Several Parties, having thanked the proponents for the Resolution, stressed that the ATCM should not prejudge how CCAMLR acts within its scope of competence.

(103) Other Parties expressed the view that the establishment of new ASMAs and ASPAs should be based on sound scientific evaluation in accordance with CEP and ATCM standard procedures for designation.

(104) The Meeting adopted Resolution 5 (2017) *Establishment of the Ross Sea Region Marine Protected Area.*

(105) South Africa presented IP 33 *Gateway Access: Transit Visa Developments in South Africa*, which responded to concerns raised in ATCM XXXIX related to difficulties experienced by foreign nationals obtaining transit visas when travelling to and from Antarctica via Cape Town. South Africa's Department of Home Affairs had issued a "special dispensation" for "[r]esearchers, specialists, and expeditions teams using Cape Town as a corridor to and from Antarctica." South Africa stated that it hoped that the matter had now been resolved satisfactorily and that it remained firmly committed to facilitating access to Antarctica for scientific purposes.

(106) The Russian Federation thanked South Africa for its paper and for making such an effective and prompt response in dealing with the issues that had been raised at ATCM XXXIX. It stressed the excellent cooperation between South African and Russian authorities during the intersessional period and considered it an example of the spirit of cooperation that formed one of the main principles of Antarctic Treaty System.

(107) As Gateway states, Chile and Argentina thanked South Africa for sharing its experiences, noting that they also had similar issues and were working to resolve them. While Chile stated it was currently dealing with them on a

case-by-case basis, Argentina noted that it had moved forward with a new immigration regulation, which was in its final steps of adoption and would address these issues. IAATO also noted that it was helpful to know that its field personnel could be accommodated in this way by Gateway ports.

(108) Turkey presented IP 94 *Ratification of Protocol on Environmental Protection to the Antarctic Treaty by Turkey*. It reported that the Grand National Assembly of Turkey had ratified the Environment Protocol, including all of its annexes, on 14 February 2017. It noted that the law on ratification of the Environment Protocol had been finalised and published in its official gazette. The Meeting congratulated Turkey on its successful ratification of the Environment Protocol.

(109) Iceland presented IP 169 *Statement by Iceland*. Iceland said that its rationale for joining the Antarctic Treaty System in October 2015 had been the importance of the scientific work related to oceans, climate change and environmental protection. It noted that all the states in the Arctic Council were now either Consultative or non-Consultative Parties to the Antarctic Treaty.

(110) In respect of intersessional consultations, the Meeting further agreed that each Party would notify the Executive Secretary of its Representative and any Alternate Representatives in accordance with revised Rule 46(a) within two weeks of the closure of the ATCM.

(111) China presented IP 175 rev. 2 *Chair's summary of the Special Meeting "Our Antarctica: Protection and Utilisation"*, which reported on the host country's special meeting held on 23 May 2017, which was not a formal agenda item of the ATCM. China reported that the special meeting was chaired by H.E. Mr Liu Zhenmin, Vice Foreign Minister of China, who underlined the important role of the Antarctic Treaty System and noted that coordinated actions were needed in response to the global challenges facing Antarctica. China reported that H.E. Mr Zhang Yesui, First Vice Foreign Minister of China, delivered a key note speech, elaborating his observation on the relationship between the protection and utilisation of Antarctica. China also reported that eight other speakers from the Russian Federation, Poland, Argentina, United States, China, the United Kingdom, Chile and Australia were invited by China to present their views on a variety of issues regarding science and management of Antarctica. China referred Parties to IP 175 rev. 2 for the Special Meeting Chair's summary of the meeting.

(112) The United States reminded the Meeting of the entitlement to designate up to three Arbitrators under Article 2 of the Schedule to the Protocol on

Environmental Protection to the Antarctic Treaty. Designations should be conveyed to the Secretary General of the Permanent Court of Arbitration.

(113) The following background paper was submitted under this agenda item:

- BP 23 *Ingreso no Autorizado a la Estación Machu Picchu Período 2016 - 2017* (Peru).

Item 7: Operation of the Antarctic Treaty System: Matters related to the Secretariat

(114) Turkey presented IP 89 *Antarctic Treaty Secretariat Internship Grant for Republic of Turkey*, describing a four-week internship at the Antarctic Treaty Secretariat for the Legal Advisor of the Istanbul Technical University Polar Research Center, Mr Onur Sabri Durak. The internship assisted Turkey in gaining a greater understanding of the mechanisms and functions of the Antarctic Treaty Secretariat.

(115) The Executive Secretary introduced SP 4 rev. 4 *Secretariat Report 2016/17*, detailing the Secretariat's activities in the Financial Year 2016/17 (1 April 2016 to 31 March 2017). He thanked the Embassy of China in Buenos Aires and the Embassy of Spain with its programme "Antártida Educa" and the Instituto Fueguino de Turismo for cooperating with the Secretariat in organising an arts competition for students from schools in Argentina and Chile on the occasion of the commemoration of the 25th anniversary of the signing of the Environment Protocol. A publication on the 25th anniversary of the adoption of the Protocol was launched by the Secretariat on 4 October 2016, and was available in the four Treaty languages online on the Secretariat's website and in hard copy through an internet retailer.

(116) The Executive Secretary updated the Meeting on issues related to coordination and contacts, information technologies, publication of the Final Report of ATCM XXXIX, public information, personnel and financial matters. He noted that there were no changes in Secretariat personnel. The Executive Secretary said there had been changes and improvements to the Electronic Information Exchange System (EIES) following the outcomes of the ICG on Reviewing Information Exchange Requirements and other discussions held at ATCM XXXIX. He reiterated that the Secretariat would continue to supplement its online document databases with translations to all documents.

(117) The Executive Secretary introduced SP 5 rev. 2 *Secretariat Programme 2017/18*, outlining the activities proposed for the Secretariat in the Financial

Year 2017/18 (1 April 2017 to 31 March 2018). The Executive Secretary noted that the cost of living in Argentina continued to rise in 2016, and proposed to award a six percent rise to the General Staff to compensate for this. There would be no increase for the Executive Staff.

(118) The Executive Secretary also introduced SP 6 rev. 1 *Five-Year Forward Budget Profile 2017/18-2021/22*. While noting that the budget profile anticipated moderate cost rise adjustments in US dollar terms, the budget profile assumed no major changes in the years 2017/18 to 2021/22 and maintained a zero nominal increase in contributions in that period.

(119) The Meeting thanked the Executive Secretary for these detailed reports and acknowledged the important work undertaken by the Secretariat. China thanked the Secretariat for the valuable support it had received in the preparations of ATCM XL.

(120) Following further discussion the Meeting adopted Decision 5 (2017) *Secretariat Report, Programme and Budget*. The Meeting requested the Executive Secretary to develop a separate Secretariat Paper on Human Resource Policy for the Antarctic Treaty Secretariat Staff.

(121) The Meeting agreed that it would be desirable for the next Executive Secretary to examine the website and consider appropriate changes to make it more user friendly and report back to the ATCM.

Item 8: Liability

(122) As agreed at ATCM XXXIX, the Executive Secretary reported that the Secretariat had renewed the invitation of the Meeting to the IOPC Funds, the IGP&I Clubs and to IMO to provide advice on issues relating to Annex VI to the Protocol. The Meeting welcomed the participation of these groups.

(123) Consultative Parties provided updated information on the status of their approval of Annex VI, and implementation of Annex VI in domestic legislation. Of the Parties that had approved Annex VI (Australia, Ecuador, Finland, Italy, the Netherlands, New Zealand, Norway, Peru, Poland, the Russian Federation, South Africa, Spain, Sweden, and the United Kingdom), five reported that they were applying domestic legislation implementing Annex VI pending the entry into force of Annex VI (Finland, the Netherlands, Norway, The Russian Federation and Sweden). Other Parties noted that their legislation would enter into force when Annex VI came into force.

(124) Several Parties advised that they were in the process of implementing Annex VI in domestic legislation and for some Parties, implementation might be completed within the current legislative period. Germany advised that its ratification procedure was expected to take effect later this year.

(125) Among non-Consultative Parties, Turkey advised that it had ratified Annex VI on 14 February 2017.

(126) Parties that had yet to approve Annex VI were encouraged to do so as a matter of priority. It was noted that while the halfway point had now been reached (14 out of the required 28 approvals) it had been 12 years since the Annex was adopted.

(127) The Meeting agreed to continue to monitor implementation of Annex VI.

(128) Parties that had already approved Annex VI to the Protocol, offered to share their experience with other Parties.

(129) The IOPC Funds presented IP 88 *The International Oil Pollution Compensation Funds*, which aimed to provide an overview of the function of the IOPC Funds to facilitate a comparison with the mechanism envisaged under Article 12 of Annex VI to the Environment Protocol. IOPC Funds provide financial compensation for oil pollution damage that occurs in its Member States, resulting from spills of persistent oil from tankers. While noting that shipping has experienced fewer incidents in recent years, it confirmed that the risk of a major spill remains with some 1,800 million tonnes of oil transported by sea every year. It reported that 114 States had joined the 1992 Fund as members, and 31 States had joined the Supplementary Fund which offers compensation for larger oil spills. Since their establishment, the 1992 Fund and the preceding 1971 Fund had been involved in 150 incidents of varying sizes all over the world. No incidents had occurred so far that had involved, or were likely to involve the Supplementary Fund.

(130) The IOPC Funds described how its compensation system works. It noted that the shipowner has strict liability for any pollution damage caused by the oil and that the shipowner could normally limit its financial liability to an amount determined by the tonnage of the ship. This amount was guaranteed by the shipowner's liability insurer and, if the loss was larger than what was covered by liability insurance, the IOPC Funds provided compensation to those who stood to lose. IOPC Funds were funded by the oil industry and managed by Governments. The governing bodies of the organisations, consisting of each Fund's Member States, met twice per year to make decisions on

compensation payments, policy matters and budgetary matters, including the amounts to levy in contributions. It highlighted that Article 3 of the 1992 Fund Convention stated that the Convention applied exclusively to pollution damage caused in the territory (including the territorial sea of a Contracting State) and in the Exclusive Economic Zone (EEZ) of a Contracting State.

(131) The IOPC Funds explained that an oil pollution incident could generally give rise to claims for five types of pollution damage: property damage; costs of clean-up operations at sea and onshore; economic losses by fishermen or those engaged in mariculture; economic losses in the tourism sector; and costs for the reinstatement of the environment. Pollution damage was defined as the cost of reasonable measures of reinstatement actually undertaken, or to be undertaken, and the costs of preventive measures and further loss or damage caused by preventive measures. It further defined preventive measures as any reasonable measures taken by any person after an incident has occurred to prevent or minimise pollution damage. The IOPC Funds noted that while compensation was payable for the costs of reasonable reinstatement measures aimed at accelerating natural recovery of environmental damage, compensation was not paid for damages of a punitive nature on the basis of the degree of fault of the wrong-doer. The objective of the fund was to work with insurers to provide prompt payment to victims. Members of the IOPC Funds had established a policy of claims that was reflected in the 1992 Fund's Claims Manual which, together with other publications, developed the definition of pollution damage and the claims process in practice.

(132) The IOPC Funds described how the fund was administered, noting that the General Funds cover the administration expenses of the respective Funds, including the costs of running the Secretariat and, in respect of the 1992 Fund, for compensation payments and claims-related expenditure. Separate claims funds were established for major incidents. It explained that the claims fund were funded by oil receivers, not the government, in the member state in which the incident occurred. It stressed that IOPC Funds were financed by contributions levied on any entity that received in the relevant calendar year more than 150,000 tonnes of contributing oil. These contributions were scaled based on the amount of oil received. Governments of member states had an obligation to report any incidents.

(133) The IOPC Funds advised that it provided several services to stakeholders to ensure the prompt and equitable payment of compensation. Specifically it: assisted with the correct implementation of the Conventions; delivered

national and regional workshops on the international liability and compensation regime; delivered an annual short course in conjunction with the IMO and IGP&I Clubs; and provided education and outreach activities including conference presentations and exhibitions at institutions.

(134) The IOPC Funds explained that it formed a part of an international liability and compensation regime that has proven successful, efficient, and invaluable for 40 years. The IOPC Funds offered to share its experience, and to provide further assistance to Parties in the creation of the Fund envisaged in Article 12, Annex VI.

(135) In response to a query from Spain on the maximum amount of payment for a very large incident the IOPC Funds informed the Meeting that based on the 1992 Civil Liability Convention, the 1992 Fund Convention, and the 2003 Supplementary Fund Protocol, civil liability for a larger tanker was limited to approximately 90 million SDR or 130 million US dollars. The maximum payment allowed under the compensation regime was approximately one billion US dollars. It noted that the first part of the payment was derived from the shipowner's payment of premiums through the IGP&I Clubs (90 million SDR) and the remainder was funded by the oil industry of member states, not the member states themselves. The IOPC Funds stated that in its 40 year experience, one billion dollars would be sufficient to cover the costs associated with any of the spills that had occurred to date.

(136) In response to a query from the Netherlands, the IOPC Funds stated that it had no experience with reinstatement measures in the polar regions, as there had been no spills in those regions. The IOPC Funds noted that spills in polar regions was a topic that was being actively discussed in a number of fora. It noted that cleaning up oil spills in an ice-covered environment would be extremely complicated.

(137) In response to a question posed by the United States regarding 'reasonable reinstatement measures' aimed at accelerating natural recovery of environmental damage in general, the IOPC Funds made two points. First, 'reasonable reinstatement' had the same meaning as 'restoration' and the two terms were used interchangeably. Second, despite not having had the practical experience of implementing 'reasonable reinstatement measures' in the context of polar areas, the reasonableness of environmental reinstatement would be science based. When asked for examples of cases in which reinstatement might be neither necessary nor feasible, the IOPC stated that any reinstatement response would be entirely based on the particular factual circumstance. The IOPC Funds gave various examples of the flexibility of

such a response in different environments, including arrangements in which natural processes were deemed to be less harmful to the environment than more interventionist strategies.

(138) The Parties thanked the IOPC Funds for its helpful and informative presentation.

(139) The IGP&I Clubs presented IP 87 *Liability Annex: Financial Security*, which described the financial security provisions and the scope of third party liability cover provided by its members. It explained that each club was a mutual agreement where the insured were collectively the insurer. The insured were members of the club, paid premiums to the club, and the club did not operate to make a profit or loss. Surplus funds would either be returned to members or be put in a reserve fund, whilst deficient funds were met by requiring higher premiums from the members. While noting that each club provided insurance cover in accordance with its own rule book, the IGP&I Clubs observed that had been little difference in the rules between clubs, as all clubs focused extensively on safety and loss prevention issues related to the operation of ships.

(140) The IGP&I Clubs stated that the range of liabilities covered by each Club is comprehensive and includes most of the liabilities a shipowner was likely to encounter in the operation of his ship including: pollution liability; liability to cargo; liability to crew, collision liability, liability for damage to property, and liability for wreck removal. It observed that the liabilities related to both pollution and wreck removal could correspond to an environmental emergency as defined by Annex VI. The IGP&I Clubs informed the Parties that the protection and indemnity (P&I) cover provided by the Clubs underpinned the liability and compensation regime established by the International Maritime Organization (IMO) for ship-sourced pollution damage. With reference to the 1992 International Convention on Civil Liability for Oil Pollution Damage and the International Convention on Civil Liability for 2001 Bunker Oil Pollution Damage, it noted that these are currently in force in 136 and 83 States, respectively. It further noted that many of the non-state vessels operating in Antarctic waters maintained P&I cover with a member of the IGP&I Clubs.

(141) The IGP&I Clubs recalled that Annex VI applied to "environmental emergencies" and that these are defined as accidental events that resulted in, or imminently threatened to result in, any significant and harmful impact on the Antarctic environment. It suggested that there were essentially three aspects of obligations and liability under Annex VI, reflecting those

outlined in the Environment Protocol itself: the prevention and mitigation of environmental emergencies; responding to such emergencies; and assigning liability for meeting the costs of such response. The IGP&I Clubs also stated that Article 6 of the Annex made an operator that failed to take the required response action strictly liable for the costs of actions taken by any Parties. It pointed out that when an operator should have taken prompt and effective response action but failed to do so, and no response action was taken by any Party, the operator would be liable to pay the costs of the response action which should have been undertaken into a fund administered by the Secretariat of the Antarctic Treaty. Alternatively, in the case of the non-state operator, it would need to pay the estimated costs of response to the Party taking enforcement action against it under Article 7(3) of the Annex.

(142) From an insurance perspective, the IGP&I Clubs observed that the Parties must require their operators to maintain adequate insurance or other financial security up to the applicable limits contained in Annex VI. This should cover: their liability to Parties that step in to take the required response actions; their liability to make a payment to the Fund; or their liability where a Party takes enforcement action against it in circumstances where no Party steps in to address the emergency. Noting that the limits prescribed by Annex VI are identical to the property damage limits contained in the Protocol of 1996 to Amend the International Convention on Limitation of Liability for Maritime Claims, the IGP&I Clubs recorded its concern that this could mean that in a jurisdiction where wreck removal claims are carved out of the limitation regime, the shipowner or operator may incur an unlimited liability.

(143) The IGP&I Clubs said that its insurance would, in principle, cover the liabilities of a "commercial operator" as defined in Article 6 of Annex VI. The definition of "operator" in Article 2 (c) of Annex VI was much wider and encompassed "any natural or judicial person, whether governmental or non-governmental, which organises activities to be carried out in the Antarctic Treaty area". Such a definition might encompass actors other than the shipowner and may include parties that did not have P&I cover with the IGP&I Clubs. It observed that the insurance provision contained in Article 11 of Annex VI required those parties that fall within the definition of "operator" to maintain adequate insurance or other financial security.

(144) The IGP&I Clubs noted that certificates of insurance (known as 'certificates of entry') that were issued by the IGP&I Clubs to all ships entered for P&I cover should be sufficient evidence that a ship had insurance in place that met the requirements of Annex VI. On the basis that the compulsory insurance

provision does not provide for a right of action directly against the insurance provider, nor a requirement that insurers waive policy defences contained in the Clubs' Rules, the IGP&I Clubs noted that insurers would be able to invoke defences contained in Club Rules as well as the defences available to the insured in Article 8 of Annex VI.

(145) Noting that the limits of liability contained in Article 9 of Annex VI appeared to represent a minimum requirement, the IGP&I Clubs suggested that jurisdictions with lower limits would be superseded by the Annex VI limits and that jurisdictions with higher limits would prevail.

(146) The IGP&I Clubs also advised that it was unclear how Article 7 and 9 (2) of Annex VI would operate in concert with existing international limited liability regimes. Pointing out that Article 9 (2) of Annex VI provided that the Annex shall not affect the liability or right to limit liability under any applicable international limitation of liability treaty, the IGP&I Clubs noted that this primarily referred to existing international limited liability regimes that were in force, and that existing regimes did not contain their own jurisdiction clauses. It also noted that Article 7 of Annex VI addressed where actions may be commenced, but it was unclear how this related with Article 9(2) and existing international limited liability regimes.

(147) In concluding, the IGP&I Clubs commented that Article 12 used the term "reasonable and justified costs" in relation to seeking reimbursement from the Fund without defining the costs, which posed concerns.

(148) The Meeting thanked IGP&I Clubs for attending and for its useful and detailed input.

(149) Several Parties welcomed the confirmation provided by the report that the P&I insurance required under Annex VI was available. Some Parties noted that insurance was a complicated matter that would require further discussions, some of which may be beyond the scope of the Meeting and would require an understanding of what Annex VI would look like when in force. They noted that this paper and the channel of dialogue with the IGP&I Clubs would assist internal discussions within domestic administrations.

(150) From the perspective of Antarctic operators, IAATO noted that the P&I insurance as described by the IGP&I Clubs, covered shipowners and not necessarily the operators that ATCM Parties authorised to travel to Antarctica. It noted that it would be important to clarify if the cover for the ship and the shipowners would also extend to the authorised operators.

(151) Whilst the Russian Federation noted that it had already implemented Annex VI, and that the Russian National Expedition's Antarctic ships had been insured for the last 15-20 years using BNI Services, it highlighted that there remained the issue of the insurance of existing equipment and facilities in the Antarctic. From its own practice, it noted that it was difficult to find insurance companies prepared to insure in Antarctica because they does not have the necessary abilities or capabilities, and knew that they would have to rely on National Antarctic Programmes for their expertise.

(152) Responding to the comments of IAATO and the Russian Federation relating to operators that were not shipowners, the United Kingdom noted that it defined "operator" as the organisation receiving the permit, and, that in the case of ship-based activities, once Annex VI was in force it would not issue a permit unless the operator was using a ship that had appropriate insurance in place. In relation to non-ship based-activities, the United Kingdom noted that it had engaged extensively with the United Kingdom based insurance market to discuss the implications of Annex VI. Whilst the insurance industry was open to the possibility of developing bespoke insurance products, it was waiting for Annex VI to come into force internationally, as the detail of the liability requirements would not become clear until then, and it would be difficult to undertake the necessary risk assessments on which insurance products were based.

(153) In response to a question posed by the United States regarding the responsibility of the operator to ensure any ship engaged in its operations has necessary insurance cover, the IGP&I Clubs noted that insurance could be entered in the name of the shipowner, while the operator of the ship could be co-insured to the same level of liability as the shipowner. It was noted, however, that the charterer of a vessel fell outside the scope of insurance offered by the IGP&I Clubs and therefore a Charterer would not qualify to be so insured.

(154) The IOPC Funds cautioned Parties that many ships may not be adequately/properly insured, unless they were insured by a member of the IGP&I Clubs. The IOPC Funds clarified the three events where its fund would pay compensation: where the owner was exempt from liability; where the insurance owner or shipowner could pay; and the most common case, where the damage exceeded insurance and liability.

(155) Recalling that after twelve years Annex VI had not come into force, IMO stated that it sought to provide practical advice that could aid with the development of liability issues in the Antarctic Treaty System. IMO noted

that there was already an interface between what was achievable in the Antarctic, what was already available in the market, and what was required under existing Conventions that had come into force. It noted that the International Convention on Civil Liability for Bunker Oil Pollution Damage (the Bunkers Convention) adopted by IMO in 2001, had 84 contracting states, and that the 2007 Nairobi International Convention on the Removal of Wrecks had 35 contracting states.

(156) IMO emphasised that the international shipping community relied on established liability regimes, and that the success of these regimes relied on broad support from both industry and governments. It commented that implementation of these regimes needed to have support from states and industry alike. While recognising that it was not the role of the IMO Secretariat to interpret international liability regimes or their possible overlaps, it suggested that it would be valuable to examine the differences between the Parties' expectations of Annex VI and liability conventions negotiated under IMO.

(157) IMO noted that the aftermath of the major spill that occurred from the *Torrey Canyon* in 1967 highlighted that, in order to have an adequate compensation and liability regime, adequate insurance must exist. IMO explained that while providers of relevant insurers including IGP&I Clubs were allowed certain defences to prevent payment of claims, they were under the relevant IMO Conventions not allowed to defer paying out claims for removal of a shipwreck or bunker oils until after a shipowner had paid.

(158) IMO looked forward to progress on the adoption of Annex VI and directed Parties' attention to the successful extension of the voluntary Polar Code into a mandatory instrument under SOLAS and MARPOL that also covered Antarctica. It also noted the success of extending the MARPOL ban on heavy fuel oil, both as fuel and cargo, to the Antarctic area. It suggested that if adoption of Annex VI faltered, a similar approach to extend liability conventions already in force under IMO to Antarctic waters might be effective to provide coverage in the Antarctic.

(159) In response to a question from the Russian Federation, the IGP&I Clubs informed Parties that spill response equipment is typically provided by states and may be stockpiled by oil companies. It noted that often the government organised the spill response and the shipowner paid for the reasonable cost of the response. It explained that the Clubs typically did not, however, cover the costs of purchasing response equipment as the costs of oil spill preparedness are not considered as shipowners' P&I risks or liabilities arising from the incident.

(160) The IGP&I Clubs confirmed that, in general, the requirements of Annex VI were within the scope of cover, but highlighted that wilful misconduct or presentation of a known unseaworthy vessel would prevent cover being provided.

(161) Parties warmly thanked the IGP&I Clubs, IMO, and the IOPC Funds for their attendance at ATCM XL, and for the assistance they provided in clarifying various elements of Annex VI. Some Parties noted that discussions should continue with the IGP&I Clubs, IMO, and the IOPC Funds, and that engaging in discussions with shipowners and other operational experts would also be useful for Parties during the implementation of Annex VI.

(162) The IOPC Funds, IGP&I Clubs and IMO expressed their willingness to lend their expertise and contribute to ATCM discussions relating to liability in the future. The Meeting requested the Executive Secretary to renew its invitation to the IOPC Funds, IGP&I Clubs and IMO to attend a future ATCM and to inform those bodies that the ATCM would welcome their input and advice on issues relating to insurance under Annex VI to the Protocol.

(163) The Russian Federation presented IP 144 *Russian legislation on regulation of activities in the Antarctic*, which outlined Federal Law No. 50 concerning the "Regulation of activities of the Russian citizen and the Russian legal entities in the Antarctic". This domestic law adopted Annex VI of the Environment Protocol. It said it had provided a translation of the Federal Law No. 50 in order to share its experience of implementing Annex VI. The Russian Federation said that Parties should continue to inform one another of their approaches and solutions to the challenges and tasks in the Antarctic region.

(164) In thanking the Russian Federation for this translation of its legislation, Parties noted that the sharing of information on the implementation of Annex VI was seen as a valuable tool for those still working to implement Annex VI. Some Parties noted that their domestic legislation and regulations had already been provided either through the EIES or through previous Information Papers.

(165) Several Parties commented that it would be useful for the Secretariat to establish a dedicated webpage on which Parties could voluntarily contribute legislation reflecting the implementation of Annex VI. The Secretariat agreed to collate the information it currently held on the domestic implementation of Annex VI in a central location. Parties who had not yet done so were encouraged to provide information to the Secretariat regarding their domestic legislation and other relevant instruments.

(166) The Russian Federation also presented IP 145 *Approximate list, scope and character of response actions*, which reminded Parties of their obligations

under Article 15 of the Environment Protocol, and Article 5 of Annex VI regarding emergency response action. It encouraged Parties to consider discussions on developing an approximate list of the scope and character of response actions prior to the entry into force of Annex VI. This would assist the Russian Government, which had an obligation under its domestic implementing legislation to do so. It noted that this would give Parties that had implemented Annex VI a more solid legal basis for implementation, and would be useful support for those Parties who had not yet approved Annex VI.

(167) The Russian Federation informed the Meeting that it intended to provide an approximate list of the scope and character of response actions required from operators in case of environmental emergency while carrying out activities in the Antarctic in the future.

(168) Other Parties which had enacted legislation implementing Annex VI noted that the development of a list of response actions was not required under their legislation. It was also noted that in some domestic systems, the interpretation of relevant provisions, including those regarding the scope of a reasonable response action, would ultimately be a question for the courts. Parties agreed to continue having helpful and open discussions on the domestic implementation of Annex VI.

Item 9: Biological Prospecting in Antarctica

(169) The Netherlands presented IP 168 *An Update on Status and Trends Biological Prospecting in Antarctica and Recent Policy Developments at the International Level*. Parties exchanged views about the developments reported by the Netherlands.

(170) The Netherlands also brought to the attention of Parties the status of the process of the development of an international legally binding instrument under the United Nations Convention on the Law of the Sea (UNCLOS) on the conservation and sustainable use of marine biological diversity of areas beyond national jurisdiction. The Meeting re-affirmed that the Antarctic Treaty System is the competent framework within which to address the conservation and sustainable use of biodiversity in the Antarctic region.

(171) ASOC noted that activities related to biological prospecting had relevance to environmental protection and that biological prospecting should be discussed in a transparent way.

(172) The Meeting agreed on the need for further discussion on all aspects of this topic at ATCM and included it in the Multi-year Strategic Work Plan. It noted the importance of the Antarctic Treaty System and the work already done, including Resolution 7 (2005), Resolution 9 (2009), and Resolution 6 (2013), and agreed this work would continue next year at ATCM XLI. The Meeting encouraged Parties to submit relevant Working Papers to continue this work.

(173) At the request of some Consultative Parties the Executive Secretary reported on invitations received from the United Nations, most recently in connection with the forthcoming meeting to be held in July this year. The Meeting agreed that in the event that the Secretariat received any further invitations from the United Nations Secretariat pertaining to the process referred to in General Assembly Resolution 69/292, the Secretariat would circulate the invitation immediately to all Parties. It was agreed that unless any objection was received within 14 days of the circulation, the Secretariat would respond using the following language:

> Dear Sir/Madam,
>
> I have the pleasure of acknowledging receipt of your letter of (X DATE), which has been transmitted to the Antarctic Treaty Consultative Parties. Thank you for such a kind invitation. I take this opportunity to recall that the Antarctic Treaty System is the competent framework within which to address the conservation and sustainable use of biodiversity in the Antarctic region.
>
> Executive Secretary
> Antarctic Treaty Secretariat

(174) The Meeting noted that responding to correspondence directed to the Treaty Secretariat was a sensitive matter.

Item 10: Exchange of Information

(175) COMNAP presented IP 12 *Operational information - national expeditions: Facilities & SAR categories*, in response to two information requests in regard to exchange of information made at ATCM XXXIX (Final Report, Appendix 4). COMNAP advised the Meeting of the facility categories agreed

to by COMNAP Members to use in a range of products and tools, noting these agreed categories and their definitions had a long history of use.

(176) COMNAP also presented IP 64 *Advances to the COMNAP database*, which described the recent redevelopment of COMNAP's database system to support the work of National Antarctic Programmes. The database informed a range of products including the COMNAP Antarctic Flight Information Manual (AFIM) and in support of the COMNAP Infrastructure Catalogue project. COMNAP informed the Meeting that the database was comprehensive, and invited the ATCM to consider how the data in the COMNAP database may reduce duplication of efforts to populate data across platforms and how it might assist to ensure that data was consistent and current across those platforms. COMNAP had launched a publicly available GIS interface on its website as a tool to convey information from the database.

(177) The Secretariat presented SP 10 *Report for the review of the functioning of the Electronic Information Exchange System (EIES)*. The Secretariat introduced a number of proposed improvements and changes to the EIES, including interface considerations; data exchange with other systems; considerations of authorisation and publication; and the use of EIES data for cross-party and cross-season reporting, including the development of new summarised reports to extract useful information from the system. It noted that it would be possible to make the interface work in all Treaty languages and that further ways of exchanging data between the EIES and the COMNAP database could also be considered.

(178) Belarus highlighted the importance of a user-friendly interface and the usefulness of specifically being able to fill out electronic forms in the EIES in all Treaty languages.

(179) The Meeting invited the Antarctic Treaty Secretariat and the COMNAP Secretariat to cooperate in the intersessional period and consider ways to reduce duplication and increase compatibility across their databases, particularly in relation to the permanent information provided by Parties. COMNAP confirmed that it stood ready to explore with the Antarctic Treaty Secretariat, the practical and technical possibilities and usefulness of data-sharing across organisational platforms.

(180) Also in the intersessional period, the Meeting asked the Antarctic Treaty Secretariat to continue to improve the EIES during the next intersessional period, including the provision of the website interface in the four Treaty languages.

(181) The Secretariat was also asked to consider an online photography compilation from previous ATCMs. It agreed to consider this request.

Item 11: Education Issues

(182) Bulgaria introduced WP 24 *Second report of the Intersessional Contact Group on Education and Outreach*, prepared jointly with Belgium, Brazil, Chile, Portugal, Spain and the United Kingdom. The ICG recommended that the ATCM: recognise the usefulness of the Forum on Education and Outreach; advise the Parties to keep promoting the usage of the Forum to provide information of their activities related to Education and Outreach; assess key international activities/events related to education and outreach that Parties can engage; and advise the Parties to continue to promote not only Antarctica and Antarctic research through their Education and Outreach Activities but the Antarctic Treaty and Environmental Protocol itself.

(183) Bulgaria thanked all the Parties that had participated in the ICG, and noted that its activities had been taking place both at the international and national levels. The activities of the ICG included: a celebration of the 25th anniversary of the Environment Protocol, the annual international Antarctica Day in December, biannual Polar Weeks, and the organisation of a third international workshop of polar educators.

(184) The Meeting thanked Bulgaria for leading the ICG and emphasised the importance of education and outreach activities. IAATO thanked the Parties for inviting it to participate in the ICG and noted that this forum was not only important in sharing information and ideas for education and outreach but also for the general promotion of coordination and collaboration in Antarctic issues. The Meeting agreed to support the continuation of the ICG and encouraged it to come with a concrete proposal for action next year. The Meeting reaffirmed that the section of the Secretariat website dedicated to education and outreach would link to individual Parties' websites and would not itself contain individual Parties' material.

(185) The Meeting agreed to continue the ICG on Education and Outreach for another intersessional period, and agreed to the following terms of reference:

- foster collaboration at both the national and international level, on Education and Outreach;
- identify key international activities/events related to education and outreach for possible engagement by the Antarctic Treaty Parties;
- share results of educational and outreach initiatives that demonstrate the work of Antarctic Treaty Parties in managing the Antarctic Treaty area;

- emphasise ongoing environmental protection initiatives that had been informed by scientific observations and results, in order to reinforce the importance of the Antarctic Treaty and its Protocol on Environmental Protection;

- promote related education and outreach activities by Experts and Observers, and encourage cooperation with these groups;

- discuss the possibility for creation of an Antarctic Education and Outreach section at the ATS website.

(186) It was further agreed that:

- Observers and Experts participating in the ATCM would be invited to provide input;

- the Executive Secretary would open the ATCM forum for the ICG and provide assistance to the ICG; and

- Bulgaria would act as convener and report to the next ATCM on progress made in the ICG.

(187) Venezuela presented IP 19 *Material divulgativo/educativo: Juega y aprende con el Tratado Antártico*, which referred to the education and outreach material "Play and learn with the Antarctic Treaty". This material aimed to incorporate basic knowledge of the Antarctic Treaty System into the education system in Venezuela.

(188) Venezuela introduced IP 28 *Enlace web de divulgación y educación: Antártida en la escuela*. This paper included details of the web link for the Outreach and Education project "Antarctica in the School", aimed at providing information to members of the general public.

(189) South Africa introduced IP 51 *Creating Awareness: the Role of the Antarctic Legacy of South Africa (ALSA)*, which provided an update about the ALSA project, including its establishment, further development and evolvement into South Africa's foremost Antarctic and sub-Antarctic heritage depository and its education and awareness initiatives.

(190) Colombia presented IP 60 *Campaña de Educación "Todos Somos Antártica" Actividades 2016-2017*. This paper outlined the activities of Colombia's "We are all Antarctica" education and outreach campaign in 2016 and 2017. The campaign continued to raise awareness of Antarctica in Colombia. The activities included seminars, presentations, special outreach events, documentaries and courses.

(191) Colombia also presented IP 61 *Aportes de Colombia al Conocimiento de la Cultura y Adaptación Antárticas*, which recounted the main research activities during the third Colombian scientific expedition in 2016-2017. The expedition included 27 research projects. Colombia thanked Argentina, Spain, Chile and the United States for their support.

(192) Chile introduced IP 96 *Programa de Educación Antártica* which outlined the different levels of educational activities undertaken in Chile.

(193) Argentina introduced IP 99 *Commemoration of the 25th Anniversary of the Protocol on Environmental Protection to the Antarctic Treaty – Presentation of Postage Stamps*. Argentina commemorated the 25th Anniversary of the signing of the Protocol on Environmental Protection to the Antarctic Treaty, by issuing two commemorative postage stamps on 4 October 2016. The paper contained details about the stamps.

(194) Ecuador presented IP 129 *Primeras Jornadas Antárticas, 2016* which highlighted the outreach and education activities that Ecuador viewed as being important for all generations. As Ecuador is a tropical country, the issues of Antarctica are particularly difficult to communicate. To overcome this, Ecuador organised conferences based around education and Antarctic science and events based around the 30th anniversary of the first Ecuadorian expedition to Antarctica.

(195) Peru introduced IP 134 *Actividades del Programa Nacional Antártico de Perú período 2016-2017*, which provided information about the activities of the Peruvian National Antarctic Programme during 2016-17.

(196) Bulgaria and Turkey introduced IP 138 *Polar Scientific and Outreach Cooperation Between Bulgaria and Turkey* which provided information about the signing of a Memorandum of Understanding between the Bulgarian Antarctic Institute and Istanbul Technical University Polar Research Center in October 2016. It also highlighted the event in Istanbul, held during the Turkish Polar Science Programme workshop at which Bulgarian Antarctic Institute presented an historical Antarctic map exhibition prepared for the 25th anniversary of the signing of the Environment Protocol.

(197) ASOC presented IP 148 *Collaborating on Antarctic Education and Outreach,* jointly prepared with IAATO, which reported on education and outreach activities that they collaborated upon during the 2016-2017 intersessional period. These activities included a poster produced by ASOC, IAATO and WWF for the 2016 IUCN World Conservation Congress; joining the Antarctic Treaty System community in celebrating the 25th

Anniversary of the Environment Protocol on 4 October 2016 using the hashtag #AntarcticaProtected; and collaboration on Valentine's Day related social media campaign designed to broaden awareness of lesser-known Antarctic species, specifically invertebrates. ASOC noted that coordinated, collaborative projects and media campaigns were effective at highlighting key messages and engaging with a wider audience. ASOC and IAATO hoped the example of their shared work would stimulate more shared efforts with Antarctic Treaty Parties, as well as ATCM Observers and Experts to raise the profile of the Antarctic Treaty System.

(198) Romania presented IP 171 *Romanian Antarctic Education and Outreach Activities during 2015-2017* which described a series of events related to its involvement with the ICG on Education and Outreach. These activities included: celebrations of the 25th Anniversary of the Environment Protocol; involvement in Antarctica Day events and the APECS Polar Week; publication of a book and documentary about renowned Romanian polar scientist Emil Racovita; media events; an event at the Romanian Embassy in Canberra, dedicated to the two famous explorers Racovita and Negoita; and seminars.

(199) The following background papers were submitted under this agenda item:

- BP 9 *Piloto Luis Pardo Villalón: Rescatando del olvido a un héroe chileno* (Chile).
- BP 10 *Celebración de la Semana Antártica en Punta Arenas* (Chile).
- BP 13 *The practice of holding international scientific and practical conferences on the problems of Antarctica in the Republic of Belarus* (Belarus).

Item 12: Multi-year Strategic Work Plan

(200) The Meeting considered the Multi-year Strategic Work Plan adopted at ATCM XXXIX. It addressed each priority item and considered whether to delete current priorities and to add new priorities.

(201) Following discussion, the Meeting updated the Multi-year Strategic Work Plan and adopted Decision 7 (2017) *Multi-year Strategic Work Plan for the Antarctic Treaty Consultative Meeting*.

Item 13: Safety and Operations in Antarctica

Operations: Air

(202) SCAR introduced WP 20 *State of Knowledge of Wildlife Responses to Remotely Piloted Aircraft Systems (RPAS)*, and referred to BP 1 *Best Practice for Minimising Remotely Piloted Aircraft System Disturbance to Wildlife in Biological Field Research*. In response to a request from the CEP XVIII, the paper presented a synthesis from 23 published scientific research papers on wildlife responses to remotely piloted aerial systems (RPAS). SCAR noted that responses to RPAS were not consistent across species, flight path parameters, or the type of RPAS, and that data on demographic effects are lacking. SCAR noted that this review supported the conclusion that there would not be a one-size-fits-all solution to the mitigation of wildlife responses to RPAS. As result, SCAR indicated that guidelines would need to be site and species specific and consider both the type of RPAS used, and the noise output. SCAR recommended that the CEP implement preliminary best practice guidelines as described in the paper and that future studies on wildlife responses to RPAS in the Antarctic should consider a range of species, responses and variables as described in the paper.

(203) The Meeting thanked SCAR for its work and agreed that finding site, species, and equipment specific guidance would probably be needed to effectively manage RPAS use around wildlife.

(204) COMNAP presented IP 77 *Update from the COMNAP Unmanned Aerial Systems Working Group (UAS-WG)*, and noted the quickly evolving nature of RPAS technology, especially, as noted by the United Kingdom, the Automatic Dependent Surveillance-Broadcast (ADS-B) technology, which is a useful tool in support of air operations safety. The paper also reports on the result of a COMNAP survey on RPAS use by National Antarctic Programmes over a 12-month period. The results indicate that most RPAS deployment is for science.

(205) The Meeting thanked SCAR and COMNAP for their useful contributions.

(206) The Netherlands noted that the *General Principles on Antarctic Tourism (2009)* states that in "the absence of adequate information about potential impacts, decisions on tourism should be based on a pragmatic and precautionary approach that also incorporates an evaluation of risks". On this basis and taking into account the gaps in knowledge, as well as the decision of IAATO to temporarily ban the use of RPAS for recreational purposes in

wildlife rich coastal areas, the Netherlands would have expected that the ATCM would adopt IAATO's approach until more knowledge was available.

(207) The Meeting noted the CEP Chair's advice that the Committee had not reached consensus on a proposal raised by the Netherlands during the CEP Meeting to ban the recreational use of UAVs / RPAS, and that the ICG established by the CEP to develop guidelines for the environmental aspects of UAVs / RPAS would give further consideration to the use of such devices for all purposes.

(208) The Meeting supported the recommendations provided by the CEP regarding the use of UAVs/RPAS in the vicinity of wildlife in Antarctica. It welcomed the indication from COMNAP that it would continue to work on the safety and environmental perspectives of UAVS/RPAS operations. It agreed that UAVs / RPAS would be included in air operations at ATCM XLI.

(209) Norway introduced WP 46 *Non-governmental operators Infrastructure & Operations related to Air operations – Possible impact on National programs in Antarctica*, prepared jointly with the United Kingdom and Australia. The paper noted that while air traffic in Antarctica was, in general, managed by National Antarctic Programmes, there was increasing interest by non-governmental operators to fly to, and within, Antarctica. Norway, Australia, and the United Kingdom proposed that the ATCM look into the challenges that might occur in relation to increased air operations in Antarctica and agreed to place the topic of air operations on the ATCM Multi-year Strategic Plan for further consideration at ATCM XLI in 2018.

(210) The Meeting agreed that the issue of increasing non-governmental air traffic in the Antarctic was an important issue that had implications for both safety and environmental protection. Some Parties stressed the importance of conducting broader policy discussions, including the need to have a fundamental discussion regarding the growth in the non-government air sector.

(211) The Russian Federation informed the Meeting that due to many non-governmental operations relying on National Antarctic Programme support, its national permitting system required operators to have relevant education and training to ensure that air activities are conducted in accordance with COMNAP's Antarctic Flight Information Manual (AFIM).

(212) In response, IAATO noted that some of its air operators were self-sufficient and safely conducted and supplied their Antarctic flight operations without

assistance from National Antarctic Programmes. IAATO thanked COMNAP for the work on AFIM and aircraft tracking systems that were an important contribution to air safety.

(213) The Meeting agreed that the increasing non-government air traffic was an important issue for further discussion and wished to add this topic to the Multi-year Strategic Workplan.

(214) Germany presented IP 42 *DROMLAN - Dronning Maud Land Air Network*. Germany noted that the motivation of this paper was to increase transparency about activities conducted through the Dronning Maud Land Air Network (DROMLAN). It noted that DROMLAN was a non-profit, international cooperative project of the National Antarctic Programmes of Belgium, Finland, Germany, India, Japan, the Netherlands, Norway, Russia, South Africa, Sweden and the United Kingdom with stations and scientific interests in the wider Dronning Maud Land (DML) area. It explained that, with the consent of all DROMLAN participants, the Antarctic Logistics Center International (PTY) Ltd. (ALCI) at Cape Town is responsible for most air operations and collaborates closely with the DROMLAN Steering Committee in their management. Germany stated that the use of DROMLAN has offered easier and more frequent access into DML and has significantly improved safety standards for scientific expeditions and logistics operations in the DML.

(215) The Meeting thanked Germany for its presentation and welcomed the success of DROMLAN.

(216) The Russian Federation presented IP 143 *On use of the blue ice area in the vicinity of Romnaes Mount as a reserve airstrip*, which described the need for and use of a back-up runway for aircraft accessing Novolazarevskaya station for safety reasons. The Russian Federation noted that the South African based ALCI prepared a draft Initial Environmental Evaluation (IEE) for construction and operation of the runway which was submitted to South Africa for consideration. The Russian Federation explained that South Africa did not have updated legislative procedures set up to approve a permit and thus could not approve ACLI's IEE. It informed the Meeting ALCI Nord, a Russian company had submitted a permit application to the Russian authorities for starting work on the runway, and that this permit was recently granted.

(217) The following paper was also submitted and taken as presented under this item:

- IP 27 *Procedures for Safe use of Unmanned Aerial Systems in Antarctica* (New Zealand). The paper reported on the development of an unmanned aerial system (UAS) manual relevant to flying UAS in the Ross Sea/McMurdo Sound region of Antarctica. Based on COMNAP's UAS Operators Manual, the manual set out procedures to be followed, including pre-assessment as well as on the ground operational procedures.

Operations: Maritime

(218) The United Kingdom referred to IP 139 rev. 1 *An overview of the International Code for Ships Operating in Polar Waters* by the IMO. The United Kingdom gave an overview from the perspective of an operator of the requirements of the International Code for Ships Operating in Polar Waters (the Polar Code) with regard to maritime safety and marine environment protection, and addressed the Polar Code's place in the existing global framework that regulates international shipping. The United Kingdom explained the significance of the Polar Waters Operation Manual (PWOM), and outlined how the Polar Operational Limit Assessment Risk Indexing System (POLARIS) is used in decision-making. The United Kingdom noted that the IMO paper described the associated training and certification requirements for officers and crew serving on ships operating in polar waters, as had been included in the International Convention on Standards of Training, Certification and Watchkeeping for Seafarers (STCW). In addition, the IMO paper examined what more can be done to ensure the safety of polar shipping, taking into account on-going discussions at the IMO. The United Kingdom further noted that the IMO is currently considering whether to extend the applicability of the Polar Code to other vessels not currently included via SOLAS, such as fishing vessels and yachts.

(219) ASOC presented IP 151 *Managing non-SOLAS vessels in the Southern Ocean*, which provided a brief summary of Southern Ocean shipping and the entry into force of the Polar Code. It estimated that the Polar Code was likely to be relevant to fewer than half of the vessels operating in the Antarctic Treaty area on an annual basis, since the Code was not currently applicable to "non-SOLAS" ships including fishing vessels, pleasure craft and small cargo vessels. ASOC highlighted that concerted action by the Parties would be needed to ensure the best outcome at the IMO Maritime Safety Committee meeting in June 2017. ASOC recommended that the Parties recognised that the work to date on the Polar Code did not apply to around half of the

vessels operating in the Southern Ocean; adopted a Decision on the need for concerted action at the IMO to ensure that Phase 2 of work on non-SOLAS vessels at the IMO commenced urgently; and agreed to provide views on safety standards for non-SOLAS vessels should the IMO fail to place the previously agreed output "application of the mandatory code to non-SOLAS ships in polar waters" onto its live agenda.

(220) Finland presented IP 123 *The Polar Code – Finnish Views*, which informed on the activities undertaken and planned by Finland associated with the entry into force of the Polar Code. As Chair of the Arctic Council in 2017–2019, Finland pointed out that all Arctic States had negotiated jointly and actively on the Polar Code in the IMO. Finland welcomed the entry into force of the Polar Code on the 1st of January 2017 and encouraged all Parties to support the effective implementation of the Polar Code in Antarctic waters.

(221) Finland also noted that ships strengthened in accordance with the Finnish-Swedish Ice Class Rules (FSICR), and the equivalent ice class rules of classification societies, had successfully sailed both in Arctic and Antarctic waters for decades, and that according to the Polar Code (Resolution MSC.385 (94), sections 3.3.2 and 6.3.3) icebreakers and other ships ice-strengthened in accordance with the FSICR could be used in polar waters in relevant ice conditions in the future. Finland noted that it would arrange an International Conference on Harmonized Implementation of the Polar Code in February 2018 in Helsinki, Finland, and invited interested Parties, Observers and Experts to participate.

(222) New Zealand noted that the Polar Code would be discussed at the upcoming IMO meeting, and urged Parties to talk to their national IMO delegates to voice support for the progression of Phase 2 of the Polar Code, which would regulate non-SOLAS ships in polar waters.

(223) The United Kingdom suggested that both the ATCM and CCAMLR had significant interest in the application and further development of the Polar Code, to enhance the safety of all vessels in Antarctic waters. The United States emphasised that practical experience gained though the implementation of the Polar Code would be beneficial, particularly if work to date would form the baseline for Phase 2. Also, in recognising that there are differences between non-SOLAS vessel operations in the Antarctic Treaty area and Arctic waters, the United States noted that it might be feasible for IMO to consider a work plan which focused on the development of voluntary guidelines for non-SOLAS vessels operating in Antarctic waters.

(224) While expressing support for the progression of Phase 2 of the Polar Code, IAATO cautioned that, as POLARIS is based on an Arctic system, work remains to be done to ensure it is applied in the Antarctic in an equitable and practical way. IAATO noted that it is working with POLARVIEW and the International Association of Classification Societies (IACS) to strengthen POLARIS in Antarctica, and welcomed collaborations that could lead to the long term effectiveness of the Polar Code in Antarctic waters.

(225) The WMO recalled that it is collecting weather observations from ships on a voluntary basis. Collecting more data from Antarctica, which is data sparse, and particularly from ships sailing in the region would potentially improve services delivered by WMO applications such as climate monitoring, numerical weather prediction and marine services. It invited the ATCM and the Parties to consider promoting the concept of making the collection and reporting of weather data mandatory in the Polar Code.

(226) The Meeting thanked Parties for the papers relating to the Polar Code, and noted strong support for ongoing discussions. It acknowledged the importance of the upcoming IMO meeting, which would consider how to take forward the question of non-SOLAS vessels and the Polar Code.

(227) The International Hydrographic Organization (IHO) presented IP 4 *Report by the International Hydrographic Organization (IHO) and a Proposal for a Seminar on the Importance of Hydrography in the Antarctic Region*. It focused on the limitations of hydrographic knowledge in Antarctica and the consequent risks to scientific and maritime operations. The IHO reiterated that over 90 per cent of Antarctic waters remained unsurveyed and that this posed serious risks for maritime incidents. It urged Parties to ensure that all their vessels used depth sensors and made this information available to hydrographic offices in order to improve hydrographic mapping. Recalling that at ATCM XXXIX the Meeting inserted a priority into the Multi-year Strategic Work Plan relating to hydrographic surveying in Antarctica, the IHO proposed delivering a seminar on the status and the impact of hydrography in the Antarctic as part of the programme for ATCM XLI in Ecuador in 2018. Further, the IHO urged the ATCM to encourage the measurement, recording and rendering of depth data at sea at all times as a routine environmental observing activity unless particular restrictions apply.

(228) The Meeting stressed the importance of nautical charts in the Antarctic to ensure safe navigation, and recognised the logistic and financial cost to those undertaking hydrographic surveys. Parties were encouraged to

make all bathymetric data collected from their vessels available to IHO for hydrographic purposes.

(229) The Meeting thanked the IHO for its paper and for its continued efforts in supporting safe navigation and hydrographic activities in Antarctica. Parties welcomed the IHO proposal for a seminar on the importance of hydrography in the Antarctic region at ATCM XLI.

(230) Argentina presented IP 132 *Ayudas a la navegación, balizamiento y cartografía antártica [Aids to navigation, beacons and Antarctic cartography]*, which reported Argentina's recent activities involving its Naval Hydrography Service. The paper noted activities which enhanced navigation safety in Antarctic waters through maintenance work, surveys, and investigations.

(231) Argentina presented IP 133 *Informe sobre la instalación de ayudas a la navegación en el continente antártico [Report on the installation of aids for Navigation in the Antarctic Continent]*, which described the navigation aids installation plan mainly in the Antarctic Peninsula area with the aim of increasing the safety of navigation and consequently the safety of human life at sea, and the protection of the marine environment.

(232) The following papers were also presented under this item:

- IP 167 *New IAATO Guidelines for Submersibles and Remote Operated Vehicle activities* (IAATO), which presented the Guidelines prepared by the IAATO Field Operations Committee adopted during the IAATO Meeting in May 2017. In describing the current and potential activities of submersibles and remote operated vehicles, IAATO anticipated that with recent improvements in submersible technology there would likely be more submersible activity in the future.

- IP 56 *Contribución de Colombia a la Seguridad Marítima en la Antártida [Contribution of Colombia to Maritime Safety in Antarctica]* (Colombia). This paper reported on Colombia's activities during the 2016/17 season to obtain data on hydrography and collect physical, chemical, and biological data. It also highlighted projects involving simulation of navigation in Antarctic waters and on technical submarine work in extremely cold waters.

- IP 100 *Fildes Bay Environmental Monitoring. Coastal Environment Observation Programme Chile (P.O.A.L.)* (Chile), which reported environmental monitoring work of the Chilean Navy within the Coastal

Environment Observation Programme, carried out to evaluate the trends of pollutant elements.

- IP 101 *Support to Antarctic Campaigns Meteorological Service of the Navy* (Chile), which described the Chilean Navy's support to Chile's Antarctic campaigns through technical resources including satellite information, training cruises, research activities, observation by oceanographic ships and meteorological data obtained in different stations and centres.

- IP 102 *Maintenance of Aids to Navigation in Antarctica, Summer Season 2016-2017* (Chile), which reported on a network of 70 aids to navigation managed and maintained by Chile. These aids were mainly concentrated in the area of the Antarctic Peninsula, providing safety support for the navigation of all vessels that visit the area.

- IP 104 *Production of an Antarctic Nautical Chart by the Hydrographic and Oceanographic Service of the Chilean Navy: Nautical Chart 15350 (Int 9104) "Estrecho de Gerlache - Islote Useful a Isla Wednesday"* (Chile). This paper reported that the hydrographic surveys conducted and the exchange of information with other Hydrographic Services had made possible the production of cartographic products such as SHOA Nautical Chart 15350 (INT 9104) "Estrecho de Gerlache – Islote Useful a Isla Wednesday" published in 2016.

Operations: Stations

(233) Belarus presented IP 2 *Belarusian Antarctic Research Station - the current stage of the creation and development perspectives*. Belarus informed the Meeting about the creation of its scientific station infrastructure in Antarctica. Belarus noted that it was building a modular research station near Vecherniaya Mountain, in Enderby Land, East Antarctica, and that with logistics assistance from the Russian Federation, it had built its first module in December 2015 and begun construction on the second module and some other facilities that should be completed in the 2017-18 season. Upon completing the first phase of construction the Republic of Belarus intends in 2019-20 to conduct its first all year round research expedition. Belarus informed the Meeting that a second round of construction would take place from 2021-2025 and that it would implement a set of measures to reduce pollutant emissions, wastewater discharges, prevent fuel leakages, plan research routes, and remove scrap infrastructure and other waste remaining from previous facilities.

(234) ASOC presented IP 159 *Decarbonizing Antarctic Operations (ASOC)*, which provided an updated summary on the progress of Parties towards reducing their energy consumption and replacing fossil fuel systems with renewable energy in Antarctic operations. ASOC recommended that Parties take note of the positive experiences of operators who had introduced clean energy as part of their Antarctic operations, and encouraged the Parties to implement more comprehensive renewable energy and energy efficiency policies in Antarctica.

(235) New Zealand thanked ASOC for IP 159 and noted that it is committed to managing and reducing its emissions under the Certified Emissions Measurement and Reduction Scheme (CEMARS), which it would continue to use as a measure of success in decarbonising its operations.

(236) The following papers were also taken as presented under this item:

- IP 40 *Refurbishment and Modernization of the German Antarctic Receiving Station GARS O'Higgins* (Germany), which described the facilities, status and activities undertaken at GARS O'Higgins station, and advised on refurbishment and modernisation measures as well as their technological and infrastructure aspects.

- IP 41 *Final Modernization of Gondwana Station, Terra Nova Bay, Northern Victoria Land* (Germany), which updated the Meeting on the renovation of the Gondwana Station and noted that the station was ready for future operations for at least 25-30 years as a base for research in Northern Victoria Land.

- IP 43 *EDEN ISS: A facility to provide Neumayer Station III overwinterers with fresh food while advancing space technology* (Germany). This paper reported on the international EDEN ISS project which was directed at developing a greenhouse that integrated the newest controlled environment agriculture technologies at the German Neumayer Station III.

- IP 78 *Reconstruction of the Brazilian Station in Antarctica* (Brazil), which provided an update on the reconstruction work of the Commandante Ferraz Antarctic Station, with two pre-assembly stages in Shanghai, China, and two construction stages in Antarctica.

- IP 107 *Capacidad logística de la Estación Científica Ecuatoriana "Pedro Vicente Maldonado" - Año 2017 [Logistic capability of the Scientific Station Pedro Vicente Maldonado – Year 2017]* (Ecuador). The paper informed the Meeting on the logistic capabilities of

Maldonado Station, and the logistical support provided to scientific Ecuadorian expeditions in Antarctica during the austral summer.

- IP 109 *Aplicación de la Norma de Operación en la XXI Campaña Antártica Ecuatoriana (2016-2017) [Application of the Operational Standard during the XXI Ecuadorian Antarctic expedition 2016/17]* (Ecuador), which informed the Meeting of the Operational Standard applied during the XXI Ecuadorian Antarctic expedition in 2016/17.

- IP 110 *Aplicación de la Norma de Operación en la XXI Campaña Antártica Ecuatoriana [Contingency and Risk plan during the XXI Ecuadorian Antarctic Expedition 2016/17]* (Ecuador), which described the contingency plan and personal responsibilities for Ecuador's activities at Maldonado Station, and described a risk analysis undertaken during the summer season 2016/17.

- IP 156 *Greening of established infrastructure and logistics in Antarctica* (Norway), which summarised how Norway had explored making Norwegian infrastructure and logistics in Antarctica greener. The paper pointed out that National Antarctic Programmes establishing and upgrading infrastructure shared the universal challenge of balancing the cost of capital investment, running costs, risk, and expected lifespan. It highlighted COMNAP's key role in responding to this challenge through fostering cooperative development of the systems of individual operators, and creating synergy through sharing of logistic resources.

- IP 36 *The U.S. Antarctic Program Antarctic Infrastructure Modernization for Science Project* (United States). This paper reported on the Antarctic Infrastructure Modernization for Science (AIMS), which is a project focused on modernizing the core infrastructure of McMurdo Station, the largest of three permanent stations operated by the United States Antarctic Program, and the critical support link to the United States Amundsen-Scott South Pole Station and deep-field research sites.

(237) The following papers were also submitted under this item:

- BP 5 *Plans for the revitalization of the Dobrowolski Station* (Poland).

- BP 22 *Capacidades y limitaciones de la Base Antártica "Pdte. Eduardo Frei M." en apoyo a los Programas Antárticos Nacionales y Extranjeros [Capabilities and limitations of the Antarctic Station "Pdte. Eduardo Frei M." in supporting national and foreign Antarctic Programs]* (Chile).

Safety

(238) COMNAP presented IP 10 *Search and Rescue Coordination and Response in the Antarctic: Report from the COMNAP Antarctic SAR Workshop III* held in Valparaiso, Chile, during 1-2 June 2016, and thanked co-hosts DIRECTEMAR Chile and INACH. The workshop was attended by representatives from the five Rescue Coordination Centres who shared responsibility for the coordination of SAR in the Antarctic Treaty area, National Antarctic Programmes, CCAMLR, IAATO and other relevant organisations. COMNAP encouraged the Parties to share the report of the workshop with all those involved in Antarctic activities to support the common goal of safety of human life. COMNAP noted that the next COMNAP Antarctic SAR Workshop IV would be held in New Zealand in 2019, and details would be provided to the ATCM next year.

(239) CCAMLR and IAATO noted that they would be happy to participate in further discussions of this important topic. CCAMLR stated that fishing vessels reporting to CCAMLR already support SAR in the CCAMLR Convention Area under an arrangement that authorises the CCAMLR Secretariat to release vessel monitoring system data in the event of a SAR incident. The agreement is currently under review with the view to its renewal.

(240) The United States presented IP 7 *Austral Mid-Winter Medical Evacuation from Amundsen-Scott South Pole Station, Antarctica.* The United States described the successful air evacuation of two seriously ill winter-over contract employees of the United States Antarctic Program from Amundsen-Scott South Pole Station. The United States highlighted that the smooth execution of this medical evacuation was only possible through the close coordination and support from several other National Antarctic Programmes.

(241) The United States presented IP 72 *Antarctic Mass Rescue Operations Response and Preparedness Challenges*, which provided an overview of the challenges associated with responding to a mass rescue operation (MRO) in the Antarctic Treaty area for land, air, or sea search and rescue (SAR) incidents. It noted that a successful MRO response depended upon cooperation and coordination among SAR authorities, National Antarctic Programmes, industry stakeholders, and other assets available to assist. Stressing that an effective MRO response relied upon the development of a realistic and effective contingency plan and exercises to test the plan, the United States supported COMNAP's focus on contingency planning and triennial SAR workshops.

(242) The United States thanked COMNAP for their report and noted that they were happy to assist in the conduct of a table-top mass MRO scenario at the upcoming COMNAP Antarctic SAR Workshop IV. COMNAP thanked the United States for the suggestion to include a MRO scenario on the SAR Workshop IV Agenda and welcomed the assistance offered by the United States to planning for and conducting a table-top exercise.

(243) IAATO thanked both COMNAP and the United States for their work on SAR noting that they would be pleased to take part in an MRO exercise. IAATO explained that each year they endeavour to undertake a SAR exercise with one of the Rescue Coordination Centers (RCCs) with Antarctic responsibility, thanked Chile for the opportunity to conduct a SAREX last season and welcomed any opportunity to work with other RCCs in future.

(244) Chile presented IP 103 *Search and Rescue Cases in the Area of the Antarctic Peninsula Period 2016/2017 MRCC Chile*. The paper summarised the SAR actions provided by Chile's Maritime Search and Rescue Service (MRCC Chile) during the 2016/17 period. While noting that there had been no cases of SAR incidents in the period, one medical evacuation was reported. The paper highlighted that this figure constituted a substantial decrease in maritime incidents that required the coordination of MRCC Chile from previous years.

(245) Chile presented IP 125 *Report on the 19th Edition of the Joint Antarctic Naval Patrol between Argentina and Chile*, jointly prepared with Argentina. The paper outlined the activities of the 19th Combined Antarctic Patrol (PANC), carried out jointly by Chile and Argentina, between 15 November 2016 and 31 March 2017. Chile noted that the main purpose of the PANC was to execute and practice SAR, salvage, and pollution control exercises in the area south of 60°S latitude between the meridians 10°W and 131°W. In addition, activities related to the acquisition of meteorological and navigational data, National Antarctic Programme logistics, and medical assistance were also performed.

Operations: Expeditions and Cooperation

(246) COMNAP presented IP 64 *Advances to the COMNAP database*. The paper noted that the database provided comprehensive information on National Antarctic Programmes facilities and vessels. The database further supported a range of COMNAP products including AFIM and the Station Catalogue.

A publicly available GIS interface served information from the database by way of the COMNAP website.

(247) Colombia presented IP 55 *Activities and development of the Colombian Antarctic Program – PAC*, which reported on its Antarctic expeditions for the 2014-2017 period. It informed that during its most recent expedition, "Almirante Padilla", 19 institutions and 33 researchers were involved, and that 27 projects had been undertaken in the areas of science, operations, environment, education and international cooperation. Colombia acknowledged the support of Spain, Chile, Argentina, Japan, Brazil, and Italy for its Antarctic activities.

(248) Australia presented IP 63 *Benefits of Logistic collaboration in Antarctica in support of Antarctic Science programmes: Australia's experience in 2016-17.* The paper reported on Australia's experience of the collaborative logistics and operational cooperation undertaken by Parties active in East Antarctica during the 2016-17 season. Australia noted its close relationship with other National Antarctic Programmes, and highlighted the many benefits that came from this collaboration, including: the avoidance of duplication of activities; cost reductions; and benefits related to the mutual sharing of information and experience.

(249) Chile presented IP 105 *Chile in the Southern Antarctica Joint Scientific Polar Station "Union Glacier"*, which described four campaigns carried out at the joint scientific polar station "Union Glacier" in the Ellsworth Mountains and described the logistics and operation of the station.

(250) Ecuador presented IP 130 *XXVII Meeting of Managers of Latin American Antarctic Programs (RAPAL), 2016*, which reported on the outcomes of RAPAL's latest Meeting, held in Guayaquil, Ecuador, in 2016. Ecuador noted that the meeting provided an excellent forum for coordination and exchange on the issues of science, communication, operations and outreach, and one of its main objectives was to develop efficient cooperation to help with optimising resources.

(251) Peru presented IP 135 *Antarctic expedition ANTAR XXIV Austral summer 2016/17*, which summarised the activities carried out by its XXIV Antarctic expedition. It stated that the expedition was mainly targeted at scientific research related to geochemical and hydrogeological studies and noted that a holistic maintenance plan had been developed to cover the next 10 years. It also thanked Chile for supporting its expedition.

(252) Brazil presented IP 140 *Brazilian XXXV Antarctic Operation*, which reported on Brazil's activities during the 2016-2017 season. The paper reported on the 25 scientific research projects undertaken by Brazil during the Brazilian XXXV Antarctic Operation. The activities were carried out on-board Brazilian vessels, at various camping locations, and at the stations of a number of other National Antarctic Programmes, including Chile, Argentina, and Poland, to whom Brazil offered thanks. Brazil also noted that the operation saw the removal of a damaged Brazilian aircraft stranded at the Teniente Rodolfo Marsh Martin aerodrome on King George Island in November 2014.

Item 14: Inspections under the Antarctic Treaty and the Environment Protocol

(253) The Netherlands introduced WP 40 *Report of the Intersessional Contact Group on Inspections in Antarctica under Article VII of the Antarctic Treaty and Article 14 of the Environmental Protocol*, prepared jointly with the Republic of Korea and the United States. It recalled that ATCM XXXIX agreed to establish an ICG to consider the practice of conducting inspections under Article VII of the Antarctic Treaty and Article 14 of the Environmental Protocol. Based on a number of questions, the ICG discussed the practice of inspections and explored options to enhance the effective organisation of inspections. The paper contained the questions that constituted the basis of the ICG's discussions, summarised the views expressed by the participants and provided a number of recommendations for consideration by the Parties:

> *Recommendation A) Request the Antarctic Treaty Secretariat to establish a system that would allow for a comprehensive inspection database, with information searchable via various categories such as by station, vessel, inspection dates, inspection reports, and a list of stations that had never been inspected as well as including additional information on logistic support of science, tourism facilities, HSMs, ASMAs, and ASPAs.*

(254) The Secretariat explained the various functions of the current database, that it already contained most of the information requested, and agreed to provide a list of stations that had never been inspected. Some Parties felt that an interactive map with facilities and their related inspection information would assist with the gathering of information prior to the conduct of an

inspection. The Secretariat agreed to consider the recommendations to provide mapping options and associated costs and stated it would update Parties at ATCM XLI.

> *Recommendation B) Invite Consultative Parties to encourage Consultative Parties, when planning and conducting inspection activities to give consideration to whether a facility has been inspected often or seldom in recent years, and to consider including stations never inspected in future inspections.*

(255) The Meeting agreed that consideration should be given to stations that had never been inspected when planning inspection activities, but several Parties emphasised that this should not be the only determinative factor. The Meeting agreed that consideration of the number of inspections should instead be one factor amongst a wide range of others.

> *Recommendation C) Discuss whether it would be desirable to invite Parties to update Inspection Checklist forms for its stations and facilities annually to help ensure that the most up-to-date data is available to inspection teams, even though the Inspection Checklists have a different primary aim and are not compulsory.*

(256) Some Parties pointed out that data contained in checklists could realistically change on a daily basis, and that it would be appropriate for checklists to instead be updated on a seasonal or annual basis. Parties reiterated that, while useful for inspections, checklists were not compulsory.

> *Recommendation D) Invite Consultative Parties to take into consideration the desirability that one or more inspection team members speaks the language of the staff of the inspected facilities or to work with a translator, in order to ensure good communication during an inspection.*

(257) The Meeting agreed that it was desirable to take the native language of the personnel of the inspected facilities into consideration in the planning of inspections. It noted that it could also be desirable to include in the inspection team a member who spoke an additional Treaty language. Though desirable, Parties highlighted that this requirement should not be compulsory.

> *Recommendation E) Encourage Consultative Parties to include tourism facilities in inspections and to consider whether the development of a specific Tourism/NGO Inspection Checklist would be desirable.*

(258) In response to enquiries about the need for an additional checklist, it was noted that checklists existed for the inspections of national operators and vessels, but not for non-governmental facilities. It was added that although there were few tourism facilities in Antarctica, none had been inspected to date. The Meeting encouraged Parties to consider tourism facilities in their inspections, but added that it was not necessary to have a specific Tourism/ NGO Inspection Checklist at this time.

> *Recommendation F) Encourage Consultative Parties to include other facilities and sites, such as vessels, aircrafts, HSMs, ASMAs and ASPAs, in inspections and to discuss the options discussed by the ICG to encourage this.*

(259) The Meeting endorsed this recommendation, noting that the inspection of these types of facilities and sites had been undertaken previously.

> *Recommendation G) Discuss the various options discussed in the ICG for encouraging joint inspections and involving Consultative Parties that are unable to organise inspections on their own, while acknowledging that inspections are a Treaty right and it is within the discretion of each Consultative Party whether to conduct inspections alone or with others.*

(260) The Meeting highlighted the benefit of joint inspections to the equitable distribution of the cost of inspections and for gaining access to remote areas. It was highlighted that for best results, the execution and planning of this activity needed to be well balanced between the inspecting teams.

> *Recommendation H) Discuss the option for the ATCM to designate observers and to carry out inspections under procedures to be established by the ATCM (Article 14(2)(b) of the Protocol).*

(261) The Meeting welcomed this reminder that the Environment Protocol allowed for inspections by observers to be made in accordance with Article VII of the Antarctic Treaty.

> *Recommendation I) Discuss how inspected Parties may wish to respond to findings of inspection teams.*

(262) Some Parties expressed the view that there should be greater emphasis placed on how the findings of inspection teams were followed up by those national operators whose facilities had been inspected. Others noted that

it was already common practice for inspecting and inspected parties to communicate and offer feedback throughout the course of the inspection process. It was also noted that the recommendations arising from inspections were advisory rather than mandatory but that these were nonetheless taken seriously by all Parties. It was also stated that in some cases inspection reports contained inaccurate information, and in those cases any clarification from the inspected party should be included in any compilation of data on the Secretariat website. In order to facilitate the planning stage of inspections, it was suggested that documentation relating to previous inspections could be compiled for easy access on the Secretariat website.

(263) Argentina introduced WP 43 *General Recommendations from the Joint Inspections Undertaken by Argentina and Chile under Article VII of the Antarctic Treaty and Article 14 of the Environmental Protocol*, jointly prepared with Chile. Argentina also referred to IP 126 *Report of the Joint Inspections' Program undertaken by Argentina and Chile under Article VII of the Antarctic Treaty and Article 14 of the Environmental Protocol*, also jointly prepared with Chile. On 20 January and 24 February 2017, observers from Argentina and Chile inspected two stations – Johann Gregor Mendel (the Czech Republic) and Rothera (the United Kingdom) – in the Antarctic Peninsula region. As a result of these inspections, and of previous inspection experiences, Argentina and Chile made a series of recommendations focused on availability of information, infrastructure, medicine, science and environment.

(264) Argentina thanked the Czech Republic and the United Kingdom for their warm welcome and cooperation during the inspections. It emphasised the benefits of conducting joint inspections, noting that they allowed for direct collaboration between the logistical assets of different nations. They also allowed for access to more remote, and therefore, less inspected stations. Argentina highlighted that it was important to ensure that joint inspection teams were balanced, both in terms of ensuring multidisciplinary expertise and a numeric balance between inspectors from participating countries. Argentina further noted the importance of observer appointment notification to be carried out through appropriate channels and that the notification mechanism through the Antarctic Treaty Secretariat, as established in Decision 7 (2013), is only complementary.

(265) Reiterating the comments made by Argentina, Chile added that this joint inspection had been the result of several years of preparation including the comprehensive training of inspectors. It also highlighted that inspections

could be complex and expensive to organise but proved to be valuable learning experiences, not only for those being inspected, but also for the National Antarctic Programmes involved in conducting inspections.

(266) The Meeting agreed to continue informal consultations on joint inspections during the intersessional period.

(267) Australia presented IP 30 *Australian Antarctic Treaty and Environmental Protocol inspections: December 2016*, which summarised the inspections of Amundsen-Scott South Pole Station (United States) and ASMA No. 5 (Amundsen-Scott South Pole Station, South Pole) by Australian observers. Australia thanked the United States for its warm welcome and for its cooperation during the eight-hour inspection, during which it was given access to all areas, personnel and materials requested. It noted the ambitious scientific programme being undertaken at Amundsen-Scott Station, as well as its strong culture of safety and environmental protection. Australia reported that Amundsen-Scott South Pole Station was operating in compliance with the provisions and objectives of the Protocol and that ASMA N° 5 was operating effectively and achieving the management objectives for which it was designated. Australia also noted that as part of its inspection of the ASMA it had visited the Antarctic Logistics and Expeditions (ALE) campsite and some observations on the visit were included in its inspection report in para 4.2.2.

(268) Australia reflected that inspections provided a valuable learning experience for the inspecting team's National Antarctic Programme. In addition to inspecting the Amundsen-Scott Station, the Australian inspection team also visited the United States McMurdo Station, the joint French-Italian Concordia Station and New Zealand's Scott Base, all of which allowed the observers to learn from the different approaches taken by each of these national operators. Australia thanked these countries for their warm hospitality. Australia also noted that it had experienced difficulty in finding previous inspection reports during its preparations for this inspection.

(269) The following papers were also submitted under this item:

- BP 7 *Measures taken on the recommendations by Inspection team at Arctowski Polish Antarctic Station in 2016/2017* (Poland).
- BP 14 *Follow-up to the Recommendations of the Inspection Teams at the Eco-Nelson Facility* (the Czech Republic).

Item 15: Science Issues, Science Cooperation and Facilitation

Science Cooperation and Facilitation

(270) Germany introduced WP 39 *Filchner Ice Shelf Project: Scientific and logistic cooperation between the Federal Republic of Germany and the United Kingdom*, prepared jointly with the United Kingdom. Recalling the 2017 SCAR Lecture by Professor Tim Naish, Germany highlighted that ice shelves are at risk and could provide a significant contribution to sea level rise. The paper summarised the lessons learned from the Filcher Ice Shelf project which aimed to investigate the near-future evolution of the Antarctic Ice Sheet in a warming world. Taking into account the cooperation between the two co-authors during the project, and recalling former recommendations on the matter by the ATCM, the two Parties endorsed a continuation and enhancement of scientific and logistic cooperation at bilateral or multilateral level between Antarctic Treaty Parties.

(271) Romania presented IP 6 *Antarctic cooperation between Romania and Korea 2015-2017*, which described the scientific cooperation between Romania and the Republic of Korea to study microbial communities and the effects and adaptations of organisms in extreme environments. It highlighted the importance of such research within the life sciences.

(272) Romania presented IP 172 *Cooperation of Romania with Australia, China, India and Russian Federation within ASMA Nº 6 Larsemann Hills, East Antarctica*. The paper provided a brief report on recent Romanian cooperation with Australia, China, India, and Russian Federation in the Larsemann Hills area, East Antarctica. It emphasised the willingness of Romania to continue this scientific, logistical and environmental cooperation with these Parties in the Management Group of ASMA 6 Larsemann Hills, East Antarctica.

(273) Romania presented IP 173 *Cooperation of Romania with Argentina in Antarctica - Romanian RONARE 2017 Expedition in cooperation with Argentina*. The paper provided a summary of events leading up to the establishment of the Romanian RONARE 2017 Expedition, as undertaken in cooperation with Argentina. Romania thanked Argentina for its support.

(274) The United States presented IP 13 *U.K./U.S. Research Initiative on Thwaites: The Future of Thwaites Glacier and its Contribution to Sea-level Rise*, prepared jointly with the United Kingdom. The paper reported on a joint NSF-NERC scientific programme established with the objective of substantially improving both decadal and longer-term (century-to-multi-

century) projections of ice loss and sea-level rise originating from Thwaites Glacier. The United States noted that considerable uncertainty remained in projections of global sea-level rise, and that reducing this uncertainty was an international priority that had been underlined in the SCAR "Horizon Scan 2020" and by the National Academies of Sciences, Engineering, and Medicine. The United States welcomed further international collaboration with other Parties in relation to this research area.

(275) Spain presented IP 21 *Absorbing Aerosols Monitoring over Remote Regions*, which described a project aimed to measure black carbon and other aerosol concentrations at different wavelengths in remote regions of the planet using light aircraft. Spain reported that the collected data was currently being analysed in detail, and several articles were being prepared to present findings. It also thanked several Parties for their support throughout the project.

(276) Portugal presented IP 24 *Future Challenges in Southern Ocean Ecology Research: another outcome of the 1ˢᵗ SCAR Horizon Scan*, jointly prepared with Belgium, Brazil, France, Germany, the Netherlands, the United Kingdom, the United States and SCAR. The paper reported on an output of the SCAR Antarctic and Southern Ocean Science Horizon Scan. It focused on high-interest research areas related specifically to Southern Ocean life and ecology. Portugal highlighted the finding that Southern Ocean ecological research would require a long-term commitment by Parties to conduct international and interdisciplinary research, aided by the development of technology, and should be conducted in cooperation with COMNAP, SCAR, and CCAMLR as appropriate. It further noted the relevance of linking science to policy, and the value of education and outreach activities.

(277) Australia presented IP 26 *Australian Antarctic Science Program: Highlights of the 2016/17 season*. This paper summarised the science programme undertaken under the Australian Antarctic Science Strategic Plan 2011-12 to 2020-21, across four Antarctic science themes. It highlighted the International Collaborative Exploration of the Cryosphere through Airborne Profiling (ICECAP II) project; the Antarctic Free Ocean Carbon Enrichment (AntFOCE) project; and the successful transportation of live krill to the Australian Antarctic Division's krill research aquarium. Australia also noted the value that international collaborators added to these efforts.

(278) Canada presented IP 29 *Preliminary overview of Canadian Antarctic Research Contributions (1997-2016)*, which provided an overview of the wide-ranging Canadian Antarctic research contributions over the last

20 years. Results were based on a preliminary analysis of bibliographic information. Canada stated that much of the research was conducted in collaboration with researchers from other Antarctic Treaty nations, and noted that Canadian researchers had made significant contributions to Antarctic research across a range of research themes.

(279) Colombia presented IP 57 *Austral summer 2016/17 activities, Antarctic Marine Mammals Research Program: with special attention to migratory cetaceans to Colombian waters and Antarctic pinnipeds*, which reported on a scientific programme intended to generate knowledge and scientific information on the marine mammal fauna of the Antarctic continent and its connection with South America.

(208) Colombia presented IP 59 *Colombia's contribution to the knowledge of biodiversity and ecosystems in some areas of the Antarctic Peninsula and Dronning Maud Land*. It reported on a variety of scientific projects that Colombia had undertaken in line with SCAR objectives, aimed at contributing to the knowledge of biodiversity and marine and coastal ecosystems in Antarctica.

(281) Malaysia presented IP 65 *Malaysia's Activities and Achievements in Antarctic Research and Diplomacy*, which reported on the progress of its activities and achievements in Antarctic research and diplomacy. It highlighted that Malaysian polar scientists continued to undertake research in Antarctica, and had been involved in collaborations with researchers from the British Antarctic Survey (BAS), the Korean Polar Research Institute (KOPRI), and the Argentine Antarctic Institute (IAA) over the previous year. It announced that Malaysia had ratified the Protocol, and that this came into force for Malaysia on 16 September 2016.

(282) Japan presented IP 67 *Japan's Antarctic Outreach Activities*, which reported on a workshop on outreach organised by the Ministry of the Environment of Japan in October 2016 to explain obligations and guidelines for environmental protection for environmental protection to travel agents based in Tokyo providing Antarctic tours.

(283) China presented IP 82 *Summary of the major research achievements of Chinese Arctic and Antarctic Environment Comprehensive Investigation & Assessment Program for the past five years since its implementation*. The paper gave a summary of the major research achievements of the Chinese Arctic and Antarctic Environment Comprehensive Investigation and Assessment Program for the past five years since its implementation

in 2011. China noted that it looked forward to future collaborative projects between China and other Parties.

(284) Turkey presented IP 90 *The experience of having SCAR photo exhibition in Turkey as of a new SCAR member*, which provided information on the SCAR photographic exhibition which was hosted in Turkey by the Ministry of Foreign Affairs and Istanbul Technical University Polar Research Centre in 2016, and thanked SCAR, COMNAP, and Mr David Walton for their assistance in bringing the exhibition to Turkey. It also announced that Turkey became an associate member of SCAR in August 2016.

(285) Turkey presented IP 92 *Turkey-Chile Scientific Collaboration in Antarctica.* The paper highlighted the collaboration between the Istanbul Technical University Polar Research Center and the Chilean Antarctic Institute. In the framework of the first Turkish Antarctic Expedition, a cooperation scheme was developed between the Chilean Antarctic Institute and the Istanbul Technical University Polar Research Center. Turkey noted that this arrangement may have been of interest to non-Consultative Parties that did not have a station, but that strived to undertake ongoing research in order to gain Consultative status.

(286) Turkey presented IP 93 *Turkey-Czech Republic Scientific Collaboration in Antarctica*, which outlined the context of the First Turkish Scientific Expedition to Antarctica, which Turkey took part in collaboration with the Czech Republic Antarctic Research Programme. Turkey noted that support such as that offered by the Czech Republic was particularly helpful for those Parties with no stations who sought to undertake research in Antarctica.

(287) The Meeting thanked the Parties who submitted papers, and noted that sharing infrastructure was an ideal option that allowed for those without their own station to conduct research in Antarctica. The Meeting further highlighted the importance and many examples of international cooperation across scientific activities.

(288) Chile presented IP 95 *Opening of Chile-Korea Antarctic Cooperation Center*, jointly prepared with the Republic of Korea. The paper introduced part of the activities in the first month of the operation of the "Chile-Korea Antarctic Cooperation Center" in Punta Arenas. It noted that the Centre contributed to developing cooperative projects and enhancing experts' mobility between the two countries. It also suggested that this bilateral collaboration provided an example of how links could be improved between National Programs outside Antarctic boundaries.

(289) Chile also presented IP 97 *Programa de Publicaciones Antárticas del INACH [INACH Antarctic Publications Program]*, which provided a summary of the Antarctic Publications Programme of the Chilean Antarctic Institute to inform the international Antarctic community. These included the biannual Antarctic Chilean Bulletin (Boletín Antártico Chileno), Iliaia - Advances in Chilean Antarctic Science and "Pasaporte Antártica".

(290) Belarus presented IP 98 *The experience in using a remote unmanned underwater vehicle in the Belarusian Antarctic Expedition in 2016-2017.* The paper described the use of a portable remote-controlled pilotless underwater vehicle in the Antarctic, which was used for the purpose of researching marine and freshwater flora and fauna during the Belarusian Antarctic Expedition in 2016-17. It commented that the expedition provided excellent practical experience in the use of this technology, which was highly versatile, mobile and compact. Belarus noted that it planned to share its experiences of the expedition at upcoming SCAR and COMNAP meetings.

(291) Finland presented IP 120 *Finland's international collaboration in the Antarctic field work with different stations and other actors.* The paper informed Parties that the Finnish research station Aboa had served since 1988 as the Finnish scientific centre in Antarctica, and had also supported international projects from various countries. It reported that international collaboration would be further enhanced during the Year of Polar Prediction from austral winter 2017 to austral winter 2019. Finland thanked its research partners for their excellent cooperation.

(292) Finland also presented IP 121 *Status Report 2017: Ongoing and Recently Ended Antarctic Research Funded by the Academy of Finland*, which identified the Academy of Finland as the main financier of Finnish Antarctic research projects. It noted that, in accordance with Finland's Antarctic Research Strategy (2014), the purpose of its Antarctic programme was to focus on interactive, multidisciplinary and high-impact research in order to promote the renewal and regeneration of science.

(293) Peru presented IP 134 *Actividades del Programa Nacional Antártico de Perú Período 2016-2017 [Activities of the Peruvian National Antarctic Programme during the period 2016/17]*, which reported on the main Antarctic activities of Peru's National Antarctic Programme, including outreach activities, participation in Antarctic Treaty System forums, training of young scientists and international cooperation. Peru thanked the institutions which assisted it in these training activities. It also noted that

it had signed a Memorandum of Understanding on Antarctic scientific and logistical cooperation with Colombia and Poland.

(294) COMNAP presented IP 136 *COMNAP Antarctic Station Catalogue Project,* which directly related to the COMNAP database (IP 64) and which supported the goal of information exchange and international collaboration. The project was on-going, and importantly, future catalogue information would be automatically updated online in the COMNAP GIS as National Antarctic Programmes updated their database information. COMNAP welcomed feedback from the ATCM on other data fields which might be useful to include in future revisions of the GIS or the database.

(295) Bulgaria presented IP 138 *Polar Scientific and Outreach Cooperation Between Bulgaria and Turkey,* jointly prepared with Turkey. It informed the Meeting of a Memorandum of Understanding between Bulgarian Antarctic Institute and Istanbul Technical University Polar Research Centre, Turkey, through which an exchange of scientists had been arranged between both programmes. Scholars from both states also visited each other and participated in Association of Polar Early Career Scientists (APECS) events.

(296) Peru presented IP 155 *Creando espacios de colaboración: Reunión de Administradores de Programas Antárticos Latinoamericanos [Creating spaces for collaboration: Meeting of Managers of Latin American Antarctic Programs],* prepared jointly with Argentina, Brazil, Chile, Ecuador and Uruguay. It reported that the co-authors participated annually in the Meeting of Administrators of Latin American Antarctic Programs (RAPAL), which was the forum for coordination in Latin America on scientific, logistical and environmental topics in Antarctic matters. Peru also noted that 27 RAPALs had taken place to date, facilitating coordination and cooperation among countries in the development of Antarctic operations. Outcomes of the meetings included an Antarctic accident prevention manual, a first aid manual (Recommendation XXI-12) and a guidelines manual for Antarctic Environmental Protection (Recommendation XXIII-2).

(297) Kazakhstan presented IP 170 *The Kazakh Geographical Society,* which referred to the three Antarctic and Arctic expeditions undertaken by the Kazakh Geographical Society since 2011. It noted that the Kazakh Geographical Society was representing Kazakhstan for the second time at the ATCM. It reported that, in conjunction with scientific, educational and other organisations, the Kazakh Geographic Society was researching the possibility of establishing an automatic scientific station in Antarctica.

(298) The following papers were also submitted under this item and taken as presented:

- IP 18 *Participación Venezolana en la Antártida 2017 [Venezuelan participation in Antarctica in 2017]* (Venezuela). It outlined the second stage of the bilateral project "Estudio de la reflectancia espectral en Península Fíldes, Isla Rey Jorge, Antártida marina", with the Chilean Antarctic Institute (INACH), the University of Santiago de Chile (USACH) the Venezuelan Institute of Science (IVIC). Venezuela thanked Chile for their collaboration and support during this project.

- IP 62 *IV Expedición Científica de Colombia a la Antártica Verano Austral 2017-2018 "Almirante Tono" [IV Colombian Antarctic expedition "Almirante Tono" in the austral summer 2017-18]* (Colombia). This paper reported on a planned Antarctic expedition for the season 2017/18, its scientific objectives and the international cooperation involved.

(299) The following papers were also submitted under this item:

- IP 174 *Report from Asian Forum for Polar Sciences to the ATCM XL* (China).

- BP 2 *Scientific and Science-related Cooperation with the Consultative Parties and the Wider Antarctic Community* (Republic of Korea).

- BP 6 *South African National Antarctic Program (SANAP): Science Highlights 2016/7* (South Africa).

- BP 11 *Monitoring of Antarctic flora – new Ukrainian-Turkish cooperation, a key for understanding biodiversity in the Argentine Islands, West Antarctica* (Ukraine and Turkey).

- BP 12 *Sightings of cetaceans during the First Joint Ukrainian-Turkish Antarctic Scientific Expedition 2016* (Ukraine and Turkey).

- BP 15 *Incidencia de factores bióticos y abióticos en la composición y abundancia de la comunidad fito planctónica y las migraciones zoo planctónicas en la Antártida, las islas Galápagos y el Ecuador continental [The effect of biotic and abiotic factors on the composition and abundance of phytoplankton communities and on zooplancton migration in Antartica, Galápagos Islands and mainland Ecuador]* (Ecuador).

- BP 16 *Estudio de la dinámica poblacional y adaptación al cambio climático de microorganismos acuáticos de los cuerpos de agua dulce* en la Isla Dee, Islas Shetland del Sur [Study of population dynamics and adaptation to climate change of aquatic microorganisms in fresh water bodies on Dee Island, South Shetland Islands] (Ecuador).

- BP 17 *Estudio comparativo de la diversidad liquénica antártica versus andina con fines de bioprospección y biomonitoreo [Comparative study of Antarctic versus Andean lichen diversity for bioprospecting and biomonitoring purposes]* (Ecuador).

- BP 18 *Inventario y caracterización preliminar de la biodiversidad de moluscos marinos en transeptos litorales de la estación antártica ecuatoriana Pedro Vicente Maldonado [Inventory and preliminary characterization of the marine molluscs biodiversity in coastal transepts of the Ecuadorian Antarctic station Pedro Vicente Maldonado]* (Ecuador).

- BP 19 *Tratamiento de lodos de la planta de aguas residuales de la Estación Científica Pedro Vicente Maldonado (2016-2017) [Mud treatment at the Pedro Vicente Maldonado station wastewater treatment plant]* (Ecuador).

- BP 21 *The Polish Programme on Polar Research and Strategy of Polish Polar Research – concept for years 2017-2027* (Poland).

Expeditions

(300) Colombia presented IP 58 *Colombian Antarctic scientific expeditions* and IP 62 *IV Colombian Antarctic Expedition "Almirante Tono" in the Austral summer 2017-2018*. These papers illustrated Colombia's continuing efforts in the realms of environmental protection and scientific investigation in Antarctica. Colombia highlighted that its fourth Antarctic expedition would take place from November 2017.

(301) Japan presented IP 85 *Japan's Antarctic Research Highlights 2016-17*. It described various research activities carried out by the Japanese Antarctic Research Expedition (JARE) in the Syowa Station area, including: a large-scale atmospheric radar at Syowa Station (PANSY) conducting the second Inter-hemispheric Coupling Study by Observations and Modelling (ICSOM2) for better forecasting future climate change; comprehensive observations on aerosol transportation using UAVs; and a joint geological survey in East Antarctica inviting geologists from Indonesia, Mongolia and Thailand, under the umbrella of the Asian Forum for Polar Sciences for reconstructing the past geological history of the Antarctic.

(302) Turkey presented IP 91 *Turkish Antarctic Expedition 2016-2017 (TAE - I) Experiences*, which outlined the very first national and independent Turkish Antarctic Expedition between 24 February and 4 April 2017. The expedition consisted of nine scientists from four different universities from around Turkey. It noted that researchers focused on four scientific fields: physical sciences, life sciences, geosciences, and humanities and social sciences.

(303) Ecuador presented IP 111 *XXI Expedición Científica Ecuatoriana a la Antártida (2016-2017) [XXI Scientific Ecuadorian Antarctic expedition (2016/17)]*, which described various projects pertaining to the development of Ecuador's Antarctic station "Pedro Vicente Maldonado". These included three logistical programmes as well as several scientific investigations focusing on climate and applied technologies. Ecuador thanked Spain and Chile for their support in these endeavours.

Climate

(304) SCAR presented IP 68 *Update on activities of the Southern Ocean Observing System (SOOS)*, on behalf of SOOS. It reminded Parties that SOOS was a joint initiative of SCAR and the Scientific Committee on Oceanic Research (SCOR), launched in 2011 with the mission to facilitate the collection and delivery of essential observations on dynamics and change of Southern Ocean systems. SCAR highlighted that SOOS was primarily funded by the Australian Research Council's Antarctic Gateway Partnership, and that this funding was due to end in mid-2018. It also reported that SOOS had developed a 5-Year Business Plan (draft available on request) that articulated the resources required to deliver the 5-Year Implementation Plan *(http://soos.aq/activities/implementation)*. Interested Parties were encouraged to contribute to this international initiative.

(305) The WMO emphasised the importance of the work conducted by SOOS, noting that it was endorsed by the Climate Variability and Predictability (CLIVAR) and Climate and Cryosphere (CliC) projects of the World Climate Research Programme (WCRP). WMO thanked Australia and Sweden for their continued financial support, noting that funding was only guaranteed for this initiative until mid-2018.

(306) The WMO presented IP 113 *The Global Cryosphere Watch and CroNet*, which noted that the Global Cryosphere Watch (GCW) is directly related to priorities 9 and 10 of the ATCM's Multi-year Strategic Work Plan. The WMO noted that it had started implementation of the GCW in 2015 to address

the demand for authoritative information on the state of the world's past, current and future cryosphere. It highlighted that when fully operational, GCW would provide wide access to cryosphere information, for example to support infrastructure design in cold climates, improved management and protection of terrestrial, coastal and marine ecosystems, and an improved understanding of environmental factors affecting human health.

(307) The WMO noted that it was working with partners to develop the GCW observing network including its core CryoNet. It encouraged Parties and other organisations to contribute to the GCW by considering if any of the observing stations they managed and operated in Antarctica could be proposed as CryoNet Sites or Stations, and informing GCW if they were aware of existing sources of cryospheric data for Antarctica that could contribute to GCW and be made discoverable through the GCW Data Portal.

(308) The WMO presented IP 114 *The Polar Space Task Group: Coordinating Space Data in the Antarctic Region.* It noted that the mandate of the Polar Space Task Group (PSTG) was to provide coordination across Space Agencies to facilitate acquisition and distribution of fundamental satellite datasets, and to contribute to, or support the development of, specific derived products for cryospheric, polar, and high-mountain scientific research and applications. It outlined several Antarctic Satellite Products, including those related to ice sheets, sea ice, and the atmosphere.

(309) WMO presented IP 116 *Southern Hemisphere Key Activities and Special Observing Periods during the Year of Polar Prediction.* The paper summarised key activities of the Year of Polar Prediction (YOPP), which aimed to improve environmental prediction capabilities for the Polar Regions and beyond. The WMO reported that key YOPP activities included: intense observation periods dedicated to routine measurements and investigations of physical phenomena; the development and improvement of numerical forecasting models; and the verification and enhancement of forecasting services. It reported that YOPP would implement Special Observing Periods (SOPs), and that the Southern Ocean SOP was planned for 16 November 2018 to 15 February 2019.

(310) The WMO presented IP 117 *The Antarctic Observing Network (AntON) to facilitate weather and climate information: an update*, prepared jointly with SCAR. This paper reported on the Antarctic Observing Network (AntON), a surface meteorological and upper air observing network operated by WMO in partnership with SCAR and contributing data to Numerical Weather Prediction, climate and other cryospheric applications in Antarctica. While

AntON gave visibility to its observing stations and to what observations were made, the WMO noted that it relied on WMO being made aware of any new installations, or sites that were no longer functioning. The co-authors encouraged Parties to notify AntON (*AntON@wmo.int*) if they were aware of any changes regarding stations or platforms in the Antarctic region where meteorological (and related e.g. snow depth) data were collected.

(311) Norway presented IP 154 *MADICE – Joint Initiative of Scientific Programme at CDML by India and Norway*, prepared jointly with India. This paper provided information on the joint Indian-Norwegian Mass Balance Dynamics and Climate of Central Dronning Maud Land (CDML) coast, East Antarctica (MADICE) project. MADICE encouraged collaborative work to investigate ice dynamics, current mass balance, millennial-long evaluation of the coastal region at Central Dronning Maud Land and past changes in atmospheric dynamics and sea-ice in the region using satellite remote sensing, geophysical field measurement and ice-cores. Norway reported that the programme would operate for four years starting in 2016 and ending in 2020, and included two joint field seasons in the austral summers of 2016-17 and 2017-18.

Item 15a: Future Antarctic Science Challenges

(312) The United Kingdom introduced WP 1 *Future Antarctic Science Challenges – A UK Perspective*, and noted that it was intended to achieve two main objectives: to encourage all Parties to submit information about their Antarctic science priorities over the next few years to enable them to identify synergies and new opportunities for collaborative working and logistical cooperation; and to encourage the ATCM to reflect on when and how it receives and commissions scientific advice. It also noted the utility of the ATCM considering whether it would be helpful to identify some key priorities over the coming few years, where specific scientific advice would be helpful, possibly drawing on the Multi-year Strategic Work Plan.

(313) The Meeting thanked the United Kingdom for its paper and reaffirmed the importance of scientific cooperation and collaboration among Treaty Parties. Several Parties reported that their National Antarctic Programmes had developed, or were in the process of developing, strategic scientific plans for their research work in Antarctica. Some Parties highlighted that there was a history within the ATS of sharing information about national Antarctic science plans and priorities, which had fostered successful synergies and

collaborations in the past. It also noted that cooperation opportunities often became clearer when Parties were able to identify the overlaps and gaps between each other's scientific programmes. There was broad agreement that this kind of information sharing on Antarctic science priorities, and collaboration on science programmes, should continue in the future.

(314) With respect to the question of how the ATCM received and commissioned scientific advice, some Parties expressed the view that SCAR had continued to demonstrate its capacity to deliver sound, evidence-based scientific advice to the CEP and ATCM. These Parties considered that the ATCM should be careful not to overlap with the work of SCAR. In response to these concerns, the United Kingdom clarified that its intention was not to duplicate or interrupt current processes but rather to encourage the ATCM to consider whether it was being clear enough about its scientific needs and whether it was being as open as possible to welcoming contributions from science. It was also noted that such a reflection on the ATCM science priorities would help to foster synergies, not only among Parties, but also between the ATCM and SCAR, as well as between the ATCM and external bodies.

(315) SCAR reported that it was in the process of developing new science research programmes and that this process would provide an opportunity for Parties, through their national adhering bodies, to influence the policy-relevant science that they may wish to see in their programmes.

(316) COMNAP reminded the Meeting of its Science Expert Group, which was tasked with screening SCAR and national Antarctic science programmes in order identify areas of logistic support that could be facilitated jointly. In order to facilitate ATCM discussions on this matter, COMNAP encouraged the ATCM to provide feedback as to what information might be required to assist with future science challenges discussions.

(317) CCAMLR reported that a two-day symposium, held during the SC-CAMLR meeting in October 2016, had considered how SC-CAMLR could prioritise its research in order to provide advice to the CAMLR Commission. It noted that the symposium had produced a clear five-year work plan for SC-CAMLR and its associated working groups. CCAMLR encouraged the ATCM to provide feedback as to what information might be required from the Science Expert Group to assist with future science challenges discussions.

(318) SCAR introduced WP 4 *Future Antarctic Science Challenges*, which summarised SCAR's Strategic Plan 2017-2022 and identified key future research challenges. SCAR encouraged the Parties to: draw on SCAR's

considerable efficacy in identifying emerging science priorities; developing, facilitating and coordinating international research in, from and about Antarctica and the Southern Ocean; enabling complex interdisciplinary research; distilling research outcomes into policy-ready evidence; growing research capacity; enhancing awareness of the value of research in, from and about Antarctica and the Southern Ocean; and facilitating interactions with other international science-based agreements. SCAR also encouraged Parties to continue to recognise the value of SCAR and its science advisory role in the Antarctic Treaty System, including by encouraging national adhering bodies and scientists to grow their support of and participation in SCAR's activities.

(319) COMNAP introduced WP 15 *The SCAR Antarctic Science Horizon Scan & the COMNAP Antarctic Roadmap Challenges projects*, prepared jointly with SCAR. The SCAR Antarctic and Southern Ocean Science Horizon Scan identified the 80 highest-priority scientific questions that researchers aspired to answer. This was followed by the COMNAP Antarctic Roadmap Challenges (ARC) project, which was a community effort to determine the steps necessary to answer those 80 critical questions. The ARC project reported on the technology, access, infrastructure, logistics, costs and levels of international collaboration that would be required.

(320) COMNAP and SCAR recommended that the ATCM: draw on the outcomes of these projects as a basis for its deliberations about Future Antarctic Science Challenges; make use of these outcomes to demonstrate and communicate the global importance of Antarctic research and its support to decision-makers and to the public; and consider that success would be dependent on national investment in science and science support technologies, as well as the availability of logistics and infrastructure.

(321) Parties thanked COMNAP and SCAR for their important work in identifying key research challenges shared by the Parties as well as condensing important research findings to sound policy advice. Some Parties noted that differences in the organisation and financing of National Antarctic Programmes may make it harder to coordinate research efforts. It was also noted that the ATCM needed to be clear in communicating shared research priorities both to the research community active in Antarctica and to national governments financing Antarctic research.

(322) Australia introduced WP 30 *International cooperation to advance shared Antarctic science objectives*, and recalled the Multi-year Strategic Work Plan priority to "share and discuss strategic science priorities, in order to identify

and pursue opportunities for collaboration as well as capacity building in science, particularly in relation to climate change". Australia commented that broader engagement by Parties would be necessary to advance this priority. It also noted that the inclusion of a specific agenda item on Future Antarctic Science Challenges presented a valuable opportunity for dedicated discussions of these matters during ATCM XL. Australia suggested that the Parties consider initiating intersessional work to build on the deliberations in ATCM XL, and to prepare a report to inform further discussions at ATCM XLI.

(323) Parties thanked Australia for the concrete proposal taking the discussion further. While noting the more general challenge of maintaining an effective interface between science and policy, some Parties referred to the work of SCAR and COMNAP in identifying key research challenges, and stated that it is up to the ATCM to derive the policy priorities based on this work.

(324) Several Parties highlighted the importance of continuing discussions about scientific cooperation and scientific priorities, and stressed that the discussions should focus on identifying areas of mutual scientific interest. They noted that such discussions would facilitate potential future collaboration and ensure that the ATCM remained informed regarding shared scientific priorities.

(325) The Meeting welcomed Australia's offer to lead an informal intersessional group to discuss the topic of Future Antarctic Science Challenges. Several Parties recognised the value of work done by SCAR and COMNAP, and highlighted the importance of finding the best ways to bring science into the ATCM Forum, rather than duplicating processes. The Meeting agreed to include Future Antarctic Science Challenges under Item 15 for future ATCMs and to amend the name of the item to "Science issues, future science challenges, scientific cooperation and facilitation".

(326) WMO confirmed that they would be happy to be involved in future science discussions.

(327) Recognising the value of the SCAR science lecture in addressing science challenges Parties supported a proposal to schedule the lecture early in the ATCM Plenary session rather than over lunch. SCAR confirmed that they would welcome suggestions for the topic of the lecture which would be considered by the SCAR Executive Committee.

(328) Finland presented IP 122 *The Future Challenges of Antarctic Research – The Finnish Perspective*, which presented the priorities and key future science questions of Finnish Antarctic research. Finland highlighted several

key research questions related to: the Antarctic ice sheet, ice shelves and the sea-level rise; meteorology, oceanography, and sea ice; climate forcing parameters, atmospheric composition and atmosphere-cryosphere-ocean interactions; biodiversity; mantle dynamics, large magma eruptions, and continental breakup; as well as human activities in the Antarctic. Finland noted that Antarctic research required well-coordinated international efforts in in-situ observations, in analyses of existing and new data, and in experiments applying a range of models.

(329) SCAR presented IP 161 *What does the United Nations Paris Climate Agreement mean for Antarctica?* The key issues identified in this paper and in BP 20 included: the relationship between the United Nations Framework Convention on Climate Change (UNFCCC) and the ATS, its agreements and SCAR; the consequences for Antarctica and the Southern Ocean of 1.5°C, 2°C, and more than 2°C of global warming based on the latest international science; as well as the poorly understood and potentially underestimated contribution of Antarctic ice loss to future global sea-level rise as a major uncertainty in policy-relevant climate science. SCAR also noted the importance of understanding the impacts and avoided impacts of achieving the goal of the Paris Climate Agreement, and noted it as a key Future Science Challenge identified by SCAR and COMNAP.

(330) The Russian Federation presented IP 141 *Russian-Swiss Antarctic Circumnavigation Expedition 2016-2017*, which described the Antarctic Circumnavigation Expedition carried out in 2016-2017 and organised through the Swiss Polar Institute. The paper noted that the expedition demonstrated the major role of international scientific and logistical cooperation in the study of the Antarctic and the sub-Antarctic area. It noted that many scientists from different countries had an opportunity to perform their studies outside the traditional regions of activity of National Antarctic Programmes. It also highlighted that the expedition contributed to the enhancement of scientific knowledge of the sub-Antarctic islands.

(331) The Russian Federation presented IP 142 *To question on the project of the international scientific drifting station "Weddell-2"*. The paper highlighted that 25 years had passed since the opening of the Russian-United States' drifting scientific station in the southwestern part of the Antarctic Weddell Sea. It informed the Meeting of the scientific achievements at the "Weddell-1" drifting station, and noted that in February 2017, during a meeting in St. Petersburg, participants had considered a proposal to repeat this experiment.

The Russian Federation invited all interested Parties to form an organising committee.

(332) The following paper was also submitted under this item:

- BP 20 *The SCAR Lecture: What does the United Nations Paris Climate Agreement mean for Antarctica?* (SCAR).

Item 16: Implications of Climate Change for Management of the Antarctic Treaty Area

(333) The United Kingdom presented IP 71 *Agreement by CCAMLR to establish time-limited Special Areas for Scientific Study in newly exposed marine areas following ice shelf retreat or collapse in the Antarctic Peninsula region*, prepared jointly with Belgium, Finland, France, Germany, Italy, Netherlands, Poland, Spain and Sweden. This paper described CCAMLR Conservation Measure CM 24-04, which provides a mechanism for the designation of Special Areas for Scientific Study, and the management measures that would apply in these areas. The paper also noted that the ATME on Climate Change (2010) recommended that "the CEP consider, and advise the ATCM accordingly, as to means by which automatic interim protection might be afforded to newly exposed areas, such as marine areas exposed through ice-shelf collapse" (Recommendation 10). The co-proponents of the paper invited the ATCM to take note of CCAMLR Conservation Measure CM 24-04, as summarised in the paper, as a positive contribution towards the delivery of this recommendation.

(334) SCAR presented IP 80 rev. 1 *Antarctic Climate Change and the Environment – 2017 Update*. SCAR highlighted the new format of this report which was designed to be accessible to a broad readership. This paper presented an update on the Antarctic Climate Change and the Environment Report. It presented perspectives on recent scientific advances, rather than a synthesis report through looking at changes in the Antarctic physical environment and changes in the Antarctic biological environment. SCAR highlighted studies showing evidence that: the Southern Ocean is warming much more rapidly and at greater depths than elsewhere in the world; non-native species invasions in the marine realm; and of Adélie penguin breeding declines being tied to decreases in sea ice.

(335) The United Kingdom thanked SCAR for continuing to provide an annual update on Antarctic Climate Change and the Environment. Noting that

climate change impacts in Antarctica, in particular ice shelf collapse and retreat, are of global significance, the United Kingdom encouraged SCAR to continue to provide these updates in a similarly clear and understandable format as IP 80 rev. 1.

(336) The WMO presented IP 118 *Progress Update on WMO Polar Regional Climate Centres.* Referencing successful developments for the Arctic, the WMO informed the Meeting that it is taking steps to develop an Antarctic Polar Regional Climate Centre network to provide centres of excellence that would operationally generate regional climate products, including climate monitoring and prediction, in support of regional and national climate activities. It highlighted that one important goal is to address the needs of National Antarctic Programmes for routine, targeted and authoritative climate information to support effective decisions and mitigate risks to people and the environment. It noted the relevance of this WMO initiative to the ATCM Multi-year Strategic Work Plan, particularly to priorities 9 and 10. It encouraged ATCM Consultative and non-Consultative Parties to assist WMO in connecting with their national meteorological services and National Antarctic Programmes; and invited Observers, Experts and other interested Parties to participate at the 2018 scoping workshop that it was planning to organise on the Antarctic Polar Regional Climate Centres (APRCC) network, and to provide their guidance and input to clarifying user requirements and priorities.

(337) ASOC presented IP 147 *Climate Change Report Card*, which provided an update on Antarctic climate science research findings and news headlines. ASOC noted that this paper had already been discussed in detail in the CEP. It briefly recommended that Parties and related bodies including SCAR and WMO continue to: develop a mechanism for ATCM reporting of Antarctic climate information to the broader public; develop precautionary or rapid-response management plans in place to address sudden climate-related events; and establish protected areas that can be used as reference areas to attribute changes to climate change with no or minimal interference from local and regional activities.

(338) The Secretariat presented SP 8 *Actions taken by the CEP and the ATCM on the ATME recommendations on climate change* (ATS), and asked for guidance on future preparations on this Secretariat Paper. The Secretariat reminded the Meeting that it had been updating the ATCM and the CEP on the status of the recommendations produced by the ATME on Climate Change (2010) since 2011. It called the Parties' attention to the CEP incorporating the

recommendations under its purview into the CEP's Climate Change Response Work Plan. While noting that recommendations 4-6 are not under the CEP's purview, it suggested there was little material to analyse. The Secretariat stated, that in its opinion, Recommendation 4 had been fulfilled.

(339) The Meeting thanked the Secretariat for its paper, and suggested that the Meeting accept the work of the CEP and allow it to continue its work.

(340) The following papers was also submitted and taken as presented under this agenda item:

- IP 152 rev. 1 *Tracking Antarctica - A WWF report on the state of Antarctica and the Southern Ocean* (ASOC).

Item 17: Tourism and Non-Governmental Activities in the Antarctic Treaty Area

Review of Tourism Policies

(341) The Secretariat presented SP 9 *Update on the current state of recommendations of the 2012 CEP Tourism Study*. Recalling a request from ATCM XXXIX to the Secretariat (ATCM XXXIX Final Report, para. 245), the paper analysed the state of the eight recommendations proposed by the CEP Tourism Study (CEP XV, 2012), and highlighted those matters that were still pending further consideration. It noted that most recommendations were pending further action by Parties or the CEP.

(342) In relation to the recommendations to establish a database of tourism activities managed by the ATCM (Recommendation 1 and 2), the Secretariat noted that, although the EIES provided most of the functionality expected from a database on tourism activities, it did not include a centralised repository of visited sites.

(343) Following a request made by New Zealand to expand on the technical steps to develop and implement a centralised tourism database, the Secretariat demonstrated to Parties that although some information was available through the Antarctic Secretariat website, the information had gaps, and there was no historical record of site visitation available.

(344) IAATO reported on its own experience in developing an electronic database on its member's activities and noted that it had specified a nomenclature for site names, and a method of using drop down menus to maintain coherence.

It also highlighted that it remained committed to informing the Meeting on any updates to its systems which may help inform the Secretariat's work.

(345) Argentina considered that having more detailed information available on tourist activities would be beneficial to all Parties. It pointed out that if the Meeting agreed on the need for a centralised tourism database, further consideration would be required on what precise information it should contain. It highlighted that, if that was the case, coordinates and site names should be standardised; and information regarding the availability of Site Guidelines should be included. It mentioned that the issue of different languages should also be considered.

(346) The United Kingdom noted that IAATO had a very comprehensive database, covering the activities of their members. While this did not include non-IAATO operators or information about visits to sites by national Antarctic Operators, it included a wealth of information from previous years, to give very good indications about overall visitation activity in Antarctica, including to specific sites. Whilst a comprehensive ATS database might be desirable, it would clearly be complicated and expensive, and the United Kingdom suggested that there was sufficient information already available on which to make progress on a range of tourism issues.

(347) The Meeting did not reach consensus on what steps the Secretariat should take in relation to a centralised depository of tourist sites and activities, and agreed that Parties should reflect on this issue through the following intersessional period and be prepared to address it at to ATCM XLI.

(348) New Zealand introduced WP 31 *A Strategic Approach to Environmentally Managed Tourism*. New Zealand recalled that ATCM XXXIX agreed to commence work to develop a common vision of Antarctic tourism (ATCM XXXIX - WP 28). It noted that WP 31 laid out a general framework that builds on the ATCM's previous work on tourism, including the framework provided by Resolution 7 (2009) *General Principles of Antarctic Tourism*, to present a strategic approach focussed on active and effective management of tourism activities by the Parties. While noting Resolution 7 (2009) remained relevant and represented the agreed common values of the ATCM as they relate to tourism, New Zealand stressed that a strategic approach to environmentally managed tourism required further operationalization of these principles.

(349) New Zealand noted that a strategic approach to environmentally managed tourism should be supported and guided by comprehensive monitoring and

useable data that is well-managed, standardised and able to be easily shared between Parties. It highlighted that a strategic approach must be agile and responsive, with regular reviews of existing Measures, implementation of existing Measures and recommendations and the development of new Measures in response to environmental monitoring data or analyses of operator generated post-visit reports. New Zealand reinforced that Antarctic tourism should be regulated by the Antarctic Treaty Parties. It also noted that the collective expertise of tourism operators would be beneficial in providing an operational lens on the development of new measures. WP 31 contained two recommendations: that the ATCM adopt its proposed strategic approach, and that it populate the Multi-year Strategic Work Plan to begin operationalising that strategic approach from ATCM XLI onwards.

(350) The Meeting thanked New Zealand for its paper, and reiterated its commitment to a strategic approach to tourism management. In relation to the proposed implementation of the General Principles of Antarctic Tourism, Parties exchanged a range of views.

(351) Argentina noted that as tourism had not grown drastically over the last decade, it considered there was no call for urgency to work on the development of a shared and common approach to tourism management. Other Parties stressed that tourism management required urgent consideration.

(352) China highlighted the importance of dealing with the tourism issue in the framework of the Antarctic Treaty System, and emphasised that actions in this regard should be taken based on solid data and scientific assessment.

(353) Several Parties preferred a strategic 'vision' to an 'approach' as this would provide more clarity as to where the Parties were headed and what the final outcome might be. Other Parties preferred a strategic approach, considering the strategic vision had been articulated through the General Principles in 2009. Several Parties emphasised the importance of considering tourism as a dynamic and permanently changing activity and highlighted the need for an equally dynamic and efficient response from the ATCM.

(354) Some Parties referred to the specific importance of developing a strategic approach on the issues of Antarctic tourism monitoring and data management. Canada noted that during its national permit issuing process it required a commitment from applicants to monitor activities and provide post-visit reports, but noted that a standardised monitoring approach would improve the usability and the opportunities to share data. Some Parties agreed that

a broader information exchange on existing permits for tourism and non-governmental organisations within national jurisdictions could be useful.

(355) The United Kingdom suggested that SCAR may be able to assist with further work relating to monitoring and systematic data collection of visited sites.

(356) SCAR informed the Meeting that, together with IAATO, it has commenced a two-year project to develop a systematic conservation plan (SCP) for the Antarctic Peninsula, particularly with a view to managing the long-term sustainability of Antarctic tourism (described in IP 166). SCAR explained that the SCP approach has the ability to show what the best spread of sites could be for different activities to arrive at an optimal solution that balances the different interests of stakeholders. SCAR also noted that there was currently a wealth of data and technologies that could be used for developing the SCP, such as data gathered via remote sensing.

(357) The Russian Federation expressed concern that many Measures relevant to tourism and non-governmental activities adopted during ATCMs were not yet in effect and stressed the need for a uniform approach by Parties to issues related to tourism and non-governmental activities. It also highlighted the need to share information regarding unauthorized activities taking place in Antarctica.

(358) Other points raised by Parties included: the need to consider the diversification in tourist activities; the need to consider additional regulations regarding permanent facilities for tourism; the importance of maintaining a dialogue with IAATO and the industry; and the importance of securing safe and environmentally friendly tourism in Antarctica. Several Parties considered that the Meeting should evaluate to what extent the General Principles had been progressed before reviewing Recommendation 7 (2009).

(359) ASOC thanked New Zealand for the paper and noted that it had followed the issue of Antarctic tourism with great interest for a number of years during which this industry had changed substantially. ASOC highlighted the dynamic nature of Antarctic tourism and stressed its opinion that it was time for the Parties to take greater action on the matter and that WP 31 provided a way forward. In this regard, ASOC emphasised its belief that Parties needed to undertake a 'whole spectrum' review of Antarctic tourism that included both IAATO and non IAATO operators and modalities, such as land based and fly-sail operations tourism as well as shipborne tourism. ASOC concluded by emphasising its view that it was important that tourism

developments in Antarctica not take place below the collective radar of the Parties.

(360) IAATO thanked New Zealand for the paper and encouraged the Parties to continue to work towards the development of a strategic approach to Antarctic tourism. IAATO highlighted Measure 15 (2009) and Resolution 7 (2009) as important and positive developments that had helped frame developments in the field and develop guidance material for tourist operators. It highlighted that ongoing collaboration was important, particularly given the status of the Parties as the competent authorities for the issuing of permits for tourism activities in the Antarctic Treaty Area. While noting that as an industry group it possessed the ability to respond to challenges quickly, IAATO reflected that its ultimate penalty for rule breakers was expulsion from the Association. It considered that the Parties and the ATCM had an important role to provide a robust legal framework to ensure that tourism in Antarctic remained both safe and environmentally responsible. IAATO thanked the Parties for their ongoing cooperation and committed themselves to continue to work with the Meeting.

(361) Taking these reflections into account, New Zealand, in consultation with several Parties, proposed to advance the General Principles on Antarctic Tourism (2009) and make them practical and operational through six tracks of action:

- Ensure that tourism activities remain under the governance of the Antarctic Treaty System.
- Implement a consistent approach to managing tourism activities that utilises the best available science, builds on the common understanding that these activities should have no more than a minor or transitory impact, and takes into consideration the precautionary approach.
- Be informed of the environmental impact of tourism activities in Antarctica through targeted systematic environmental monitoring and data collection, including through sharing information from EIAs.
- Ensure the ATCM takes a systematic, proactive and precautionary approach to assessing and managing sites used by visitors and applying appropriate management tools.
- Work with the tourism industry on the identification and resolution of issues arising from tourism activities.
- Implement and uphold any instruments relating to tourism activities in a timely manner.

(362) The Meeting thanked New Zealand for its considered efforts. Some Parties noted their concern that the six items identified raised a number of new issues that required further reflection and discussion before they could be endorsed by the ATCM. The Meeting welcomed further discussion on mechanisms to give effect to the General Principles on Antarctic Tourism (2009) at ATCM XLI.

(363) The Russian Federation introduced WP 22 *Non-governmental activity in the Antarctic - current reality, requiring legal regulation*, which described current issues with non-governmental activity in Antarctic, and the need for regulation. While noting that non-governmental organisations had been successfully cooperating with Parties in the Antarctic Treaty area for many years, it documented challenges that may arise when the organiser was an international group without a clear legal address, or when non-governmental activities involved the building or operation of stations. It reminded Parties that private property could be sold, leased, inherited, or mortgaged, and that the legal owner would be free to use the property to pursue goals that contravened the role of Antarctica in the world community. Highlighting the easier access to the Antarctic, and that new and non-traditional types of activity were emerging, the Russian Federation noted that the increase of risk associated with non-governmental activity presented a new challenge to the Antarctic Treaty System.

(364) The Russian Federation highlighted the "Antarctic Biennale" art event of March 2017, where it had refused to permit an activity, and the activity took place regardless using the ship's existing permit for tourism. It also reported on the erection of an Antarctic station using a private source of funds. The Russian Federation proposed that the ATCM establish a permanent ICG, hosted on the ATCM forum, where participants could exchange opinions, discuss the development of non-governmental activity in the Antarctic and prepare practical proposals to be considered at ATCM.

(365) Several Parties welcomed the identification of issues associated with involving a private partner in the establishment of a station. Parties noted that the nature of non-governmental activity in Antarctica was not static, that the number and types of activities were growing, and that effective regulation should be able to respond to new developments. They also highlighted the importance of safety as a prime concern. ASOC expressed the view that these developments should be considered in the strategic management of tourism.

(366) The Meeting thanked the Russian Federation for its helpful presentation and agreed to progress discussions on this topic through the existing Competent Authorities Sub-Forum.

(367) The Russian Federation introduced WP 23 *New challenges of Antarctic yachting to the Antarctic Treaty System*. The Russian Federation noted both the difficulty and interest in regulating yachts that travel to Antarctica. It gave as an example the Russian sailing yacht Peter I which repeatedly made unauthorised trips to the Antarctic in the 2016-17 season. It thanked Chile for intercepting the yacht and informing Russia that the yacht had been seen in the Antarctic without permitting documentation. It noted that CCAMLR has a "blacklist" of IUU fishing vessels that are unpermitted, and proposed that Parties establish a similar list for yachts that travel to the Antarctic without proper authorisation.

(368) Several Parties reiterated the importance of effective information exchange. They noted that such exchange could be conveyed through the EIES, the Competent Authorities Sub-Forum, or through formal diplomatic channels. They noted that the port state and flag state had different responsibilities, but that both needed to be kept informed. They further highlighted the importance of reporting sightings of unauthorised vessels in a timely fashion to allow for enforcement actions to be taken.

(369) While Parties and IAATO noted the importance of enforcement, some Parties considered that there could be legal issues with the implementation of a "Black List".

(370) South Africa informed the Meeting that it had during the 2016/7 Antarctic summer season dealt with a renowned South African adventure tourist who refused to follow due process, ignored their advice and decided to complete an unauthorised solo Antarctic crossing. South Africa further informed the Meeting that as a result thereof, it had listed the expedition in their 2016/7 pre-season report on the EIES as an activity that had been denied authorisation. They also noted that the same individual had also on a previous expedition in 2008 entered an ASPA and an HSM without any prior authorisation. This individual also confirmed that he would not require any assistance from any National Antarctic Programme but, in the end, did need help to be re-united with his yacht after it could not negotiate the pack ice to collect him. South Africa additionally notified the Meeting of a second planned unauthorised airborne expedition that they had convinced not to travel to Antarctica as the operator had not met the requirements for consideration of support. South Africa, following these recent experiences, questioned whether the simple

listing of an activity on the EIES as unauthorised was sufficient, and as a result, supported the Russian Federation's proposal of a blacklisting system.

(371) Argentina noted that while it encouraged the continuous exchange of information among Competent Authorities on unauthorised vessels, the fact that information is provided to the port state does not remove flag state responsibility. Argentina recalled that the port state did not have the necessary authority to prevent the departure of a foreign vessel to Antarctica if this vessel complied with international law. It also indicated that it did not see clearly what consequences a vessel would face if included in a "blacklist" of the kind suggested by WP 23. Argentina encouraged the Parties to continue exchanging information on these matters, both in their EIES as well as in the Competent Authorities Sub-Forum or through diplomatic channels.

(372) France reflected on its own experiences with an unauthorised Antarctic expedition that was routed close to Concordia Station and ended at Dumont D'Urville Station. France stated that it was not informed officially about the expedition at any stage, and highlighted the potential risks to safety posed by such unauthorised activities. It further noted that there were no legal consequences in this case. France concluded that all countries should have at their disposal tools to react and respond to such situations through their national legislation.

(373) IAATO reiterated that unauthorised activity is a significant concern to IAATO. It explained that IAATO had decided to accept the operator of the yacht "Peter I" as a member but membership was contingent on successful authorisation from the Russian Federation for subsequent Antarctic voyages. IAATO emphasised that the reason for this decision was that it was likely the operator would return to Antarctica, and had the potential to become a strong advocate for the Antarctic Treaty System and comply with the requirements of the Russian Federation in the future. IAATO further emphasised that it was willing to work with any previously unauthorised operators undertaking tourism related activities in the Antarctic to make sure they did reform and acquire the correct permitting documentation.

(374) The Meeting thanked the Russian Federation for its presentation of WP 23. It observed that legally complex situations arise when a vessel operator may be headquartered in one country, but the vessel is flagged to another. Parties expressed interest in pursuing a vessel "Black List" once legal implications had been discussed and possibly resolved. Noting that both WP 22 and WP 23 raised issues related to liability, safety, cooperation, regulation, and

environmental management responsibilities, many Parties expressed an interest in working together to continue discussions of such issues during the intersessional period and the Meeting agreed the appropriate method would be through the Competent Authorities Sub-Forum.

(375) New Zealand introduced WP 33 *Updating Resolution 4 (2004) on contingency planning, insurance and other matters for tourist and other non-governmental activities, to reflect the IMO Polar Code* which was prepared jointly with France and Norway. New Zealand recalled that Measure 4 (2004) *Insurance and Contingency Planning for Tourism and Other Non-governmental Activities in the Antarctic Treaty Area* was adopted in response to concerns about the potential impacts of tourist or other non-governmental activities on National Programmes and the safety of those involved in SAR operations. It recalled that Resolution 4 (2004) had been adopted to promote the objectives of Measure 4 (2004) until the Measure enters into force. It noted that the Polar Code came into Force on 1 January 2017. New Zealand highlighted the requirement under the Polar Code to carry out an assessment of the ship and its equipment, taking into consideration the anticipated range of operating and environmental conditions, hazards specifically listed in the introduction to the Polar Code, and any additional hazards identified and that this assessment formed the basis of a Polar Water Operational Manual (PWOM), which ships must carry on board. The paper proposed that Resolution 4 (2004) be replaced by a new, updated Resolution that notes the entry into force of the Polar Code and enables ship-based tourism operators to provide or draw on the contents of their PWOM to fulfil obligations under the new resolution. New Zealand explained that the aim of their proposal was to simplify documentation for operators, and not to provide an opportunity for Parties to second guess PWOM approvals issued by another Party. The co-authors recommended that the Meeting: note the entry into force of the Polar Code; adopt a new Resolution to update and replace Resolution 4 (2004); and encourage Consultative Parties that had not yet approved Measure 4 (2004) to do so as a matter of priority.

(376) IAATO thanked New Zealand for clarifying that ship operators may provide only the relevant sections of their PWOM, as it was likely that much of this information would be folded into the operators' larger Safety Management System, required under the IMO's International Safety Management (ISM) code, which included sensitive and strictly confidential information. IAATO further noted the importance of ensuring that it was explicit that the operators would not be required to amend any parts of the PWOM as part of gaining

their Antarctic authorisation, as the PWOM was a critical component that was part of the vessel's assessment by flag state and classification societies in order to gain their Polar Ship Certificate under the IMO's Polar Code.

(377) The Meeting thanked New Zealand, Norway, and France for their paper, and adopted Resolution 6 (2017) *Guidelines on Contingency Planning, insurance and other matters for tourist and other non-governmental activities in the Antarctic Treaty Area.*

(378) France presented IP 124 rev. 1 *Action taken following unauthorized presence of a French yacht in the Treaty Area during the 2015/2016 season,* which updated the Meeting on the administrative and judicial proceedings initiated by the unauthorized presence of a French flagged yacht in Antarctic waters during the 2015-16 season. France thanked the Parties that alerted it to the yacht's unauthorised presence in the Antarctic, allowing it to gather evidence and pursue penalties. France noted that in a decision made on 23 September 2016, the Prefect, High Administrator of the French Southern and Antarctic Lands, issued the leader of the "Ch'timagine III" expedition with a warning, and the yacht was prohibited from penetrating Antarctic waters for a period of five years (*ie* until 22 September 2021). France reiterated its intention, wherever possible and appropriate, to prosecute those who infringe on the provisions of the French Environment Code applicable to the Antarctic continent.

(379) The Meeting welcomed the report from France, and noted the timely exchange of information had allowed France to initiate legal action in this case.

(380) ASOC presented IP 150 *Options for Visitor Management in the Antarctic.* The paper explored options for visitor management in the Antarctic. ASOC noted that although the ATCM had undertaken extensive discussions on tourism in recent years, few decisions had been made about the management of activities. It suggested one way to deal with aspects of the matter was through the establishment of a system for visitor management. ASOC highlighted that it is the responsibility of the Antarctic Treaty Parties to make binding rules for tourism to preserve the environment, and that this is particularly relevant in the context of climate change. It noted that several Parties have developed successful visitor management frameworks domestically and suggested that these successful programmes which shared a number of common approaches could inform the development of an Antarctic visitor management framework. ASOC noted that the paper provided a sample ten year time line for developing such a framework, which would focus on developing strategic goals for the management of tourism.

(381) Australia welcomed ASOC's paper and noted that it is useful to consider examples and lessons from tourism management in other places where tourism occurs in natural areas. It considered that even though Antarctica is unique, the ATCM could learn from successful visitor management regimes in other natural areas.

(382) IAATO presented IP 167 *New IAATO Guidelines for Manned Submersibles and Remote Operated Vehicle Activities*. The paper introduced and presented the new *IAATO Guidelines for Submersibles and Remote Operated Vehicle Activities*. It noted that to date in the Antarctic, submersibles have only been used by a few operators. With recent improvements in submersible technology, IAATO anticipated there may be further submersible activity in the future. It also noted that the guidelines had been developed with encouragement from some Antarctic Treaty Parties and that IAATO stood ready to collaborate on the development of best practice guidelines for any new activities.

(383) The United Kingdom indicated that it had been encouraging IAATO to develop a range of guidelines to cover their activities. The United Kingdom thanked IAATO for presenting their new guidelines for marine submersibles and remote operated vehicles, which added to the suite guidelines they had already developed. The United Kingdom considered that these peer-reviewed industry guidelines were very helpful to promote consistency and to assist Competent Authorities consider best practice in a range of tourism activities.

Competent Authorities

(384) Norway presented IP 66 *Blue Ice Runway by Romnæsfjellet* which was prepared jointly with Belgium. Norway noted that IP 66 was written in response to the request of ATCM XXXIX to "conduct further inquiries on the development of the blue ice runway... and to report back to ATCM XL" (ATCM XXXIX Final Report, paragraph 282). Norway reported that they and Belgium had conducted inquires with the involved Parties and non-governmental operators and determined that: Antarctic Logistics Centre International (ALCI) is the operator in charge of construction and operation of the runway; there is no built infrastructure on the runway at present; there are containers, construction vehicles, building materials and other equipment present in the vicinity of the runway. There were concrete plans to establish infrastructure before an EIA was submitted to an appropriate authority, but that work has been suspended. It further explained that two separate EIA documents had now been submitted one for flight activity which had been

submitted and gained prior approval form the Russian Federation, and a second for the construction and operation of the runway, which the Russian Federation informed the Meeting that it had recently approved. Norway stressed that establishment of the runway in and of itself was not necessarily a problem, rather the problem was that work began before an EIA had been prepared and had been approved. Norway emphasised the importance of clarity, transparency, and following established procedures, particularly in projects that involve multiple Parties and private entities.

(385) The Russian Federation confirmed that, after a cumbersome bureaucratic processes, it had recently issued a national permit to cover the blue ice runway construction and operation activities. The Russian Federation stressed that it is responsible for the safety of flights in DROMLAN, and that because of this it was very interested in establishing a back-up runway in the area. It reported that it would monitor the work and runway operations closely and if there was any evidence of wrongdoing it would revoke the permit and notify the Antarctic Treaty Parties. The Russian Federation stated that it has not carried out any work on the preparation of the runway and had not delivered any equipment for its construction.

(386) Belgium informed the Meeting that its contribution to IP 66 consisted *inter alia* of observation of the vehicles and equipment staged at the runway from an aerial survey that was part of the Dutch-Belgium inspection of Princess Elisabeth and Romnoes. Belgium also reported that due to the proximity to its station, it was likely that station operations and science activities would be impacted by construction and operation of the new runway. Belgium emphasised that it would have preferred if the Russian authorities had consulted with the Belgian authorities during the planning and environmental review of the project. Belgium expressed its hope that the Russian Federation would make the approved EIA documents available through the EIA database. It also highlighted the utility of ongoing monitoring activities near stations to detect impacts caused by human activity, therefore offered to cooperate with the Russian Federation on such monitoring, and welcomed the Russian Federation's commitment to monitor activities near the runway.

(387) France welcomed the co-author's work in determining the identity of the operator and the confirmation that there were procedures in place for operating the runway in the future. France expressed surprise that this activity had been initiated without prior completion of an environmental impact assessment. France also requested if possible to have a report of the inspection carried out by Belgium and the Netherlands at the next ATCM.

(388) In response to a query from the United Kingdom, Russia confirmed that the permit it recently issued covered the construction and operation of the runway for the sole purpose of serving as a back-up runway for DROMLAN National Antarctic Programme use. It further explained, that if an operator were to use the runway for non-governmental flights, the Russian Federation would revoke that operator's permits.

(389) Norway noted that this runway project had not been formally discussed or approved by DROMLAN.

(390) The Meeting thanked Norway and Belgium for presenting this paper which covered a complex and delicate issue. The Meeting noted that the EIA process needs to be conducted prior to projects commencing, in accordance with the Environment Protocol, and that there should be good communication between stakeholder Parties during the review process. The Meeting further noted that such communication was particularly important when multiple Parties and private entities were involved or potentially impacted by the activity undergoing review.

(391) As a general note, it was noted that the Competent Authorities Sub-Forum established last year was an appropriate place to continue discussions on Competent Authorities issues. There was an exchange on technical aspects of the Sub-Forum. The Secretariat would welcome any feedback from members that might help to improve it.

(392) The Meeting agreed to task the Secretariat to create a discussion e-mail list for National Competent Authorities, with the same functionality as the one already in use for the CEP, which would enable designated contact points to immediately inform others of forum postings and any other relevant activity.

Trends and Patterns

(393) The United Kingdom introduced WP 19 *Data Collection and Reporting on Yachting Activity in Antarctica in 2016-17* which was prepared jointly with Argentina, Chile, and IAATO. This paper consolidated information from the United Kingdom, Argentina, Chile and IAATO relating to yachts sighted in Antarctica, or indicating an intention to travel to Antarctica, during the 2016-17 season. It noted that a total of 33 yachts were sighted in, or reported an intention to sail to, Antarctica during the 2016-17 season. This represented a slight decrease from 41 reported in 2015-16. It highlighted that half of these were IAATO members; 13 were non-IAATO members but had Party authorisation to travel to Antarctica; and five unauthorised vessels

were sighted. The United Kingdom highlighted the yacht outreach activities undertaken by IAATO, and noted that these proved to be beneficial in raising awareness of permitting requirements. It further stressed the importance of information sharing, particularly between competent authorities, and encouraged Parties to share information about yachts they have authorised through the EIES Pre-Season Information facility and via the post-visit reports, in line with Resolution 5 (2005).

(394) The Meeting thanked the co-proponents for their work in providing the report on yachting activity, and cited this as an important example of collaboration and information exchange between parties. It noted the need to better understand the current situation with regards to yachts in the Antarctic region, and welcomed the joint approach taken to the paper.

(395) In the case of unidentified or unverified yacht arrivals in Antarctica, Australia thanked the co-authors for bringing the issue to its attention and noted that it was currently conducting an investigation. The Netherlands reported that it understood the yacht "Geluk" was provided with a permit by another Consultative Party in the previous season, but that the vessel operator had sought authorisation in the Netherlands for the coming 2017/18 season, and that it was communicating with Germany with regards to the vessel "Sarah Vorwerk". The Netherlands announced that it was in the process of amending its own Act to ensure that Dutch nationals who organise an activity to Antarctica from another country would fall within the definition of "organiser," and that it had codified certain bylaws of IAATO in permit conditions to ensure the same legally enforceable standards apply to both IAATO and non IAATO members.

(396) IAATO welcomed the reports that Parties were taking actions to follow up on unauthorised yacht activity to the Antarctic. It noted that a variety of methods were being employed to both ensure consequences were enforced, and encourage yacht operators to follow proper authorisation procedures for potential future trips.

(397) The Meeting recalled the proposal by the Russian Federation to implement a black-list of non-governmental actors (WP 23) and observed that while it would be difficult to implement a blacklist, it is important to think about measures that non-flag states can take to prevent unauthorised voyages to Antarctica. The Meeting reaffirmed the need to keep working jointly on these complex issues through the Competent Authorities Sub-Forum and at ATCM XLI.

(398) Argentina presented IP 137 *Report on Antarctic Tourist Flows and Cruise Ships Operating in Ushuaia during the 2016/2017 Austral Summer Season.* The paper reported on the flows of passengers and vessels that visited Antarctica during the 2016/2017 austral summer season from the port of Ushuaia. It noted that such data has been collected annually since the 2008/09 season, and that the data set included information about the number of vessels departing from Ushuaia; the number of trips undertaken by each vessel; the numbers of passengers and crew on board; nationalities of those on board; and the movements of the ships. It reported that the number of passengers that had visited Antarctica from Ushuaia totalled 40,349 in the 2016/2017 austral summer season, a 3.86 per cent increase on the prior season. Argentina pointed out that such information was complimentary to data collected by other nations, and by organisations such as IAATO.

(399) IAATO noted that it could only report on the activities of its members, and that data collected by port authorities helped to build an overarching picture of tourism activities in the Antarctic region. IAATO further acknowledged and thanked Argentina for the effort put in to collect and collate such data.

(400) The Meeting thanked Argentina for its work, and for the ongoing collation of information relating to tourist flows and cruise operations in Ushuaia.

(401) Argentina presented IP 160 *El turismo marítimo antártico a través de Ushuaia desde sus inicios en 1958 hasta la actualidad [Ship-based tourism in Antarctica through Ushuaia since its beginning in 1958 until present]*, which provided a summary of maritime movements from Ushuaia since the first tourist trip, which took place in 1958, up until the 2016/17 season. Argentina noted that it had taken 30 years for the Antarctic tourism industry to consolidate, but that it had been a particularly important industry for Ushuaia since the early 1990s.

(402) The Meeting thanked Argentina for the background information on the emergence of the Antarctic tourism industry, and the insights into the patterns of tourist flows in Ushuaia.

(403) IAATO presented IP 163 rev. 1 *IAATO Overview of Antarctic Tourism: 2016-17 Season and Preliminary Estimates for 2017-18*, which reported on the overview of the Antarctic season in 2016-17 and the estimates of Antarctic tourism for the 2017-18 season. It highlighted that preliminary numbers in the 2016-17 season (44,367 persons) were slightly higher (by 500 visitors) than the forecast in ATCM XXXIX - IP 112 *IAATO Overview of Antarctic Tourism 2015-16 and Preliminary Estimates for 2016-17 Season,*

and represented a 15 per cent increase in visitor numbers. IAATO noted that the three principle nationalities of visitors were from the USA, China and Australia respectively. IAATO drew the Meeting's attention to Appendix 3, and reported that estimates for 2017-18 indicated that passenger numbers would continue to rise to approximately 46,385 individuals which exceeds the previous peak season. It reiterated that a wide range of data was available via the IAATO website.

(404) The Meeting thanked IAATO for its annual contributions outlining tourism activities in the Antarctic region. It recognised that such data allowed Antarctic Treaty Parties to have an overview of the tourism situation.

(405) Several Parties noted the importance of the role of industry in understanding Antarctic tourism, and pointed out the large amount of existing data relating to Antarctic tourism. Parties noted that this data comes from a range of sources, in a range of formats. Specifically, they identified that information pertaining to yachts had been presented systematically since 2010; that data relating to tourists departing from Ushuaia had been available since 2008; and that the continuity of data presented by IAATO was a valuable resource.

(406) Argentina suggested that a large suite of information was already available and that Parties could make better use of it. Other Parties suggested that interrogating existing data in light of specific questions could be sufficient to help Parties move towards management solutions.

(407) Several Parties suggested that at a future meeting the IAATO overview paper should be presented first, to set the scene for further discussions on the issue of tourism. They highlighted the value of the raw data on Antarctic tourism that was available via the IAATO website, and the strategic importance of considering area management as a priority as visitor numbers increase.

(408) ASOC thanked IAATO for IP 163 and expressed appreciation for the information provided by IAATO over the years, noting that this information underscored a trend towards tourism growth and the importance of taking a strategic approach to managing tourism, which had been discussed for a number of years.

(409) In response to a query regarding the cause of the increase in tourist numbers to Antarctica, IAATO explained that there were two main reasons for the increase. The first concerned the increase in air/cruise tours to Antarctica and tour operators' growing confidence in air/cruises as a reliable style of tourist operation. The second reason was that Antarctic tourist ships had increased in size and capacity since the 2007/08 season. IAATO considered

that it was difficult to forecast future trends, but IAATO believed that air/ cruise tours were not likely to continue growing at the current rate given physical constraints such as restricted access points, unpredictable weather windows and the limited capacity of the gravel runway at the Chilean Frei Station to accommodate larger aircraft.

(410) IAATO thanked Chile for allowing its operations manager to spend time at Frei Station to observe and facilitate air/cruise operations. IAATO also commented that the vessel size limits adopted by the ATCM in Measure 15 (2009) appeared to be influencing the Antarctic tourist market, and the size of new ships being built for the tourist fleet. IAATO viewed this as an indication that strategic tourism approaches were working.

(411) In response to queries about how tourism growth was being managed, IAATO highlighted its collaboration with SCAR (IP 166) which was intended to focus specifically on site management in order to ensure that Antarctic tourism was subject to the best management solutions, continued to cause no more than a minor or transitory impact, and was not in conflict with other activities in the Antarctic. IAATO also cited other programmes and initiatives intended to support these efforts, including the training and accreditation of field staff, the strengthening of its wilderness etiquette and monitoring schemes. IAATO also encouraged Parties to attend its annual meetings, noting that these meetings offered a valuable opportunity for exchange and interaction between IAATO members and Treaty Parties.

Sites

(412) Japan presented IP 67 *Japan's Antarctic Outreach Activities*, which reported on a workshop to Antarctic travel agencies held on 31 October 2016 that explained obligations when visiting Antarctica and guidelines for environment protection. The paper noted that the workshop utilised existing guidelines adopted by ATCM or issued by IAATO to describe precautions to be taken when visiting Antarctica, and when engaging in landings and wildlife viewing. Japan informed the Meeting that it requested that travel agents disseminate the presented information to their customers. Japan reported that about 700 Japanese tourists visited Antarctica annually. It encouraged interested Parties to visit the website of the Japanese Environmental Ministry to learn more about the outcomes of this workshop.

(413) The Meeting thanked Japan for sharing its experiences, and highlighted that it was important to keep the general public informed of the ATCM and its work.

(414) Argentina presented IP 131 *Areas of tourist interest in the Antarctic Peninsula and South Orkney Islands region. 2016/2017 austral summer season*, which reported on the distribution of tourist visits to the Antarctic Peninsula and South Orkney Islands region according to the voyages made by vessels during the 2016/17 summer season, operating through the port of Ushuaia. Argentina reported that during the 2016/17 summer season, a total of 225 voyages were made to the Antarctic Peninsula and South Orkney Islands region through the port of Ushuaia. The voyages were run by 33 vessels. Out of a total number of 77 visit sites distributed in 8 areas, 30 had Site Guidelines for Visitors, coinciding with the most frequently visited places, while 4 stations had internal guidelines to regulate visits.

(415) The Meeting thanked Argentina for this detailed breakdown of areas visited.

(416) SCAR presented IP 166 *Systematic Conservation Plan for the Antarctic Peninsula*, jointly prepared with IAATO. The paper reported on the recent agreement of SCAR and IAATO to undertake a collaborative effort to develop a Systematic Conservation Plan (SCP) for the Antarctic Peninsula. The plan will provide evidence to inform potential issues in landing site management, in line with IAATO's mission statement. The SCP would include: baseline data about the features to be conserved; consideration of the extent to which conservation targets were already met within the existing management regime; the development of different scenarios by setting explicit goals for conservation; and engaging with multiple stakeholders to test outcomes using different goal criteria. SCAR highlighted that SCP would allow for the inclusion of diverse expert opinion into decision-making about landing site management, and encouraged interested Parties to contact them or IAATO in relation to the further development of this plan.

(417) The Meeting thanked SCAR and IAATO for their initiative, and several Parties and ASOC expressed an interest in contributing to SCP. The Netherlands encouraged IAATO and SCAR to note the precautionary principle in the further development of this plan and expressed the view that in applying SCP to the Antarctic, the primacy of environmental protection as reflected in the Protocol and other ATS instruments should be respected.

(418) The following paper was also submitted under this agenda item and taken as presented:

- IP 164 Report on IAATO Operator Use of Antarctic Peninsula Landing Sites and ATCM Visitor Site Guidelines, 2016-17 Season (IAATO). The paper presented statistical data from the IAATO Operator Post Visit

Reports for the recently concluded 2016/17 season, and an overview of patterns of tourism for the Antarctic Peninsula region.

Item 18: Appointment of the Executive Secretary

(419) The Chair of the ATCM announced that, in accordance with the agreed procedures, Mr Albert Lluberas from Uruguay had been elected as the new Executive Secretary of the Antarctic Treaty and would take up his duties in 1 September 2017. The Meeting adopted Decision 6 (2017) *Appointment of the Executive Secretary*.

(420) The Meeting mandated the Chair to write to the Argentine Government to this effect, in accordance with Article 21 of the Headquarters Agreement for the Secretariat. A copy of this letter was attached to Decision 6 (2017).

(421) The Meeting congratulated Mr Lluberas for his appointment. The Meeting also thanked Dr Reinke for his eight years of service.

Item 19: Preparation of the 41ˢᵗ Meeting

a. Date and place

(422) The Meeting welcomed the kind invitation of the Government of Ecuador to host ATCM XLI in Quito, tentatively in June 2018.

(423) The Meeting noted the information from SCAR and COMNAP regarding the confirmed dates of their meetings (11ᵗʰ-27ᵗʰ June 2018).

(424) For future planning, the Meeting took note of the following likely timetable of upcoming ATCMs:

- 2019 The Czech Republic.
- 2020 Finland.

b. Invitation of International and Non-governmental Organisations

(425) In accordance with established practice, the Meeting agreed that the following organisations having scientific or technical interest in Antarctica should be invited to send experts to attend ATCM XLI: the ACAP Secretariat, ASOC, IPCC, IAATO, the International Civil Aviation Organization (ICAO), IHO, IMO, IOC, IOPC Funds, IGP&I Club, the International Union for

Conservation of Nature (IUCN), UNEP, UNFCCC, WMO and the World Tourism Organization (WTO).

c. Preparation of the Agenda for ATCM XLI

(426) The Meeting approved the Preliminary Agenda for ATCM XLI (see Appendix 1).

d. Organisation of ATCM XLI

(427) According to Rule II of the Rules of Procedures, the Meeting decided to propose the same Working Groups for ATCM XLI as for this Meeting. The Meeting agreed to appoint Ms Therese Johansen from Norway as Chair for Working Group 1 for 2018. It also agreed to appoint Professor Dame Jane Francis from the United Kingdom and Mr Máximo Gowland from Argentina and as co-Chairs for Working Group 2 in 2018.

e. The SCAR Lecture

(428) Taking into account the valuable series of lectures given by SCAR at previous ATCMs, the Meeting decided to invite SCAR to give another lecture on scientific issues relevant to ATCM XLI.

Item 20: Any Other Business

(429) With regard to the guidelines of the procedure to be followed with respect to Consultative Party status (Decision 2 [2017]), Venezuela indicated it will duly follow those guidelines and present the necessary documentation.

(430) Argentina referred to an event conducted on the margins of the ATCM regarding the promotion of the Swiss Polar Institute's Antarctic Circumpolar Navigation Expedition. It stated that all events conducted during, or on the margins of an ATCM, should attend adequately to any sensitive issues Consultative Parties may have. Furthermore, Argentina stated that Antarctic Treaty Secretariat personnel should be especially careful of participation in any such events. In this respect, Argentina noted that although it had approached the representative of Switzerland on the margins to avoid these sensitivities, brochures and the web page used by the Swiss Polar Institute contain erroneous references regarding the territory of the Argentine Republic. To be specific, regarding the legal-territorial condition of South

Georgias and South Sandwich Islands. Argentina rejects such representation of these islands as a separate entity of the Argentine National Territory. The Malvinas, South Georgias and South Sandwich Islands, and the surrounding maritime areas, are an integral part of the Argentine National Territory. As they are under illegal British occupation, they are the object of a sovereignty dispute between Argentina and the United Kingdom which has been so recognized by the United Nations, the Organization of the American States and numerous other organizations and international fora. Once again Argentina reaffirms its sovereignty over the Malvinas, South Georgias and South Sandwich Islands and the surrounding maritime areas.

(431) In response, the United Kingdom stated that it had no doubt about its sovereignty over the Falkland Islands, South Georgia & the South Sandwich Islands and their surrounding maritime areas, as is well known to all delegates.

(432) Argentina rejected the United Kingdom's intervention.

Item 21: Adoption of the Final Report

(433) The Meeting adopted the Final Report of the 40th Antarctic Treaty Consultative Meeting. The Chair of the Meeting, Mr Liu Zhenmin, made closing remarks.

Item 22: Close of the Meeting

(434) The Meeting was closed on Thursday, 1 June at 13:31.

2. CEP XX Report

Table of Contents

Report of the Twentieth Meeting of the Committee for Environmental Protection (CEP XX)

Beijing, China, May 22 – 26, 2017

(1)   Pursuant to Article 11 of the Protocol on Environmental Protection to the Antarctic Treaty, Representatives of the Parties to the Protocol (Argentina, Australia, Belarus, Belgium, Brazil, Bulgaria, Canada, Chile, China, the Czech Republic, Ecuador, Finland, France, Germany, Italy, Japan, Malaysia, Monaco, Netherlands, New Zealand, Norway, Peru, Poland, Portugal, Republic of Korea, Romania, the Russian Federation, South Africa, Spain, Sweden, Ukraine, the United Kingdom, the United States, Uruguay, and Venezuela) met in Beijing, China, from 22 to 26 May 2017, for the purpose of providing advice and formulating recommendations to the Parties in connection with the implementation of the Protocol.

(2)   In accordance with Rule 4 of the CEP Rules of Procedure, the meeting was also attended by representatives of the following Observers:

- Contracting Parties to the Antarctic Treaty which are not a Party to the Protocol: Colombia, Switzerland, Turkey, and the Slovak Republic;
- the Scientific Committee on Antarctic Research (SCAR), the Scientific Committee for the Conservation of Antarctic Marine Living Resources (SC-CAMLR), and the Council of Managers of National Antarctic Programs (COMNAP); and
- scientific, environmental and technical organisations: the Antarctic and Southern Ocean Coalition (ASOC), the International Association of Antarctica Tour Operators (IAATO), and the World Meteorological Organization (WMO).

Item 1: Opening of the Meeting

(3)   The CEP Chair, Mr Ewan McIvor (Australia), opened the meeting on Monday 22 May 2017 and thanked China for organising and hosting the meeting in Beijing.

(4)   The Chair recalled the 25th anniversary of the adoption of the Protocol on 4 October 2016, and noted that the related publication endorsed at CEP

XIX, *25 Years of the Protocol on Environmental Protection to the Antarctic Treaty*, had been released on that date. He also noted that many Parties and organisations had celebrated and promoted this significant milestone in international efforts to protect Antarctica.

(5) Highlighting that this was the 20th meeting of the CEP, the Chair noted that the Committee would continue to play an important role in supporting the Parties, which had reaffirmed their 'strong and unwavering commitment to the objectives and purposes of the Antarctic Treaty and its Environmental Protocol' in the Santiago Declaration on the 25th Anniversary of the signing of the Protocol on Environmental Protection to the Antarctic Treaty.

(6) The Chair acknowledged the work of the many current and past representatives of CEP Members and Observers. On behalf of the Committee, he presented awards in special recognition of those colleagues attending CEP XX who had maintained a close association with the Committee since its first meeting in Tromsø, Norway, in 1998: José Maria Acero (Secretariat, Argentina); Neil Gilbert (New Zealand, United Kingdom); Valerii Lukin (Russian Federation); Birgit Njåstad (Norway); Christo Pimpirev (Bulgaria); Ricardo Roura (ASOC); David Walton (Secretariat, SCAR) and Victoria Wheatley (United States, IAATO).

(7) The Committee joined the Chair in thanking and congratulating those long-serving colleagues, and other current and past representatives, for their contributions to the work of the Committee.

(8) On behalf of the Committee, the Chair welcomed Malaysia as a new Member, following the entry into force of the Protocol for Malaysia on 16 September 2016. The Chair noted that the CEP now comprised 38 Members.

(9) The Chair also noted the advice presented in the Depositary's report that the Protocol would enter into force for Switzerland on 1 June 2017, and Turkey's advice in IP 94 *Ratification of Protocol on Environmental Protection to the Antarctic Treaty by Turkey* that it had ratified the Protocol.

(10) The Committee joined the Chair in welcoming Malaysia as a new Member, and looked forward to welcoming Switzerland and Turkey as Members in the near future.

(11) The Chair summarised the work undertaken during the intersessional period (IP 157 *Committee for Environmental Protection (CEP): Summary of Activities during the 2016/17 intersessional period*). He noted that excellent

progress had been made on the actions arising from CEP XIX, and thanked all Members and Observers involved in this significant body of work.

Item 2: Adoption of the Agenda

(12) The Committee adopted the following agenda and confirmed the allocation of 30 Working Papers (WP), 67 Information Papers (IP), 5 Secretariat Papers (SP) and 6 Background Papers (BP) to the agenda items:

1. Opening of the Meeting
2. Adoption of the Agenda
3. Strategic Discussions on the Future Work of the CEP
4. Operation of the CEP
5. Cooperation with other Organisations
6. Repair and Remediation of Environment Damage
7. Climate Change Implications for the Environment

    a. Strategic Approach

    b. Implementation and Review of the Climate Change Response Work Programme

8. Environmental Impact Assessment (EIA)

    a. Draft Comprehensive Environmental Evaluations

    b. Other EIA Matters

9. Area Protection and Management Plans

    a. Management Plans

    b. Historic Sites and Monuments

    c. Site Guidelines

    d. Marine Spatial Protection and Management

    e. Other Annex V Matters

10. Conservation of Antarctic Flora and Fauna

    a. Quarantine and Non-native Species

    b. Specially Protected Species

    c. Other Annex II Matters

11. Environmental Monitoring and Reporting
12. Inspection Reports

13. General Matters

14. Election of Officers

15. Preparation for Next Meeting

16. Adoption of the Report

17. Closing of the Meeting

Item 3: Strategic Discussions on the Future Work of the CEP

(13) No papers were submitted under this agenda item.

CEP Five-Year Work Plan

(14) The Committee briefly considered the Five-Year Work Plan, adopted at CEP XIX (SP 2), at the end of each agenda item.

(15) The Committee revised and updated its Five-Year Work Plan (Appendix 1). The major changes reflected actions agreed during the Meeting, including: the proposed establishment of a Subsidiary Group on Climate Change Response; intersessional contact groups (ICG) on reviewing the Antarctic Clean Up Manual and developing guidelines for the environmental aspects of Unmanned Aerial Vehicles (UAV) / Remotely Piloted Aircraft Systems (RPAS); and further work on Environmental Impact Assessment (EIA) matters.

Item 4: Operation of the CEP

(16) New Zealand introduced WP 25 *Antarctic Environments Portal*, jointly prepared with Australia, Japan, Norway, the United States, and SCAR, and referred to IP 14 *Antarctic Environments Portal: Content Management Plan*. WP 25 provided an update on the operation of the Antarctic Environments Portal and highlighted developments since CEP XIX. New Zealand noted in particular recent progress in the long-term management and operation of the Portal, including the agreement by the 2016 SCAR Delegates Meeting that the SCAR Secretariat would explore cost-neutral options for SCAR to take over operational management of the Portal after 2018. A Content Management Plan for the Portal had been prepared (IP 14), with the aims of both providing a structured approach to the development of content and facilitating a dialogue with the CEP regarding topics for publication. The co-authors recommended the Committee consider opportunities for supporting SCAR's future management of the Portal, and review and provide comments and suggestions on the Content Management Plan.

(17)   The Committee expressed its continued support for the Portal as an important source of up-to-date scientific information integral to the work of the CEP, and thanked the co-authors of the papers for their continued efforts in the management and development of the Portal.

(18)   The Committee supported the decision taken by SCAR, in principle, to assume the management of the Portal after 2018. It agreed to consider further opportunities to support SCAR's management of the Portal.

(19)   The Committee welcomed France's contribution for the translation of Portal content into French as an example of support in kind, and welcomed the offer made by the Netherlands during the meeting to financially support the Portal in the future. The Committee encouraged Members to consider further opportunities to support the management of the Portal and to consult with SCAR over this.

(20)   The Committee expressed general support for the Content Management Plan, and recalled that the objectives of the Portal were to ensure that all content presented through the Portal was neutral, objective, based on peer-reviewed science, and relevant to priorities identified by the Committee. In that regard, the Committee noted the important role played by the Portal's editorial committee. The Committee also welcomed SCAR's advice that in addition to its close involvement in the development of Portal content, it would continue to provide scientific advice to the CEP through papers submitted to annual meetings.

(21)   The Committee recognised the importance of keeping the Portal content up to date through review and revision as necessary. It noted that the editorial arrangements for the Portal included periodic revision and updating of existing content, and welcomed further opportunities to consider the Content Management Plan at future CEP meetings. Regarding the issues identified in the current Content Management Plan, some Members noted their intention to encourage their scientists to participate in the preparation of summaries and it was suggested that plastics and ocean acidification were two issues of particular interest.

(22)   The CEP Chair introduced WP 34 *Supporting the work of the Committee for Environmental Protection (CEP): A paper by the CEP Chair*. In conjunction with the 20th meeting of the CEP, the paper sought to initiate a discussion among the Members about ways to ensure the Committee remained well-placed to support the Parties' efforts to comprehensively protect the Antarctic environment. It noted that the CEP, over the years, had continually developed

ways to enhance its effectiveness. It additionally highlighted the increasing importance of the CEP's work in light of the ongoing, new, and emerging environmental challenges facing Antarctica. In light of these objectives and trends, the CEP Chair invited Members to consider: whether a list of CEP 'science needs' (such as that presented in Attachment A to WP 34) could help promote and support science to better address and understand the environmental challenges facing Antarctica; and whether access to modest funding could help the Committee better deliver high quality and timely advice and recommendations on priority issues to the ATCM.

(23) Welcoming the CEP Chair's paper, the Committee agreed that it was important to continually consider ways to ensure that the CEP remained well-placed to provide high quality advice and recommendations to the Parties. Regarding the first issue raised in WP 34, Members recognised the importance to the Committee that its work retained close links to science. It agreed that a list of CEP science needs would help with promoting and supporting science to better understand and address the environmental challenges facing Antarctica, support collaboration and prioritisation of science, and help to ensure that the CEP would receive relevant science input. The Committee also agreed that such a list could be useful for highlighting to the ATCM environmental research and monitoring needs, in keeping with its function under Article 12(k) of the Protocol, and for informing Parties' ongoing discussions on Antarctic science priorities. It was noted that further consideration could be given to presenting the list in a format that would be suitable for informing ATCM discussions, and keeping it updated through annual review. Some Members noted that they were already using the list presented in WP 34 for discussions about their national Antarctic science priorities. SCAR and WMO noted their continuing efforts to conduct and support research relevant to the scientific needs of the CEP. SCAR indicated that it would take the Committee's discussions into consideration in planning its future science programmes.

(24) The Committee agreed to review the list of science needs contained in WP 34 at CEP XXI before passing it to the ATCM. It agreed that the review could consider opportunities to identify new and emerging science needs, to link the list to the CEP's Five-Year Work Plan, and to explore possible links to the Content Management Plan of the Environments Portal.

(25) The Committee also acknowledged the need for additional mechanisms to help the CEP address its increasing workload, and agreed that its work could be strengthened by access to modest financial support, particularly where

it might improve or expedite provision of advice to the ATCM. It noted, however, that it would be necessary to give further consideration to possible mechanisms for obtaining and utilising any such funding, taking into account that the source of the funds would ensure that the Committee's independence was maintained. In the discussion Members suggested also giving thought to opportunities for in-kind support and also the possibility of establishing special funds, such as those used by SC-CAMLR. While Members noted the importance of considering additional ways of involving experts in the CEP's work, a reservation was raised on whether it would be an appropriate role for the Committee to support a fellowship programme.

(26)   The Committee welcomed the Chair's offer to undertake further work during the intersessional period, in consultation with the Secretariat and interested Members, to further develop the concept of a mechanism for the CEP to obtain modest funding to support its work. The Committee looked forward to further discussions on this matter at CEP XXI.

CEP advice to the ATCM on supporting the work of the CEP

(27)   The Committee considered ways to ensure that the CEP could remain well placed to deliver high quality environmental advice and recommendations to the Parties, and agreed to advise the ATCM that:

- It had agreed that a list of science needs would help with promoting and supporting science to better understand and address the environmental challenges facing Antarctica, which would be useful for its work, as well as the ATCM's discussions on Antarctic science priorities. In this regard, the Committee would review the list of CEP science needs contained in WP 34 at CEP XXI.
- It had acknowledged the need for additional mechanisms to help the CEP address its increasing workload, and agreed that its work could be strengthened by access to modest financial support. In this regard, the Committee had welcomed the offer by the CEP Chair to undertake further work during the intersessional period, in consultation with the Secretariat and interested Members, to consider options for obtaining and managing possible CEP funding.

(28)   Turkey presented IP 94 *Ratification of Protocol on Environmental Protection to the Antarctic Treaty by Turkey*, to inform the Committee of Turkey's impending ratification of the Environment Protocol in 2017. During the meeting Turkey advised the Committee that on 24 May 2017 it had completed

its ratification process of the Protocol together with all six annexes. The Protocol and its six annexes had been published in Turkey's Official Gazette issue number 30075 and had become part of the Turkish legislation. Turkey noted that it soon hoped to become a full member of SCAR, and that it was interested to develop cooperation with other Parties.

(29) The Committee welcomed Turkey's advice that it had acceded to the Environment Protocol and that ratification would be finalised shortly. The Committee looked forward to welcoming Turkey as a member of the Committee.

Item 5: Cooperation with other Organisations

(30) COMNAP presented IP 9 *Annual Report for 2016/2017 of the Council of Managers of National Antarctic Programs (COMNAP)*, and emphasised a number of highlights from the period since CEP XIX, including the review of its Antarctic Unmanned Aerial Systems (UAS) Operator's Handbook (IP 77), a revision of the COMNAP database, and progress in updating the COMNAP Station Catalogue. COMNAP reminded the Members of its Antarctic Research Fellowship for early career researchers, technicians and engineers, and encouraged Members to publicise the Fellowship to potential applicants.

(31) SCAR presented IP 35 *The Scientific Committee on Antarctic Research Annual Report 2016-2017 to Antarctic Treaty Consultative Meeting XL* which provided a synopsis of SCAR's key outcomes and activities for the period, including those of its three science groups and six research programmes. It noted that SCAR had welcomed Austria, Colombia, Thailand and Turkey as new associate members from 2016. SCAR also drew attention to the new format of its Annual Report which was intended to make the report more accessible to a general audience.

(32) The United Kingdom presented IP 50 *Report by the CEP Observer to the XXXIV SCAR Delegates Meeting,* which highlighted aspects of the XXXIV SCAR Delegates Meeting of particular relevance to the work of the CEP. These included SCAR's continued commitment to playing an active role in supporting the Antarctic Environments Portal, and to providing updates to the Antarctic Climate Change and the Environment report. It also noted SCAR would continue to provide reports and updates on matters relevant to the work of the CEP.

(33) The Committee thanked COMNAP, SCAR and the United Kingdom for their reports. The Committee also congratulated Prof. Steven Chown for his

election as President of SCAR, and acknowledged Prof. Jeronimo Lopez-Martinez for his achievements while SCAR President.

(34) CCAMLR presented IP 53 *Report by the SC-CAMLR Observer to the Twentieth Meeting of the Committee for Environmental Protection.* The paper reported on five issues of common interest to the CEP and Scientific Committee of the Commission for the Conservation of Antarctic Marine Living Resources (SC-CAMLR): climate change and the Antarctic marine environment; biodiversity and non-native species in the Antarctic marine environment; Antarctic species requiring special protection; spatial marine management and protected areas; and ecosystem and environmental monitoring. It also noted that SC-CAMLR and its working groups had considered the report of the 2016 Joint CEP / SC-CAMLR Workshop on Climate Change and Monitoring and had endorsed the recommendations contained within the workshop report.

(35) CCAMLR also reported that a Scientific Committee Symposium had been held on 13-14 October 2016, where SC-CAMLR had agreed that a work plan with short, medium, and long-term objectives was required, and that the CEP Five-Year Work Plan would form a useful template for its development. Further, SC-CAMLR had noted the need for broader engagement with the global scientific community, and was considering joint workshops and integration of medium to long-term work priorities with organisations such as the Scientific Committee on Oceanic Research and SCAR. CCAMLR also highlighted the agreement to establish the Ross Sea Region Marine Protected Area (MPA) in Conservation Measure 91-05 and that a three day Ross Sea Region MPA Research and Monitoring Plan Workshop was held in Italy in late April 2017.

(36) The Committee thanked the SC-CAMLR observer for the report, and welcomed the Scientific Committee's endorsement of the recommendations arising from the 2016 joint CEP / SC-CAMLR workshop. The Committee looked forward to further engagement with SC-CAMLR both in this area and in other areas of mutual interest to ensure a coordinated approach to shared priorities.

(37) The CEP Chair recalled that at CEP XIX the Committee had endorsed the recommendations arising from the Joint CEP / SC-CAMLR Workshop on Climate Change and Monitoring held in Punta Arenas, Chile, in May 2016, and had recognised the importance of monitoring progress on implementation of these recommendations. He further noted that ATCM XL would consider

the outcomes of the joint workshop, and invited the Committee to consider providing updated advice to the ATCM on this matter.

CEP advice to the ATCM on outcomes from the 2016 Joint CEP/SC-CAMLR Workshop on Climate Change and Monitoring

(38)   The Committee recalled its advice to ATCM XXXIX that it had endorsed the recommendations arising from the Joint CEP / SC-CAMLR Workshop on Climate Change and Monitoring held in Punta Arenas, Chile, in May 2016, and had recognised the importance of monitoring progress on implementation of these recommendations. Noting that the ATCM Multi-Year Strategic Work Plan included an action for ATCM XL to consider the outcomes of the joint workshop, the Committee agreed to advise the ATCM that:

- SC-CAMLR had also welcomed the workshop report and endorsed the recommendations arising;
- actions by the CEP to advance the workshop recommendations were largely being addressed in conjunction with its ongoing work to implement the Climate Change Response Work Program; and
- with reference to workshop Recommendation 16, it had agreed to update its Five-Year Work Plan to include an action on planning for a future joint workshop, including a review of the implementation of the recommendations from the 2016 workshop.

(39)   The WMO presented IP 112 *WMO Annual Report 2016-2017* and IP 116 *Southern Hemisphere Key Activities and Special Observing Periods during the Year of Polar Prediction*. These papers highlighted a number of WMO initiatives of potential interest to the CEP, and in particular provided an update on the Year of Polar Prediction (YOPP), and the planned development of the Antarctic Polar Regional Climate Centre (PRCC) Network. A special Observing Period for YOPP was planned in Antarctica from 16 Nov 2018 to 15 Feb 2019, which would act as a focus to enhance routine observations in an attempt to close the gaps in the observing system over an extended period of time. The success of YOPP would depend on the enthusiasm and support of Parties.

(40)   The Committee thanked the WMO and reiterated its previous expression of support for the Year of Polar Prediction, and looked forward to further reports from the WMO to inform its discussions on the implications of climate change for the Antarctic environment.

Nomination of CEP Representatives to other organisations

(41) The Committee nominated:

- Dr Yves Frenot (France) to represent the CEP at the 29th COMNAP Annual General Meeting, to be held in Brno, Czech Republic, from 29 July to 2 August 2017; and

- Dr Polly Penhale (United States) to represent the CEP at the 36th meeting of SC-CAMLR, to be held in Hobart, Australia, from 16-20 October 2017.

Item 6: Repair and Remediation of Environment Damage

(42) Australia introduced WP 28 *Review of the Antarctic Clean-Up Manual*, jointly prepared with the United Kingdom. In keeping with an action identified in the CEP Five-Year Work Plan, the co-authors proposed the establishment of an ICG to review and revise the Antarctic Clean-Up Manual. This would provide an opportunity to consider this topic collectively and systematically.

(43) The Committee thanked Australia and the United Kingdom for their paper and agreed on the importance of keeping the Clean-Up Manual up to date to reflect the current state of knowledge.

(44) The Committee agreed to establish an ICG to review the Antarctic Clean-Up Manual, with the following terms of reference:

1. Collate information on developments and advances in matters relevant to the clean-up of Antarctic past waste disposal sites, past work sites, and contaminated sites;

2. Review the Antarctic Clean-Up Manual appended to Resolution 2 (2013), as updated in 2014, and suggest any modifications and additional guidance; and

3. Report to CEP XXI.

(45) The Committee welcomed the offer from Dr Phillip Tracey (Australia) to serve as convener.

(46) The Committee also welcomed the other papers reported under this agenda item, which reported on actions taken by Parties consistent with their clean-up obligations under Annex III to the Protocol, and also with key guiding

principles in the Clean-Up Manual. The Committee noted that these papers as well as related papers to previous meetings would be useful references for the ICG discussions.

(47) The Republic of Belarus presented IP 3 *The experience in the reduction of the sources of waste generation in the Belarusian Antarctic Expedition.* Belarus described the steps it had taken to improve the management of fuel at its new station, in compliance with Annex III to the Protocol, including installation of a double-skinned fuel tank to avoid the use of 200-litre barrels. Belarus thanked the Russian Federation for technical assistance, as well as COMNAP, and highlighted the importance of international networks for small countries and small expeditions.

(48) Italy presented IP 74 *Clean-up and removal of Italy installations at Sitry airfield camp along the avio-route MZS-DDU, Antarctica*, which described the operations to dismantle the Sitry airfield camp, a landing point between the Italian Mario Zucchelli Station and the French Station Dumont D'Urville. Italy reported that eleven buried drums and a Weatherhaven tent were left on the site and that, as the environmental impact of a dedicated traverse would be greater, no dedicated operation was planned to retrieve them. No significant leakage from the buried fuel drums was expected considering the high quality of drums used. If future activities required going near the site again, it would complete the work.

(49) The following papers were also submitted under this agenda item:

- IP 48 *Clean-up of Scientific Equipment and Infrastructure from Mt. Erebus, Ross Island, Antarctica* (United States).

- IP 49 *Report on Clean-up at Metchnikoff Point, Brabant Island* (United Kingdom).

- IP 108 *Gestión de los desechos sólidos generados en la Estación Maldonado - XXI Campaña Antártica (2016-2017)* (Ecuador).

Item 7: Climate Change Implications for the Environment

7a) Strategic Approach

(50) Referring to WP 13 *Antarctica and the Strategic Plan for Biodiversity 2011-2020*, Japan drew the Committee's attention to the fact that 22 May is the International Day for Biological Diversity.

(51) SCAR presented IP 80 rev. 1 *Antarctic Climate Change and the Environment – 2017 Update*, which provided an update on the Antarctic Climate Change and the Environment Report, initially published in 2009 and updated in 2013. The paper detailed recent scientific advances in the understanding of climate change across the Antarctic continent and the Southern Ocean, and the associated impacts on terrestrial and marine biota. Research highlights included: a reduction of sea ice around the West Antarctic Peninsula; indications of improvement with regard to the ozone hole; the warming of oceans around Antarctica; southward transport of a boreal sea-star that was a potentially high-risk invader of the sub-Antarctic and Antarctic; and fast ice changes and associated impacts upon Adélie penguin populations. The paper noted the importance of undertaking further species-specific research in clarifying ecosystem responses to climate change.

(52) The Committee thanked SCAR for continuing to provide annual updates to its Antarctic Climate Change and the Environment Report and acknowledged the considerable work that was involved in preparing IP 80 rev. 1. The Committee strongly supported SCAR's move to present the report in a format accessible to a broad audience. It was noted that the summary information presented in the IP 80 rev. 1 could usefully inform the preparation and review of content in the Environments Portal. The Committee reiterated the importance of scientific research as outlined in this paper for its work to understand and address the environmental implications of climate change. The Committee welcomed the advice that the WMO would be cooperating with SCAR on future update reports.

(53) WMO presented IP 115 *The Polar Climate Predictability Initiative of the World Climate Research Programme*. The paper reported on the work of the Polar Climate Predictability Initiative (PCPI) and on its six core themes, each related to a different aspect of polar predictability. The focus of the PCPI was on finding elements of the climate system that contribute to predictability, and how those processes could be improved in models. The PCPI aimed to advance understanding of the sources of polar climate predictability on timescales ranging from seasonal to multi-decadal. WMO noted that this work was relevant to the CCRWP, and also had links to the IPCC and the SCAR AntClim21 Scientific Research Programme.

(54) WMO also presented IP 119 *Regional climate downscaling through the Antarctic-CORDEX project*. It reported on the work of the Antarctic Coordinated Regional Downscaling Experiment (CORDEX), to develop regional climate downscaling of Antarctica to provide an accurate description

of regional- to local-scale climate phenomena and their variability and changes. WMO noted that there were currently 10 groups from 7 countries involved in CORDEX, and encouraged all interested Members to participate.

(55) WMO presented IP 118 *Progress Update on WMO Polar Regional Climate Centres*. The WMO was taking steps to develop an Antarctic PRCC network that would generate regional climate products including climate monitoring and prediction in support of regional and national climate activities. One important goal was to address the needs of National Antarctic Programmes. The WMO would organise an Antarctic scoping workshop in 2018 to explore shared objectives at the technical level and a better understanding of the necessity for and desired form and function of an Antarctic Regional Climate Centre and would extend an invitation to the CEP and other interested organisations. The WMO invited Members, Experts and Observers to support the initiative, and assist the WMO to connect with their National Meteorological Services and National Antarctic Programmes.

(56) The Committee acknowledged the wide range of climate activities undertaken by the WMO in the Antarctic region, many of which were likely to be relevant to the Committee's work on climate change issues. The Committee encouraged interested Members and Observers to engage with the WMO in support of these various initiatives.

(57) ASOC presented IP 147 *Climate Change Report Card*. ASOC noted that it annually prepared a Climate Change Report Card to summarise key events and findings related to Antarctic Climate Change. ASOC recommended that the ATCM and CEP and its Members:

- Invest in robust monitoring of the Antarctic region to understand total patterns and anomalies of the Earth's climate system.
- Invest in ecological monitoring, which is imperative for understanding responses to environmental changes among species and ecosystems, including from immediate and diffuse human impacts.
- Develop a mechanism for ATCM reporting of Antarctic climate information to the broader public.
- Develop precautionary or rapid-response management plans in place to address sudden climate-related events. For example, CCAMLR recently agreed Conservation Measure (CM) 24-04, Establishing time-limited Special Areas for Scientific Study in newly exposed marine areas following ice-shelf retreat or collapse. The ATCM may wish to

consider similar measures for terrestrial or coastal areas newly exposed by ice-shelf retreat or collapse.

- Establish protected areas that can be used as reference areas to attribute changes to climate change with no or minimal interference from local and regional activities.

(58) The Committee welcomed IP 147 and noted that ASOC may wish to consider the suggestion raised by the United Kingdom to identify possible linkages to the CCRWP in future update reports. The Committee noted that a number of the recommendations raised in IP 147 related to the ongoing work of the CEP to implement the CCRWP.

(59) ASOC also presented IP 152 rev. 1 *Tracking Antarctica - A WWF report on the state of Antarctica and the Southern Ocean*. ASOC noted that the report provided a scientific update on the state of Antarctica and the Southern Ocean. The report was launched in October 2016. ASOC highlighted that a key finding of the report was that increasing human activities would magnify the effects of climate change and increase the vulnerability of Antarctic ecosystems, mammals, fish, and birds. ASOC also noted that the report identified ways to respond to these challenges based on the latest scientific evidence. ASOC informed the Committee that the report would be updated every two years.

(60) The Committee noted that this report provided further motivation for its ongoing work on climate change, including through the CCRWP. The Committee thanked ASOC and its member organisation WWF for the paper.

(61) Australia presented IP 84 *Climate change impacts on Antarctic ice-free areas*. The paper summarised a forthcoming publication in *Nature*, which quantified the potential impacts of climate change on Antarctic ice-free areas, home to over 99% of Antarctic terrestrial biodiversity. It reported that the publication explored the potential implications of physical changes for Antarctic terrestrial biodiversity, including increased competition and the spread of invasive species. The findings of the publication were directly relevant to the CEP's work on several priority issues, particularly efforts to prepare for, and build resilience to, the environmental impacts of a changing climate.

(62) The Committee recognised that the papers submitted under this agenda item addressed priority areas in the CCRWP, and would be useful references as the Committee discusses ways to draw on the best available science to understand and address climate change implications for the environment.

(63) The Russian Federation recalled that at CEP XIX it discussed changing sea ice conditions in the Antarctic. It noted that until the 2015-16 summer, sea ice extent had been increasing in the Antarctic, but the 2016-17 season experienced a sea ice minimum. Further, it highlighted the importance of paying attention to all factors that influence sea ice dynamics in the Antarctic, to avoid drawing incorrect conclusions.

(64) WMO noted that it was well documented that sea ice extent around Antarctica had on average seen a relatively small increase until recent years, while in contrast sea ice extent in the Arctic had been consistently decreasing. WMO explained that as the ozone hole starts to repair, sea ice extent is expected to decrease further in Antarctica, though uncertainties are large.

(65) SCAR noted that the 2017 Antarctic Climate Change update (IP 80 rev. 1) addressed changes in Antarctic sea ice both in the text and in Figure 1. SCAR emphasised that the time series in Figure 1 was insufficient to make specific future predictions.

(66) The following papers were also submitted under this agenda item:

- IP 13 *U.K./U.S. Research Initiative on Thwaites: The Future of Thwaites Glacier and its Contribution to Sea-level Rise* (United States, United Kingdom).
- IP 52 *Integrating Climate and Ecosystem Dynamics in the Southern Ocean (ICED) programme* (United Kingdom).
- SP 8 *Actions Taken by the CEP and the ATCM on the ATME Recommendations on Climate Change* (ATS).

7b) Implementation and Review of the Climate Change Response Work Programme

(67) New Zealand introduced WP 2 *Informal Intersessional Discussion: Implementation of the Climate Change Response Work Programme (CCRWP)*. Noting that implementation of the CCRWP was encouraged by Parties as a matter of priority through Resolution 4 (2015), and that CEP discussions to date had not concluded on how to implement the programme, the paper contained five recommendations. These included: that the CEP consider options for establishing a Subsidiary Group to review and manage the CCRWP; and that the group develop mechanisms to support good participation and efficient handling of the work, including Secretariat support for translation of key texts and technical support for coordinating and communicating updates. New Zealand also noted that the group would provide advice to the CEP on

actions, that innovative working methods would be required to support broad participation, and that further work was required to undertake an update to the CCRWP itself to support clear communication of the CCRWP with Members, Observers, Experts and the ATCM.

(68) SCAR presented IP 69 *Mapping SCAR affiliated research to the CEPs Climate Change Response Work Programme (CCRWP)*, prepared over the 2016-17 intersessional period in response to a request from the Committee at CEP XIX. The paper noted that as SCAR affiliated research covered all the key issues of the CCRWP and was truly interdisciplinary, including the physical, biological and social sciences, SCAR groups were well placed to contribute to the CCRWP. SCAR noted that clear and timely communication between the CEP and SCAR on the priorities and objectives of the CCRWP would maximise the likelihood of the potential of SCAR's contribution to the CCRWP being realised.

(69) The Committee thanked New Zealand for leading the intersessional discussions on the implementation of the CCRWP and for preparing the report in WP 2. The Committee acknowledged all Members and Observers that actively participated in the discussions, and expressed broad support for the recommendations in the paper.

(70) Regarding operational mechanisms, it was suggested that a Subsidiary Group could utilise the CEP discussion forum, which would facilitate the desired inclusive and transparent approach to managing related intersessional work. It was also suggested that enhancing the format of the CCWRP itself could assist with the aims of improving effective communication with stakeholders and with the ATCM. It was further noted that, in addition to work that may be conducted within a Subsidiary Group, it would be important for the Committee to continue to allocate dedicated time (or even a workshop) during future meetings to consider the CCRWP in order to facilitate wide engagement by Members.

(71) The Committee agreed that key texts, for example texts for discussion and or draft annual updates of the CCRWP be translated, on a case-by-case basis. Noting that the Subsidiary Group would generally conduct its business remotely, the Committee considered that translation of key texts would meet the requirements of Rule 21.

(72) The Committee agreed, subject to ATCM approval under Rule 10 of the CEP Rules of Procedure, to establish a Subsidiary Group on Climate Change Response (SGCCR) in accordance with the framework presented in Appendix 2.

(73) The Committee agreed to appoint Ms Birgit Njåstad (Norway) as the convener of the SGCCR.

(74) CEP XX tasked the SGCCR, in addition to the agreed ToR, to develop operating mechanisms in the 2017/18 intersessionary period to support good participation and efficient handling of work, including through Secretariat support for translation of key texts and technical support for coordinating and communicating updates.

(75) CEP XX noted that the SGCCR may, in future:

- Consider innovative ways of operating that engage a wide group of Members, including, for example, facilitating dedicated sessions or workshops as needed.

- Address recommendations 18 (Give consideration to taking a more regional approach in the application of environmental; management tools, in addition to the current continent-wide approach) and 29 (Remain alert to the development of climate change related conservation tools elsewhere in the world that may also have application in an Antarctic context (eg, climate change adaptation plans, risk assessment tools and mechanisms for assisted translocation of endangered species)) from the 2010 Antarctic Treaty Meeting of Experts (ATME) on Climate Change.

(76) The Committee emphasised the importance of ensuring broad participation and engagement by CEP Members in the work of the Subsidiary Group.

(77) The Committee expressed appreciation for SCAR's significant efforts to provide a comprehensive report on the substantial body of SCAR-affiliated work related to the CCRWP. The Committee acknowledged the points raised in IP 69 and noted that SCAR-affiliated research covered all issues related to the CCRWP. The Committee also noted the challenge of feeding the results from the numerous ongoing SCAR initiatives into the framework of the CCRWP, moving from having an overview of the work to seeing how the outcomes of the work would provide answers to CCRWP tasks. The Committee agreed that effective communication between the CEP and SCAR on the implementation of the CCRWP remained important.

(78) The Committee welcomed the WMO's offer to submit a similar paper to CEP XXI, mapping its own activities to the issues and needs identified in the CCRWP.

CEP advice to the ATCM on implementation of the Climate Change Response Work Programme

(79) Noting the ATCM's request in Resolution 4 (2015) to receive annual updates from the CEP on implementation of the Climate Change Response Work Programme, the Committee requested the ATCM to:

- Approve the establishment of a Subsidiary Group on Climate Change Response (SGCCR) in accordance with Rule 10 of the CEP Rules of Procedure to support the implementation of the CCRWP, as outlined in Appendix 2.

- Request Secretariat support for translation of key texts and technical support for coordinating and communicating updates to support good participation and efficient handling of work.

- Note that it had welcomed a comprehensive report from SCAR on the work of its subsidiary and affiliated groups relevant to the issues and needs identified in the CCRWP, which clearly indicated that SCAR groups are well placed to contribute.

- Also note that it had welcomed an offer from the WMO to provide a report to CEP XXI on its activities relevant to the CCRWP.

(80) The CEP Chair referred to SP 8 *Actions Taken by the CEP and the ATCM on the ATME Recommendations on Climate Change*. The Committee noted that Recommendations 18-30 were related to the work of the CEP, and that all of these except recommendations 18 (on consideration of taking a more regional approach in the application of environmental management tools) and 29 (on remaining alert to the development of climate change related conservation tools elsewhere in the world) had been incorporated into the CCRWP. Therefore, the Committee agreed that addressing recommendations 18 and 29 would be recorded as future work for the Subsidiary Group on Climate Change Response, and that further updates from the Secretariat were not required by the CEP. The Committee noted that the ATCM may still wish to be updated on progress against recommendations, particularly recommendations 1-17.

(81) United Kingdom presented IP 71 *Agreement by CCAMLR to establish time-limited Special Areas for Scientific Study in newly exposed marine areas following ice shelf retreat or collapse in the Antarctic Peninsula region*, jointly prepared with Belgium, Finland, France, Germany, Italy, Netherlands, Poland, Spain, and Sweden. It described the mechanism for the designation

of Special Areas for Scientific Study under CCAMLR Conservation Measure 24-04, and the management measures that would apply, consistent with Recommendation 26 from the Antarctic Treaty Meeting of Experts (ATME) on Climate Change (2010).

(82) The Committee welcomed CCAMLR CM 24-04 as a positive contribution towards the delivery of Recommendation 26 from the 2010 ATME.

Item 8: Environmental Impact Assessment (EIA)

8a) Draft Comprehensive Environmental Evaluations

(83) No papers were submitted under this agenda item.

8b) Other EIA Matters

(84) The United Kingdom introduced WP 41 *Environmental Impact Assessments – Update on broader policy discussions*, prepared jointly with Australia, Belgium, New Zealand and Norway. The paper noted that informal intersessional discussions had examined the broader environment impact assessment (EIA) policy issues identified during the ICG convened during the 2014/15 and 2015/16 intersessional periods to review the *Guidelines for Environmental Impact Assessment in Antarctica*. The United Kingdom noted that the paper was not an attempt to summarise the discussions, but rather to distil and advance the salient points and areas of general agreement. The issues presented in the paper were divided into three categories, based on how easily they could be addressed. The paper presented six recommendations to the CEP relating to: the terms of reference for intersessional discussions examining CEEs; the establishment of a central repository for practical EIA guidance and resources, additional to the EIA guidelines; the effectiveness of Resolution 1 (2005); standard approaches to environmental baseline surveys; adding other EIA related tasks to the CEP Five Year Work Plan; and seeking ATCM advice on EIA priorities.

(85) The Committee thanked the United Kingdom and the co-authors for their work in the preparation of the paper and noted its importance, and expressed general support for the recommendations. In addition, a number of Members and ASOC expressed interest in participation in further discussions on the matter.

(86) The Committee agreed to update the Procedures for intersessional CEP consideration of draft CEEs (Appendix 3) to include the following standard ToR:

- Whether the CEE: i) has identified all the environmental impacts of the proposed activity; and ii) suggests appropriate methods of mitigating (reducing or avoiding) those impacts.

(87) The Committee also agreed to include the following actions in the CEP Five-Year Work Plan:

- Members and Observers work to progress and coordinate information that will assist development of guidance on identifying and assessing cumulative impacts.

- Ask SCAR to provide guidance on how to undertake an environmental baseline conditions survey, and consider their advice in due course.

- Encourage Members to provide feedback on the utility of the revised set of *Guidelines for Environmental Impact Assessment in Antarctica* in the preparation of EIAs.

- Consider potential changes required to the EIA database to improve its utility with a view to giving proposals to the Secretariat.

(88) With respect to the 2nd bullet point, SCAR indicated its willingness to support the CEP by providing this guidance, however it cautioned that the scope of the advice provided would be dependent upon the resources available to support this work.

(89) The Committee agreed on the benefit of having collated generally applicable resource material to assist in the preparation of EIAs and to be used alongside the revised EIA guidelines. As there was no consensus on how this material might be presented (whether as a centralised repository of information, an annex to the revised EIA guidelines, or as an EIA manual), no actions were added to the CEP Five-Year Work Plan. The Committee encouraged Members to share their experiences and resources and noted that the presentation of material could be considered in the future once sufficient material had been collated.

(90) The Committee agreed that Resolution 1 (2005) remained up-to-date and continued to provide highly useful information.

CEP advice to the ATCM on policy issues associated with the Environmental Impact Assessment process

(91)   The Committee considered a report on intersessional discussions about broader policy issues related to the EIA provisions of Annex I, as identified by the ICG convened during the 2014/15 and 2015/16 intersessional periods to review the Guidelines for Environmental Impact Assessment in Antarctica, and agreed to advise the ATCM that:

   •   It recommended that all Parties provide the information requested in Resolution 1 (2005) in an appropriate and timely manner.

   •   It requested advice from the ATCM on the extent to which the CEP should begin work on:

      -   Creating an appropriate and effective method within the Antarctic Treaty system of preventing an environmentally-damaging project proceeding.

      -   Potential application for Antarctica of 'screening and scoping' processes commonly applied as part of the EIA process for large projects in other parts of the world.

      -   Processes for regular independent review of CEE-level activities (including the assessment of compliance with any Permit Condition imposed by the Competent Authority).

(92)   Belarus presented IP 5 *Towards establishing of values of critical loads and thresholds for the Antarctic environment*, which noted that while the unique ecosystems of the Antarctic area are particularly sensitive to anthropogenic impact, the terms 'load', 'limit', 'threshold' and similar had rarely occurred in the CEP documents. Belarus highlighted that data from the SCAR Scientific Research Programmes, such as State of the Antarctic Ecosystem (AntEco) and Antarctic Thresholds – Ecosystem Resilience and Adaptation (AnT-ERA), could help establish thresholds. Belarus suggested that the CEP consider adding the task of developing a methodological background and informational basis for the assessment of critical load levels when it revises guidance for the preparation of Comprehensive Environmental Evaluations (CEEs).

(93)   Germany presented IP 41 *Final Modernization of Gondwana Station, Terra Nova Bay, northern Victoria Land*, which noted that the work to renovate Gondwana Station had been completed in October and November 2016. It

reported that the station was ready to support scientific research in northern Victoria Land for at least 25 to 30 years.

(94) Italy presented IP 70 *Final Comprehensive Environmental Evaluation for the construction and operation of a gravel runway in the area of Mario Zucchelli Station, Terra Nova Bay, Victoria Land, Antarctica.* The paper presented the final CEE, which had been approved by the Italian Ministry of Environment and Protection of Land and Sea, and allowed for submission by the Italian Ministry of Foreign Affairs and International Cooperation. It noted that the final CEE addressed feedback received from the Committee at CEP XIX. Italy concluded that the benefits of the proposed infrastructure, in terms of more reliable and cost effective management of the Italian scientific and logistic operations, as well as increased safety and cooperation with neighbouring Antarctic programmes, would outweigh the environmental impacts. Italy reiterated that it was committed to trying to minimise, as much as possible, potential environmental impacts related to the construction of the gravel runway.

(95) The Republic of Korea congratulated Italy for the completion of its final CEE and noted that Italy had reconsidered and withdrawn the use of explosives in the construction of the runway, to minimise impact on a nearby penguin colony. The Republic of Korea expressed a desire to collaborate with Italy to reduce the cumulative impacts of their usage of the area.

(96) The Committee thanked Italy for the presentation of IP 70, outlining its response to how the comments on the draft CEE raised at CEP XIX had been addressed in the final CEE.

(97) Ecuador presented IP 106 *Environmental Compliance Audit of the XX Ecuadorian Antarctic Expedition (2015-2016)*, which reported on its first Environmental Compliance Audit to assess the environmental impact of activities undertaken at its station Maldonado during its 20th expedition.

(98) The following papers were also submitted under this agenda item:

- SP 7 rev. 2 *Annual list of Initial Environmental Evaluations (IEE) and Comprehensive Environmental Evaluations (CEE) prepared between April 1st 2016 and March 31st 2017* (ATS).
- BP 3 *Information on the Progress of the Renovation of the King Sejong Korean Antarctic Station on King George Island, South Shetland Islands* (Republic of Korea).

Item 9: Area Protection and Management Plans

9a) Management Plans

    i) Draft Management Plans which have been reviewed by the Subsidiary Group on Management Plans

(99)   The convener of the Subsidiary Group on Management Plans (SGMP), Patricia Ortúzar (Argentina) introduced the first part of WP 45 *Subsidiary Group on Management Plans Report of activities during the intersessional period 2016-2017* on behalf of the SGMP. The convener thanked all active participants in the SGMP for their hard work and reminded the Committee that all Members were welcome to join the SGMP. In accordance with terms of reference #1 to #3, the SGMP had been prepared to consider the following five draft Antarctic Specially Protected Area (ASPA) management plans referred by the CEP for intersessional review:

- ASPA 125: Fildes Peninsula, King George Island (25 de Mayo) (Chile).
- ASPA 144: Chile Bay (Discovery Bay), Greenwich Island, South Shetland Islands (Chile).
- ASPA 145: Port Foster, Deception Island, South Shetland Islands (Chile).
- ASPA 146: South Bay, Doumer Island, Palmer Archipelago (Chile).
- ASPA 150: Ardley Island, Maxwell Bay, King George Island (25 de Mayo) (Chile).

(100)   The SGMP advised the CEP that the five management plans were still under review by the proponent, so revised versions of the plans were not yet available for the SGMP for review.

    ii) Revised draft Management Plans which have not been reviewed by the Subsidiary Group on Management Plans

(101)   The Committee considered revised management plans for seven ASPAs and one Antarctic Specially Managed Area (ASMA). In each case the proponent(s) summarised the suggested changes to the existing management plan and recommended its approval by the Committee and referral to the ATCM for adoption.

- WP 7 rev. 1 *Revision of the Management Plan for Antarctic Specially Protected Area (ASPA) No. 111 Southern Powell Island and adjacent islands, South Orkney Islands* (United Kingdom).

- WP 8 *Revision of the Management Plan for Antarctic Specially Protected Area (ASPA) No. 140 Parts of Deception Island, South Shetland Islands* (United Kingdom).

- WP 9 rev. 1 *Revision of the Management Plan for Antarctic Specially Protected Area (ASPA) No. 129 Rothera Point, Adelaide Island* (United Kingdom).

- WP 10 rev. 1 *Revision of the Management Plan for Antarctic Specially Protected Area (ASPA) No. 110 Lynch Island, South Orkney Islands* (United Kingdom).

- WP 11 rev. 1 *Revision of the Management Plan for Antarctic Specially Protected Area (ASPA) No. 115 Lagotellerie Island, Marguerite Bay, Graham Land* (United Kingdom).

- WP 12 rev. 1 *Revision of the Management Plan for Antarctic Specially Protected Area (ASPA) No. 109 Moe Island, South Orkney Islands* (United Kingdom).

- WP 14 rev. 1 *Updated Management Plan and maps for Antarctic Specially Managed Area No. 5 Amundsen-Scott South Pole Station, South Pole* (United States and Norway).

- WP 38 *Revision of the Management Plan for Antarctic Specially Protected Area (ASPA) No. 165 Edmonson Point, Wood Bay, Ross Sea* (Italy).

(102) With respect to WP 7 rev. 1 (ASPA 111), WP 8 (ASPA 140), WP 9 rev. 1 (ASPA 129), WP 10 rev. 1 (ASPA 110), WP 11 rev. 1 (ASPA 115) and WP 12 rev. 1 (ASPA 109), the United Kingdom noted that the management plans had been reviewed and revised with reference to the *Guide to the Preparation of Management Plans for Antarctic Specially Protected Areas* (the Guide), and only minor changes to the existing plans were proposed. Plans for ASPAs that included bird colonies had been updated with a statement clarifying that overflight of bird colonies within the Area by remotely piloted aircraft systems (RPAS) shall not be permitted unless for scientific or operational purposes, and in accordance with a permit issued by an appropriate national authority. References to the Antarctic Conservation Biogeographic Regions (Resolution 6 [2012]) and to the Antarctic Important Bird Areas (Resolution 5 [2015]) had been added. The management plan for ASPA 140 was revised to better protect botanical values; specifically, the status of Site J Perchuć Cone was changed to a Prohibited Zone (as has been done already at other geothermal sites) and reference to the SCAR Code of Conduct for Activity within Terrestrial Geothermal Environments in Antarctica was added.

(103) With respect to WP 14 rev. 1 (ASMA 5) the United States and Norway noted that revisions had been made in consultation with more than 50 members of the science community, with the Amundsen-Scott South Pole Station management team, and with input from non-governmental visitor groups including IAATO. Revisions to the management plan included adjustments to sector boundaries to reflect new survey data, the renaming of several pre-existing zones to "restricted zones" to maintain consistency with CEP discussions on zoning, the simplification of the quiet sector by removing the "quiet circle", and providing a list and locations of designated HSMs in lieu of the Historic Zone.

(104) With respect to WP 38 (ASPA 165) Italy noted that only minor changes were proposed, including a revision of Map 4 to highlight the penguin colonies and add a new seasonal campsite and a walking path. Other changes made included updating activities, references, and census information to reflect recently conducted scientific studies.

(105) To address comments raised during the meeting regarding the revised provisions relating to the use of UAV / RPAS, the Committee agreed minor changes to the revised management plans for ASPA 109, ASPA 110, ASPA 111, ASPA 115, and ASPA 129. The Committee also agreed a minor change proposed during the meeting to a map contained in the revised management plan for ASMA 5. With these changes, the Committee approved all of the revised management plans that had not been reviewed by the SGMP.

CEP advice to the ATCM on revised management plans for ASPAs and ASMAs

(106) The Committee agreed to forward the following revised management plans to the ATCM for approval by means of a Measure:

#	Name
ASPA 109	Moe Island, South Orkney Islands
ASPA 110	Lynch Island, South Orkney Islands
ASPA 111	Southern Powell Island and adjacent islands, South Orkney Islands
ASPA 115	Lagotellerie Island, Marguerite Bay, Graham Land
ASPA 129	Rothera Point, Adelaide Island
ASPA 140	Parts of Deception Island, South Shetland Islands
ASPA 165	Edmonson Point, Wood Bay, Ross Sea
ASMA 5	Amundsen-Scott South Pole Station, South Pole

iii) New draft Management Plans for protected/managed areas

(107) No new draft Management Plans for protected/managed areas were submitted.

iv) Other matters relating to Management Plans for protected/managed areas

(108) China introduced WP 35 *Report of the Informal Discussion for the intersessional period of 2016/17 on the Proposal for a new Antarctic Specially Managed Area at Chinese Antarctic Kunlun Station, Dome A.* Following discussions at previous CEP meetings, and informal intersessional discussions, on China's proposal to designate an ASMA at the Chinese Antarctic Kunlun Station, Dome A, the paper reported on further informal discussions led by China during the 2016/17 intersessional period, regarding management options for the Dome A area. China expressed its thanks to the seven Members who participated in the informal discussions.

(109) The paper presented China's responses to comments provided by several participants, noting that: it considered that the protection and management of Dome A should be maintained within the framework of the Antarctic Treaty system and its management tools; it agreed that the Committee should encourage Members planning to carry out activities in the area to consult China early in the planning stages, consistent with the provisions of Article 6.1 of the Protocol and Recommendation XV-17 (1989); and it appreciated that several Members had shared their experiences with managing their Antarctic stations, but it continued to have some concerns about the suggestion of applying China's national procedures.

(110) China indicated its willingness to learn about potential alternative management options for the region and reiterated its view that an ASMA was the most appropriate tool to proactively manage and protect the scientific and environmental values at Dome A. China informed the Committee that it intended to develop a draft Code of Conduct as the first possible management option for Dome A, and offered to lead informal intersessional discussion during 2017/18 based on the draft. China recommended that the CEP support the proposal, and encouraged interested and concerned Members and organisations, such as SCAR and COMNAP, to participate.

(111) The Committee thanked China for leading the intersessional discussions and for the report presented in WP 35. It also thanked Members who had contributed to the discussions. The Committee recalled earlier discussions on this topic and welcomed the progress that had been made. The Committee

also welcomed China's continuing engagement with others on options for the management of the Dome A area.

(112) Argentina expressed its view that all areas needed to be protected by tools provided in the Protocol and those adopted by the ATCM, rather than relying on national procedures, and that any code of conduct should relate to the management of activities and conduct of personnel in an area rather than management of the area itself.

(113) The Committee welcomed China's offer to draft a Code of Conduct for Dome A and to lead intersessional discussions based on that draft. Some Members expressed reservations about the idea that a Code of Conduct would be approved by the means of a Resolution. China clarified that it did not intend the Code of Conduct to be adopted by Resolution at this stage, but noted that international interest in scientific research at Dome A was increasing, and that it may be appropriate to consider such a procedure in the future. The Committee encouraged interested Members and Observers to contribute to this work, and looked forward to receiving a further report on progress.

9b) Historic Sites and Monuments

(114) Norway introduced WP 47 *Report of the intersessional contact group established to develop guidance material for conservation approaches for the management of Antarctic heritage objects*, jointly prepared with the United Kingdom. It reported on the first period of the ICG established at CEP XIX to develop guidance for conservation approaches for the management of Antarctic heritage objects. The ICG discussed overarching principles, inputs and considerations for the list of themes presented in ICG term of reference #2, fine-tuned some key overarching principles, and started discussions on a framework for the guidance material to be developed. It reported on some key issues discussed during the ICG including: that the understanding of the terms "sites" and "monuments" needed further consideration; that considering the concepts of general heritage values and specific historic values separately could be useful; that the introduction of concept of the universality must be treated carefully; and that guidance material should provide an overview of the broad suite of management options available, with an emphasis on how to assess site/monuments against these various options. The co-authors recommended that the Committee: request the ICG to continue its work in the 2017-2018 intersessional period; and agree to modified terms of reference for the further work of the ICG ahead of producing guidance material for CEP XXI.

(115) The Committee thanked Norway and the United Kingdom for leading the first period of intersessional work in the ICG, and acknowledged the contributions of other Members and Observers that had participated. The Committee welcomed the report on the progress of the ICGs discussions. It recognised that the ICG was dealing with complicated issues and discussions.

(116) The Committee noted that the need to balance between the provisions of Annex III regarding clean-up and Annex V regarding the protection of historic sites was integral to the work of the ICG.

(117) The Committee noted that several points raised during the meeting could be given further consideration during the continuing ICG discussions, including: that an overarching vision would be useful; further discussion would be required on identifying levels of significance for sites and monuments and on the concept of universality; further consideration of how to share and commemorate events and actions represented by sites and monuments; and the importance of considering environmental impacts during further work in the context of heritage management.

(118) The Committee agreed that the ICG would continue during the 2017/18 intersessional period, with the following terms of reference:

1. To finalise discussions and draft guidelines for the consideration of the CEP relating to the assessment of Heritage and Historic Sites in Antarctica, based on the discussion conducted in the 2016-17 intersessional period and informed by the discussions at CEP XX. These guidelines should cover:

    • providing guidance for considering whether a site/object merits HSM designation; and

    • providing guidance to management options for HSMs.

2. To liaise in this work with international and national heritage experts as appropriate.

3. To produce guidance material for consideration at CEP XXI.

(119) The Committee thanked Norway and the United Kingdom for their agreement to continue leading the work of the ICG during the next intersessional period, encouraged broad participation during the second round of exchanges and looked forward to receiving a further report at CEP XXI.

(120) The following paper was also submitted under this item:

- BP 4 *Antarctic Historic Resources: Ross Sea Heritage Restoration Project. Conservation of Hillary's Hut, Scott Base, Antarctic HSM 75* (New Zealand).

9c) Site Guidelines

(121) IAATO presented IP 164 *Report on IAATO Operator Use of Antarctic Peninsula Landing Sites and ATCM Visitor Site Guidelines, 2016-17 Season*, which reported the data collected by IAATO from IAATO Operator Post Visit Report Forms for the 2016-2017 season. IAATO noted that overall tourism levels in Antarctica had increased from the peak season of 2007-08, and were likely to exceed these numbers during the 2017/18 season. It noted the increase was not uniform, with a few sites providing the majority of the increase, and others seeing a decrease in activity. IAATO emphasised that over 95% of all landed tourism activity in the Antarctic Peninsula continued to be focused on traditional commercial ship-borne tourism. It mentioned that the increase in passenger numbers was largely due to new vessels being operated with higher passenger capacity. IAATO highlighted that all of the top visited sites were covered either by ATCM Visitor Site Guidelines or National Programme management guidelines.

(122) The Committee thanked IAATO for the report and welcomed its continued commitment to reporting to the CEP on IAATO operater landing site and Visitor Site Guidelines use.

9d) Marine Spatial Protection and Management

(123) Argentina presented IP 127 *Update on the process of designation of a Marine Protected Area (MPA) in the West Antarctic Peninsula and Southern Arc of Scotia (Domain 1)* jointly prepared with Chile. It reported on the activities led by Argentina and Chile to identify priority areas in the West Antarctic Peninsula and Southern Scotia Arc (Domain 1). The activities were a result of multinational efforts with multiple contributions of data and experiences. The co-authors hoped to present an MPA proposal for Domain 1 at the upcoming Meeting of the CCAMLR Working Group on Ecosystem Monitoring and Management (WG-EMM), and encouraged the Committee to support CCAMLR's activity with regards to the process of designation of MPAs. They further encouraged the Committee to note the importance of the work led by Argentina and Chile, in collaboration with several Members, with the purpose of identifying priority conservation areas in Domain 1, and invited more Members to collaborate with Argentina and

Chile in achieving a greater understanding of extraction activities in Domain 1, so as to achieve an effective MPA design.

(124) Welcoming Argentina and Chile's proposed presentation to WG-EMM, ASOC, on behalf of the International Union for Conservation of Nature (IUCN), informed the Committee of the upcoming fourth International Marine Protected Areas Congress (IMPAC4) in La Serena-Coquimbo, Chile, in September 2017, and a special session on Antarctic MPAs to be held at the meeting.

(125) The Committee thanked Argentina and Chile for presenting the paper. It noted that substantive discussion on the designation of MPAs in the Convention Area appropriately occurred within CCAMLR, but welcomed the report on the progress of the planning work in Domain 1 led by Argentina and Chile.

(126) The United Kingdom and the United States noted that they had already contributed to developing the proposal along with other Members, and expressed their interest in contributing and collaborating with Argentina and Chile in the ongoing work. The Committee noted comments raised during the discussion, including an encouragement to the co-sponsors of the work to consider flexibility in the further development of proposals. It encouraged interested Members to collaborate with Argentina and Chile on the ongoing work in the areas highlighted in the paper.

(127) The Committee noted that it might be useful in the future to consider and discuss means and opportunities to look at the connectivity between ocean and land, and if and how complementary measures within the framework of the Environment Protocol, in particular Annex V, could support and strengthen marine protection initiatives.

(128) Several Members also took the opportunity to note the progress on marine spatial protection by CCAMLR including the designation of the Ross Sea Region MPA.

9e) Other Annex V Matters

(129) The SGMP convener, Patricia Ortúzar (Argentina), introduced the second part of WP 45 *Subsidiary Group on Management Plans Report of activities during the intersessional period 2016-2017*. The SGMP had continued work on developing guidance documents for ASMAs, in accordance with terms of reference 4 and 5 on improving management plans, and the process for their intersessional review. This work was led by the SGMP Members from Norway and the United States and was reported in WP 16 *Guidance*

Material for Antarctic Specially Managed Area (ASMA) designations. Argentina also presented the proposed SGMP work plan for the 2017/18 intersessional period.

(130) Norway introduced WP 16 *Guidance Material for Antarctic Specially Managed Area (ASMA) designations*, prepared jointly with the United States. The paper presented the results of the SGMP's work, in accordance with the work plan agreed at CEP XIX, to finalise the development of guidance on determining whether an area could merit designation as an ASMA, and to initiate development of guidance on how to prepare and present a management plan if an ASMA designation is warranted. It reported that discussions were constructive and fruitful and that nine Members and Observers were involved in the process. It proposed that the Committee consider the two sets of guidelines, adjust them as appropriate, and agree to adopt and submit them to the ATCM to encourage their dissemination and use by means of a Resolution.

(131) Noting its role as an non-governmental organisation in issues of environmental protection and management in Antarctica, ASOC expressed its interest in continuing to be involved in discussions about potential ASMAs.

(132) The Committee endorsed the *Guidance for assessing an area for a potential Antarctic Specially Managed Area designation* and the *Guidelines for the preparation of ASMA management plans*, as modified to address comments raised during the meeting.

(133) The Committee agreed that in a future revision of the *Guidance for assessing an area for a potential Antarctic Specially Managed Area designation* it could be useful to include a schematic or table that would illustrate / summarise the process of assessing and drawing conclusions with regard to assessing an area for potential ASMA designation. It was noted that this could further improve the guidelines and facilitate the decision-making process.

(134) The United Kingdom noted that while it was prepared to remove a paragraph relating to place names from the original draft of the *Guidelines for the preparation of ASMA management plans*, in order to ensure the adoption of those Guidelines, it nevertheless wished to highlight the excellent work conducted by SCAR in the development and maintenance of the SCAR Composite Gazetteer of Antarctica. It also noted that it highly valued the gazetteer and believed it was the appropriate place for submitting new place names.

(135) The Committee thanked the SGMP for its advice, encouraged further participation among Members, and adopted the following SGMP work plan for 2017/18:

Terms of Reference	Suggested tasks
ToR 1 to 3	Review draft management plans referred by CEP for intersessional review and provide advice to proponents (including the five postponed plans from the 2016/17 intersessional period)
ToR 4 and 5	Work with relevant Parties to ensure progress on review of management plans overdue for five-yearly review
	Consider further improvements to the Guidance for assessing an area for a potential Antarctic Specially Managed Area designation
	Review and update SGMP work plan
Working Papers	Prepare report for CEP XXI against SGMP ToR 1 to 3
	Prepare report for CEP XXI against SGMP ToR 4 and 5

CEP advice to the ATCM on guidance material for Antarctic Specially Managed Areas (ASMAs)

(136) The Committee endorsed the *Guidance for assessing an area for a potential Antarctic Specially Managed Area designation* and the *Guidelines for the preparation of Antarctic Specially Managed Area management plans* and agreed to forward to the ATCM for approval a draft Resolution encouraging their dissemination and use.

(137) The CEP Chair recalled that CEP XIX had endorsed *SCAR's Code of Conduct for Activities within Terrestrial Geothermal Environments in Antarctica,* and had agreed that it would be beneficial to similarly encourage the dissemination and use of other SCAR Codes of Conduct through a Resolution of the ATCM.

(138) SCAR introduced WP 17 *SCAR's Code of Conduct for the Exploration and Research of Subglacial Aquatic Environments,* which provided reviewed and revised guidance on the planning and undertaking of exploration and research in subglacial aquatic environments. SCAR highlighted that broad and extensive consultation had been undertaken in the review and revision of this non-mandatory Code of Conduct, including with policy makers, environmental managers and scientific experts, and through SCAR subsidiary bodies, including the Standing Committee on the Antarctic Treaty System (SCATS). Noting that no substantive changes had been made, SCAR recommended that the CEP consider the revised Code of Conduct, and if agreed, encourage the dissemination and use of the Code of Conduct when planning and undertaking activities in subglacial aquatic environments.

(139) The Committee thanked SCAR for submitting the paper and for the broad consultation with stakeholders to review and improve the non-mandatory Code of Conduct. With minor modifications to incorporate proposals raised

during the meeting, the Committee agreed to encourage the dissemination and use of the Code of Conduct when planning and undertaking activities in subglacial aquatic environments.

CEP advice to the ATCM on SCAR's Code of Conduct for the Exploration and Research of Subglacial Aquatic Environments

(140) The Committee endorsed *SCAR's Code of Conduct for the Exploration and Research of Subglacial Aquatic Environments*, and agreed to forward it to the ATCM for approval by a draft Resolution on encouraging its dissemination and use.

(141) SCAR introduced WP 18 *SCAR's Environmental Code of Conduct for Terrestrial Scientific Field Research in Antarctica*, which presented reviewed and revised guidance on the planning and undertaking of terrestrial scientific field research in Antarctica. SCAR informed the Committee that broad and extensive consultation was undertaken in the review and revision of this non-mandatory Code of Conduct, including with policy makers, environmental managers and scientific experts, and through SCAR subsidiary bodies, including the SCATS. SCAR reported that minor edits, additions and improvements had been made to the Code of Conduct. It recommended that the CEP consider the Code of Conduct and, if agreed, encourage its dissemination and use when planning and undertaking terrestrial scientific field research in Antarctica.

(142) The Committee thanked SCAR for its work to review and improve this Code of Conduct. It emphasised the importance of having such a Code of Conduct, noting how such guidance for specific types of activities in Antarctica contributed to enhancing the overall protection of Antarctica. It also noted that the current version of the Code had been valuable.

(143) Although some Members expressed support for the Code of Conduct to be adopted as it was presented, other Members considered that further consultation was required, including by National Antarctic Programmes, which support the activities of field researchers.

(144) The Committee welcomed SCAR's willingness to undertake further consultations, including with COMNAP, with a view to presenting a new revision for consideration at CEP XXI.

(145) The Committee also welcomed SCAR's advice that it would present its *Code of Conduct for the Use of Animals for Scientific Purposes in Antarctica* for the Committee's consideration at CEP XXI.

(146) Argentina noted the usefulness of having these Codes presented to the Committee as working papers, in that way allowing for their official translation into the four official languages of the Antarctic Treaty.

(147) The United Kingdom introduced WP 21 *ASPA/ASMA prior assessment process*, prepared jointly with Norway. Recalling discussions at CEP XIX, the co-authors reported on intersessional consultations that had been held with interested Members, and presented a revised non-mandatory template for prior assessment of ASPAs. They recommended that the CEP recognise the benefits of providing for a standardised presentation of information on proposed new ASPA designations, where the proponent(s) decide it would be helpful to engage the Committee in a prior assessment discussion, and agree that the *Guidelines: A prior assessment process for the designation of ASPAs and ASMAs* (Appendix 3 to CEP XVIII report) should be amended to include the non-mandatory ASPA prior assessment template.

(148) The Committee thanked the United Kingdom and Norway for the paper and for the intersessional consultation with interested Members. The Committee emphasised that the purpose of the template was to provide a practical and non-mandatory means of facilitating provision of information consistent with the prior assessment guidelines and not to delay or impede proposals to designate new areas, nor to imply prior approval of a new area designation.

(149) In response to a query from IAATO, the United Kingdom stated that the intention was that information provided in the template in general would be based on sound scientific evidence. Some minor changes were suggested and incorporated in the final version of the template.

(150) The Committee noted that an ASMA template, although a more complex matter, could also be of value, and encouraged interested Members to consider the development of such a template.

CEP Advice to the ATCM on the Guidelines: A prior assessment process for the designation of ASPAs and ASMAs

(151) The Committee agreed to advise the ATCM that it had updated the *Guidelines: A prior assessment process for the designation of ASPAs and ASMAs* adopted at CEP XVIII, to include a non-mandatory ASPA prior assessment template to facilitate the provision of information consistent with the Guidelines (Appendix 4). This new version of the Guidelines replaced the version that had been appended to the CEP XVIII report in 2015.

(152) Australia introduced WP 29 *Proposed update to the Antarctic Conservation Biogeographic Regions,* and referred to IP 15 *Antarctic biogeography revisited: updating the Antarctic Conservation Biogeographic Regions*, both jointly submitted with New Zealand and SCAR. The papers summarised a recent revision of the Antarctic Conservation Biogeographic Regions (ACBRs) adopted under Resolution 6 (2012). The revision reflected updates in underlying spatial layers, including the most current representation of Antarctica's ice-free areas, together with the results of new analyses justifying the inclusion of an additional (16th) biologically distinct area in the Prince Charles Mountains region. It reported that the revised spatial layer was available from the Australian Antarctic Data Centre and would be provided to the Antarctic Treaty Secretariat for general access and use. The co-authors recommended that the CEP endorse the revised Antarctic Conservation Biogeographic Regions (ACBRs Version 2), forward the draft Resolution presented in WP 29 to the ATCM for adoption, and request that the Antarctic Treaty Secretariat make the updated data layer available via its website.

(153) The Committee thanked Australia, New Zealand and SCAR for their work on WP 29 and IP 15 and recalled its endorsement at CEP XV of the ACBRs as an important framework for its discussions relating to spatial values and environmental protection in Antarctica, and the ATCM's subsequent adoption of the ACBRs through Resolution 6 (2012) as a dynamic model to guide the work of the Committee.

(154) The Committee agreed on the importance of continuing to update the framework, including to ensure that it incorporated up-to-date information about the biodiversity of Antarctic ice-free areas, drawing on the best available sources. Accordingly, the Committee agreed to endorse the revised ACBRs, and requested the Antarctic Treaty Secretariat to make the updated spatial data layer available on its website. The Committee also noted the advice from New Zealand that the updated spatial data layer would be made available through the map presented on the Antarctic Environments Portal website.

CEP advice to the ATCM on an update to the Antarctic Conservation Biogeographic Regions

(155) The Committee considered the results of recent research to revise the Antarctic Conservation Biogeographic Regions adopted under Resolution 6 (2012). To ensure that the work of the CEP and Parties is based on the most up-to-date understanding of the spatial distribution of Antarctic terrestrial biodiversity, the Committee recommended that the ATCM adopt the revised Antarctic

Conservation Biogeographic Regions (ACBRs Version 2) and forwarded a draft Resolution to the ATCM for adoption to replace Resolution 6 (2012).

(156) The United Kingdom introduced WP 37 *Antarctic Specially Protected Areas and Important Bird Areas*, jointly submitted with Australia, New Zealand, Norway and Spain. Recalling that Resolution 5 (2015) requested the CEP to update the ATCM on the extent to which Important Bird Areas (IBAs) in Antarctica were, or should be, represented in the network of ASPAs, this paper reported that two recent analyses of IBAs had examined the extent to which representative and potentially vulnerable bird colonies were currently represented within the ASPA Network. Those analyses were presented in IP 16 *Representation of Important Bird Areas in the network series of Antarctic Specially Protected Areas* (submitted by the United Kingdom, New Zealand and Norway) and IP 17 *High resolution mapping of human footprint across Antarctica and its implications for the strategic conservation of bird life* (submitted by the United Kingdom and Spain). The co-authors of WP 37 highlighted the importance of protecting bird colonies across a range of Antarctic bird species, and that a more consistent approach needed to be taken to protect all native Antarctic bird species. The co-sponsors also clarified that it should not be assumed that all IBAs should receive ASPA designation nor that bird colonies which were not IBAs should not be considered for ASPA designation. The co-authors recommended that the Committee consider these analyses and encouraged further intersessional work between interested Members to: develop criteria for assessing the suitability of bird colonies for ASPA designation, including identifying what constitutes "major colonies of breeding birds" as set out in Article 3(2)(c) of Annex V to the Protocol; and recommend to the Committee IBAs that meet those criteria.

(157) The Committee thanked the authors of the papers submitted to the meeting for their work to support and advance the Committee's consideration of the request in Resolution 5 (2015). The Committee agreed with the recommendation in WP 37 to undertake intersessional work to develop criteria for assessing the suitability of bird colonies for ASPA designation, including to identify what constitutes 'major colonies of breeding birds' as set out in Article 3.2(c) of Annex V to the Protocol, and to recommend to the Committee a list of IBAs that meet those criteria.

(158) The Committee welcomed the offer of the United Kingdom to lead discussions during the intersessional period in consultation with interested Members and Observers. Many Members expressed their interest in participating in such

intersessional work. The Committee noted that points raised by Members in the discussion during the meeting could be considered further during the intersessional work, including: the importance of also considering relevant information other than presented in IP 16 and IP 17, including peer-reviewed, ground-truthed studies and ongoing research such as that referred to by several Members; current protection and management mechanisms at sites that were not designated as ASPAs; and the relevance of the mechanisms available in Annex II, which played an important role in the protection of Antarctic bird colonies. On the latter point, the Committee welcomed the recent entry into force of the revision of Annex II.

(159) With reference to IP 17, the Committee highlighted the importance of considering the assessment presented in the light of the results of ground truthing through field research and monitoring, and also with consideration to the characteristics of particular sites, and the results of human impact studies. The Committee also noted the comment made by the Netherlands regarding the potential wider relevance of the results presented in this paper for the Committee's further discussions on the issue of the expanding human footprint and protection and wilderness in Antarctica, and its call for further work.

(160) The Committee noted comments made by Argentina regarding the methods and results contained in the scientific paper attached to IP 17. Argentina expressed that the values for human footprint associated with the bird colony near Esperanza Station did not incorporate ground-based data and other relevant information, which could lead to misleading results. Argentina considered that this assessment should therefore be used with caution.

(161) Belgium introduced WP 42 *Prior assessment of a proposed Antarctic Specially Protected Area (ASPA) in the Sør Rondane Mountains*. Belgium notified the Committee that it had carried out a prior assessment for a proposed ASPA, in accordance with the provisions of Annex V to the Protocol and the *Guidelines: A prior assessment process for the designation of ASPAs and ASMAs* (see Appendix 3 to the CEP XVIII Report). Belgium requested further guidance from Members regarding the next steps in the process, including the drafting of a Management Plan. Belgium recommended that the Committee: agree that the values within the proposed ASPA in the Sør Rondane Mountains merit special protection; endorse the development of a Management Plan for the Area to be led by Belgium; and encourage interested Members to work with Belgium informally during the intersessional period in the development of a Management Plan for potential submission at CEP XXI.

(162) The Committee welcomed the information presented by Belgium consistent with the *Guidelines: A prior assessment process for the designation of ASPAs and ASMAs* and the associated non-mandatory template. The Committee noted that the paper provided an early opportunity for the Members to engage in the process of considering the proposal and aiding its development. At the same time, the Committee emphasised that the Guidelines were non-mandatory and were not intended to provide or imply prior designation approval by the Committee.

(163) The Committee agreed that the environmental and scientific values found at the Sør Rondane Mountains site, including generally poorly studied organisms, merited further consideration for potential designation as an ASPA enhancing the representation of ASPAs in ACBR 6. It was also noted that information provided to ATCM XL indicated a potential increase in traffic in the area in the future, which could underpin the need to protect pristine areas in this region. The Committee welcomed Belgium's intention to further consider the development of a draft management plan for the area, and noted that several Members had expressed an interest to contribute to the work. It encouraged other interested Members and Observers to work with Belgium in the intersessional period.

(164) The Committee noted a range of areas and topics for possible further consideration by Belgium. These included: consideration of further explanation of the values of the area in light of the provisions of the Annex V, including its 'outstanding values'; consideration of the merit of designating the area as an ASPA in light of existing management arrangements; consideration of the implications of a possible increase of activities in the area; consideration of historical activities which could inform the identification of possible inviolate areas that may warrant further specific protection; the possible exclusion of ice-covered areas between the ice-free areas; the possible inclusion of Utsteinen Ridge within the proposed area; the identification of possible risks associated with interactions between the station activities and the area in question; and the provision of further information about the presence of a petrel colony and the possible presence of endemic microbes, invertebrates and lichens.

(165) As a general observation, the Committee suggested that Members using the prior assessment template in future could provide a description of the values of the area under consideration, in addition to identifying the presence or absence of particular types of values.

(166) The Committee thanked Belgium for its work and looked forward to hearing about future progress. Belgium thanked the Committee for the positive response to WP 42 and noted that it intended to take all observations into account.

(167) ASOC presented IP 149 *ASOC update on Marine Protected Areas in the Southern Ocean 2016-2017*, which reported on the discussions of Marine Protected Areas (MPAs) that took place at CCAMLR XXXV in October 2016. ASOC observed that with the adoption of the Ross Sea Region Marine Protected Area, CCAMLR could now address the adoption of additional MPAs in the Southern Ocean. ASOC stated that further progress on the designation of MPAs for East Antarctica and the Weddell Sea could be made at CCAMLR XXXVI in October 2017, and noted that the MPA proposals for these two regions were first submitted in 2010 and 2016 respectively. ASOC also noted that an Antarctic tour operator had issued a statement supporting current and future MPAs in the Southern Ocean, and expressed its hope that other tour operators would follow suit. ASOC recommended that the CEP note the progress made by CCAMLR on the adoption of the MPAs in the Southern Ocean and encourage CCAMLR to continue its work on this issue to completion, and recommended that the CEP consider developing a similar process of systematic conservation planning with a view to expanding the network of terrestrial and marine protected areas in Antarctica. ASOC further noted that in due time, the ATCM, CEP and CCAMLR should look at further harmonisation of their work on marine spatial protection.

(168) IAATO thanked ASOC for providing a useful summary that could be of interest for those outside the CCALMR processes. Acknowledging ASOC's comment, IAATO reported that its Secretariat was collecting information on this issue to facilitate decision making among IAATO Members.

(169) ASOC presented IP 153 *Considerations for the systematic expansion of the protected areas network*, in which ASOC noted that the system of ASPAs was still inadequate to protect the values listed in Annex V to the Protocol. ASOC suggested that in order to expand the ASPA system, the ATCM should initiate a systematic conservation planning process to identify and designate new ASPAs. ASOC advised the CEP that it had compiled an online database of datasets that it hoped could be useful in designating new ASPAs. ASOC recommended that the Committee: continue to populate the list of relevant available metadata to improve the classification of Antarctic Environments created using Environmental Domains Analysis and its application to protected area systematic development; initiate a five to ten year systematic

conservation planning process aiming to establish a network of protected areas in the Antarctic Treaty area in accordance with Annex V, Articles 3 (1) and (2); and complement this process with the use of other area-based protection instruments, including ASMAs and those available under other instruments of the Antarctic Treaty system (such as CCAMLR MPAs).

(170) The Committee thanked ASOC for its papers and noted that some of the matters addressed in IP 153 were already raised in the CCWRP as a subject for future attention. The Committee agreed that the expansion of the protected areas network was an important issue that it was committed to examine in the future.

(171) SCAR presented IP 166 *Systematic Conservation Plan for the Antarctic Peninsula*, jointly prepared with IAATO. SCAR and IAATO noted that they had recently agreed to undertake a collaborative effort to develop a systematic conservation plan for the Antarctic Peninsula, particularly with a view to managing the long-term sustainability of Antarctic tourism. In noting this was a new initiative, SCAR invited interested Members to collaborate in the process.

(172) The Committee thanked SCAR and IAATO for the advice presented in IP 166. Several Members and Observers expressed interest in contributing to the initiative including through sharing experiences from other relevant work, and also to contribute to discussions on setting conservation goals and considering interactions between this work and other work underway or planned by the CEP and its Members. The Committee noted IAATO's advice that the initiative was part of a multi-dimensional strategy IAATO was developing for managing future growth, including site management, and encouraged interested Members to contact SCAR or IAATO, which had welcomed collaboration.

(173) Portugal presented IP 23 *Historical and geo-ecological values of Elephant Point, Livingston Island*, South Shetland Islands, jointly submitted with Brazil, Spain, United Kingdom. It provided information on the high ecological value and historical significance of the ice-free area of Elephant Point (Livingston Island, South Shetland Island, Antarctica), and highlighted the importance of all five values outlined in Annex V to the Protocol (environmental, scientific, historic, aesthetic and wilderness). Portugal noted that the paper was intended to inform the Committee's considerations on the protection and management of this area, possibly by designation as an ASPA, or by incorporating it within the nearby ASPA 126 Byers Peninsula, Livingston Island.

(174) IAATO informed the Committee that the site at Elephant Point, Livingston Island was used by tour operators. IAATO reported that the site had received about 1900 visitors last season, and that, in the absence of specific site guidelines, landings were managed using the *General Guidelines for Visitors to the Antarctic* (annexed to Resolution 3 (2011)), and IAATO mechanisms. IAATO offered to contribute expert knowledge of the site to future discussions, as required.

(175) The Committee expressed its interest in receiving further updates as the co-authors continued to develop protection and management options for Elephant Point.

(176) Australia presented IP 25 *Report of the Antarctic Specially Managed Area No. 6 Larsemann Hills Management Group*, jointly submitted with China, India, and the Russian Federation. The paper briefly reported on the activities carried out during 2015-16 by the Management Group established to oversee the implementation of the management plan for ASMA 6 Larsemann Hills. Key issues addressed by the group included: aviation coordination; collaboration on scientific research; and planned improvements to the main access route in the area. Australia also noted that China would chair the next period of the Management Group.

(177) New Zealand presented IP 86 *Use of UAS for Improved Monitoring and Survey of Antarctic Specially Protected Areas*, which presented a summary of recent work undertaken by New Zealand scientists who used remotely piloted aircraft systems to conduct high resolution surveys at two Antarctic Specially Protected Areas in the Ross Sea region: Botany Bay (ASPA 154) and Cape Evans (ASPA 155). New Zealand reported that the survey work at Botany Bay would be completed in the 2017/18 season, and an updated management plan would be prepared on the basis of the survey results and submitted to CEP XXI.

(178) The United Kingdom noted that New Zealand's approach in using UAV / RPAS to monitor and survey ASPAs pointed the way to the future for monitoring protected areas in Antarctica, and that such technology would enhance the opportunity to develop better understanding of protected areas.

(179) The following papers were also submitted under this agenda item:

- IP 34 *Workshop on Environmental Assessment of the McMurdo Dry Valleys: Witness to the Past and Guide to the Future* (United States).

- IP 44 *Significant change to ASPA No 151 Lions Rump, King George Island (Isla 25 de Mayo), South Shetland Islands* (Poland).
- IP 73 *Deception Island Antarctic Specially Managed Area (ASMA No. 4) - 2017 Management report* (United States, Argentina, Chile, Norway, Spain, and the United Kingdom).

Item 10: Conservation of Antarctic Flora and Fauna

10a) Quarantine and Non-native Species

(180) The United Kingdom introduced WP 5 *Non-native Species Response Protocol*, prepared jointly with Spain, which presented a non-mandatory Response Protocol to facilitate decision-making in the event that a suspected non-native species is discovered in the Antarctic Treaty area. The paper noted that the CEP had repeatedly recognised the importance of developing further guidelines to help Parties respond to potential non-native species introductions.

(181) The co-authors recommended that the Committee discuss the Response Protocol over the intersessional period, with the aim of adopting the Response Protocol into the CEP Non-native Species Manual at CEP XXI.

(182) The Committee thanked the United Kingdom and Spain for presenting the proposed non-mandatory Response Protocol, and noted that this work related to needs and actions identified in the CEP Non-native Species Manual, the CEP Five-Year Work Plan and the Climate Change Response Work Programme. The Committee highlighted the value of including such a Response Protocol in the Non-native Species Manual.

(183) Several Members indicated that they would agree to adopt the Response Protocol as presented in WP 5. Other Members wished to undertake further discussions on the document. The Committee welcomed the offer by the United Kingdom and Spain to consult with interested Members during the intersessional period to further revise the Response Protocol, with the aim of incorporating it into the CEP Non-native Species Manual at CEP XXI.

(184) The Committee noted that, as appropriate, a number of comments raised by Members could be given further consideration during the intersessional discussions, including: requirements relating to environmental impact assessment of response actions; questions about non-native species that may be recently discovered but may have been in place for some time; and the

idea of developing an illustrative guide to aid identifying particular species in the field to complement the manual.

(185) As a broader comment, Norway suggested that the Committee might in the future consider circumstances under which non-native species response actions could constitute emergency response actions, in accordance with provisions of the Protocol, and thus not require prior environmental impact assessment.

(186) The Committee noted the very kind offer from SCAR to bring forward information to CEP XXI regarding existing work and expertise that would be available for identifying non-native species.

(187) Regarding the process for updating the Non-native Species Manual, the Committee agreed that:

- the manual was intended to be a dynamic tool, able to be readily updated to reflect best practice;

- it would request the Secretariat to update the online version of the manual following each meeting, as appropriate, to reflect any changes agreed by the Committee;

- such changes would be marked in a way that indicated that they had been endorsed by the Committee, but had not been formally adopted by the ATCM;

- the Committee would include an action in its Five-Year Work Plan to periodically undertake a full review of the manual, and would present the resulting revision to the ATCM for adoption by means of a Resolution.

(188) In accordance with this agreement, the Committee requested the Secretariat to update the online version of the Non-native Species Manual as appropriate to reflect the Committee's agreement to:

- update the Antarctic Conservation Biogeographic Regions (WP 29);

- endorse *SCAR's Code of Conduct for the Exploration and Research of Subglacial Aquatic Environments* (WP 17); and

- incorporate a link to the Non-native Species manual developed by Argentina for its national Antarctic programme activities (IP 128 rev. 1).

(189) The Republic of Korea introduced WP 26 *Non-native flies in sewage treatment plants on King George Island, South Shetland Islands*, prepared jointly with the United Kingdom, Chile and Uruguay. It noted that at CEP XIX, the Committee agreed that Parties with stations on King George Island

should check their waste water treatment plants for non-native invertebrate infestations and, if present, should join collaborative research efforts to determine the origin of these species and identify practical and coordinated management response for fly eradication or control. It reported on the distribution of flies in the natural environment and within stations and the first steps in a coordinated international response to manage the flies.

(190) The Committee welcomed WP 26 and thanked the co-authors for the update on matters discussed at CEP XIX. The Committee congratulated the Parties involved for their ongoing efforts to eradicate this non-native fly from sewage treatment plants in certain stations on King George Island. The Committee encouraged Parties with stations on King George Island to check their facilities for non-native flies and to undertake both continuous and periodic monitoring to indicate if there are any non-native flies inhabiting the environment. It also encouraged Parties to jointly develop coordinated standardised monitoring and eradication programmes to effectively control the spread of the flies and to join the collaborative research project. In that regard the Committee noted that Argentina and China, which also had stations on the island, had expressed their willingness to be involved in this collaborative effort.

(191) The Committee also noted the advice from COMNAP that its Members had developed a non-native species checklist and training modules on non-native species matters, and that it would stand ready to assist in these ongoing efforts, if requested.

(192) In response to a query, the Republic of Korea noted that it had cleaned the sewage tanks at its station and used insect traps, but that these actions had unfortunately proven unsuccessful in eradicating the flies, so it would be undertaking further work to consider other eradication options. The Committee looked forward to receiving a report on these matters at a future meeting.

(193) Poland presented IP 47 *Eradication of a non-native grass* Poa annua L. *from ASPA No 128 Western Shore of Admiralty Bay, King George Island, South Shetland Islands*. This paper presented the results of a research study on the eradication of the non-native species *Poa annua* from ASPA 128 and from Arctowski station. Follow-up activities from the 2016/2017 Antarctic season were also reported, and it was noted that if eradication were to be completed, it must be a long term project.

(194) The Committee thanked Poland for presenting this paper. Recalling its earlier request to receive updates on this activity and welcoming the ongoing eradication and monitoring activities, the Committee congratulated Poland on its continuing efforts, and noted that it was looking forward to further updates from Poland on the success of this activity.

(195) Argentina presented IP 128 rev. 1 *Prevention of the Introduction of Non-native Species to the Antarctic Continent: Argentine Antarctic Program Operations Manual*. The paper reported that Argentina had developed a manual to prevent dissemination of non-native species by its National Antarctic Programme, which conducted a broad range of scientific and logistics operations. The manual was developed in specific fact-sheets and organised in relation to logistic means (cargo storage depots, aircrafts and vessels) and in relation to the assigned personnel (logistic and scientific). It highlighted that this was the first written document on this topic in this language, and that all original material was presented in Spanish, making it useful for other Spanish speaking programmes. Argentina wished to share this tool with other Members, and proposed that the CEP consider this Manual and include it in the Guidelines and Resources section of the CEP Non-native Species Manual.

(196) The Committee thanked Argentina for presenting its manual for preventing the introduction of non-native species through its National Antarctic Programme activities. Several Members noted that having this material available in Spanish was a very useful and valuable contribution that could be used and adopted by other Spanish speaking National Antarctic Programmes as they deemed appropriate. The Committee supported Argentina's proposal to include the manual in the CEP Non-native Species Manual in the Guidelines and Resources section.

(197) The following papers were also submitted under this agenda item:

- IP 54 *Detection and eradication of a non-native Collembola incursion in a hydroponics facility in East Antarctica* (Australia).

10b) Specially Protected Species

(198) No papers were submitted under this agenda item.

10c) Other Annex II Matters

(199) SCAR introduced WP 13 *Antarctica and the Strategic Plan for Biodiversity 2011 to 2020*, prepared jointly with Monaco and Belgium. The paper provided a summary of the outcomes and recommendations from the meeting held by SCAR, the Principality of Monaco and partners in June 2015 to assess Antarctic and Southern Ocean biodiversity and its conservation status in the context of the Strategic Plan for Biodiversity 2011-2020 and its Aichi Targets. The main conclusions of the assessment were that: the five goals of the Strategic Plan and the Aichi Targets resonated well with the extensive and inclusive work being undertaken through the ATS to ensure comprehensive protection of the Antarctic environment; and that the ATS agreements offered an unparalleled opportunity to improve conservation over the next five years, especially given the Santiago Declaration of ATCM XXXIX-CEP XIX and support for conservation from all organisations involved in the region. The co-authors recommended that the Committee consider the development, in collaboration with its partners, of an integrated biodiversity strategy and action plan for Antarctica and the Southern Ocean. This would help give effect to the pledge of the Antarctic Treaty Consultative Parties to further strengthen their efforts to preserve and protect the Antarctic terrestrial and marine environments, and form the basis for an Antarctic and Southern Ocean contribution to a truly global assessment of the state of biodiversity and its management in 2020. Belgium suggested that the portal *biodiversity.aq* could play a key-role in this process.

(200) The Committee thanked SCAR, Belgium and Monaco for the paper and their continuing efforts to assess the status of biodiversity in Antarctica and the Southern Ocean. Some Members supported the recommendation that the CEP consider the development of an integrated biodiversity strategy and action plan for Antarctica and the Southern Ocean. Some of those Members noted that this work was in-line with Article 3(2) of the Treaty. Other Members, while not supporting this recommendation, expressed their support for work at the CEP towards an improved understanding of biodiversity and its conservation in the Antarctic, including the continuation of the planned work by SCAR, Monaco and Belgium, and welcomed the advice by SCAR that it was progressing with its conservation strategy.

(201) The Committee noted that an enhanced understanding of the state of Antarctic biodiversity would also contribute to global efforts to conserve biodiversity, and emphasised that the Antarctic Treaty system was the appropriate framework for the conservation of biodiversity in the Antarctic

Treaty area. It underlined that many measures were currently in place to ensure that all of Antarctica had a high level of protection and conservation in accordance with the provisions of the Environment Protocol and the CAMLR Convention. The Committee recalled that much of its work was directed to the protection and conservation of Antarctic biodiversity including actions identified in the Five-Year Work Plan and the CCRWP. The Committee welcomed the efforts by SCAR, Belgium, Monaco, and other Members to develop evidence-based tools and approaches, including through a further workshop planned for July 2017, to assist the CEP in addressing challenges to Antarctic biodiversity conservation, and encouraged those involved to bring back their findings for its consideration.

(202) ASOC expressed its appreciation for the co-authors' work in assessing the state of biodiversity in Antarctica, and drawing attention to where more work was needed. It particularly noted that the warming and acidification of the Southern Ocean, and the related impacts on ecosystem services, made it imperative to work to manage and safeguard these global services. ASOC highlighted the need for more work in designating protected areas for both land and marine environments, and in particular ensuring that those areas designated at land and sea are representative of areas important for biodiversity. ASOC supported the co-author's recommendation of having the CEP develop an integrated biodiversity strategy and action plan for Antarctica and the Southern Ocean. ASOC noted that by 2020 it hoped significant progress would have been made on implementing the strategy and action plan.

Unmanned Aerial Vehicles / Remotely Piloted Aircraft Systems

(203) The Committee recalled that it had discussed the environmental impacts of the use of unmanned aerial vehicles (UAV) / remotely piloted aircraft systems (RPAS) in Antarctica, had welcomed SCAR's earlier agreement to report to CEP XX on the impacts of such devices on wildlife, and had agreed to give further consideration at CEP XX to developing guidance for the environmental aspects of the use UAV / RPAS in Antarctica. Recalling that the topic had been discussed for a number of years, the Committee additionally noted that the ATCM Multi-Year Strategic Work Plan included an action for ATCM XL to consider related advice from the CEP.

(204) SCAR introduced WP 20 *State of Knowledge of Wildlife Responses to Remotely Piloted Aircraft Systems (RPAS)*, and referred to BP 1 *Best Practice for Minimising Remotely Piloted Aircraft System Disturbance to Wildlife in*

Biological Field Research, which presented a synthesis from 23 published scientific research papers on wildlife responses to RPAS. Consistent with the SCAR recommendations in ATCM XXXVIII - WP 27, the paper supported the conclusion that there would not be a one-size-fits-all solution to the mitigation of wildlife responses to RPAS, and that guidelines would clearly need to be site- and species-specific and consider the type of RPAS used, including noise output. SCAR recommended that the Committee consider implementation of preliminary best practice guidelines for all RPAS use in the vicinity of wildlife in Antarctica, as presented in WP 20, until further information became available. It also identified priorities for future studies on wildlife response to RPAS in the Antarctic.

(205) Germany presented IP 38 *Use of UAVs in Antarctica: A competent authority's perspective and lessons learned*, which gave the perspective of the German national competent authority on the different aspects of the use of UAVs in Antarctica. Based on its experiences on the authorisation and use of drones in Antarctica by different stakeholders, Germany noted that it considered that there was a need for guidelines for the use of UAVs in Antarctica. It also encouraged other National Competent Authorities to share their experiences with their own authorisation or permitting procedures for UAV operations.

(206) Poland presented IP 45 *UAV remote sensing of environmental changes on King George Island (South Shetland Islands): update on the results of the third field season 2016/2017*, which provided an update on the third successfully completed field season of a monitoring programme using fixed-wing UAVs to collect geospatial environmental data. Polish scientists had used a piston engine UAV for collecting data on penguin and pinniped population size and distribution and for mapping vegetation communities, and had made observations of overflight impact on elephant seals. Poland thanked Chile for its assistance in the performance of its UAV activities.

(207) Poland presented IP 46 *UAV impact – problem of a safe distance from wildlife concentrations*, which discussed a research study on the disturbance of nesting Adélie penguins by UAVs, as well as experiences gained during three Antarctic seasons of using fixed-wing UAVs for collecting diverse environmental data. On environmental grounds, it noted that much of the applicable pre-testing of camera and sensors was done in Poland prior to its use in the field. Affixed to the paper, Poland also presented draft guidelines prepared by the Polish Antarctic Program for the future use of fixed-wing UAVs near wildlife colonies.

(208) COMNAP presented IP 77 *Update from the COMNAP Unmanned Aerial Systems Working Group (UAS-WG)*. It noted that the paper had two points of particular relevance to CEP discussions. First, the survey of National Antarctic Programmes' RPAS use in Antarctica showed that 80% of the countries had domestic legislation related to RPAS and of those, 33% applied them in their Antarctic operations. Second, the paper highlighted the many scientific and environmental management uses of RPAS.

(209) SCAR noted that considerable research was presently underway on the use of RPAS in the Antarctic. With regard to the matter of RPAS distances from bird colonies, SCAR stressed the guidelines presented in WP 20 were of a precautionary nature although at the same time based on scientific evidence. SCAR noted that it would continue to focus on evidence-based science, and welcomed support for further research on the issue.

(210) The Committee thanked SCAR for the comprehensive report on the state of knowledge of wildlife responses to RPAS use in the Antarctic, and also thanked the authors of the other papers submitted to inform the Committee. The Committee again recognised the benefits of using UAV / RPAS for research and monitoring, including the potential reduction of environmental risks. It acknowledged the value of the precautionary best-practice guidelines for RPAS use in the vicinity of wildlife in Antarctica presented in WP 20 and agreed to encourage the dissemination and use of those guidelines as an interim measure pending the further development of broader guidance on the environmental aspects of UAV / RPAS use in Antarctica. The Committee noted that further intersessional work might consider: the environmental impacts associated with the use of UAV / RPAS in the Antarctic other than those associated with wildlife disturbance; site- and species-specific guidance on their use; and how scientific project use of UAV / RPAS could be assessed in the future.

(211) The Committee supported SCAR's recommendation that future studies on wildlife response to UAV / RPAS in the Antarctic should consider:

- A range of species including flying seabirds and seals.
- Both behavioural and physiological responses.
- Demographic effects, including breeding numbers and breeding success.
- Ambient environmental conditions, for example, wind and noise.
- The effects of RPAS of difference sizes and specifications.
- The contribution of RPAS noise to wildlife disturbance.

- Comparisons with control sites and human disturbance.
- Habituation effects.

(212) The Committee noted that the list of science needs identified in WP 34 could be updated accordingly as part of the review of the list at CEP XXI.

(213) COMNAP noted that it had welcomed SCAR's advice, which it had shared with its members, and which it would use as a reference for future reviews of the COMNAP UAS Handbook, adding that it agreed that situation specific RPAS guidelines were encouraged. IAATO advised that its members had agreed to continue the ban on recreational use of UAV / RPAS in coastal areas.

(214) The Committee decided to establish an ICG to develop guidelines for the environmental aspects of the use of UAVs / RPAS in Antarctica. It noted that the work of the ICG could draw on ATCM XL - WP 20 (SCAR), ATCM XL - IP 77 (COMNAP) and other papers submitted on the subject to CEP meetings, as well as the results of ongoing scientific research and experiences of national competent authorities.

(215) The Committee agreed that the ICG would operate in accordance with the following terms of reference:

1. review and update the available information regarding the environmental aspects of UAV / RPAS including experiences on the use by national programmes and IAATO;

2. collect information from Competent Authorities regarding the environmental aspects of their authorisation/permitting procedures for UAV / RPAS operations;

3. develop, on the basis of a precautionary approach, guidance for the environmental aspects of UAV / RPAS use in Antarctica, taking into account different purposes (eg, scientific, logistic, commercial and leisure) and the type of UAV / RPAS, including site- and species-specific conditions;

4. report the outcome including a proposal for guidelines to CEP XXI.

(216) The Committee welcomed the offer from Dr Heike Herata (Germany) to act as ICG convenor.

(217) SCAR, COMNAP and IAATO expressed their commitment to continue to contribute the work of the Committee on these matters, including through the ICG.

CEP advice to the ATCM on Unmanned Aerial Vehicles (UAV) / Remotely Piloted Aircraft Systems (RPAS)

(218) Noting the ATCM Multi-Year Strategic Work Plan included an action to consider advice from the Committee on UAVs / RPAS, the Committee agreed to advise the ATCM that it had:

- encouraged the dissemination and use of the precautionary best-practice guidelines for unmanned aerial vehicles (UAV) / remotely piloted aircraft systems (RPAS) use in the vicinity of wildlife in Antarctica, as presented in WP 20;

- agreed that future studies on wildlife response to UAV / RPAS in the Antarctic should consider the matters identified in WP 20; and

- agreed to establish an intersessional contact group to develop guidelines for the environmental aspects of the use of UAVs / RPAS in Antarctica for consideration for CEP XXI.

(219) Argentina introduced WP 44 *Protection Mechanisms for the Snow Hill Island Emperor Penguin Colony, North East of the Antarctic Peninsula,* which proposed the evaluation of different mechanisms of protection for the Snow Hill Island emperor penguin colony, in the current context of climate change and anthropogenic pressures. Argentina noted that it was necessary to start a debate on the different mechanisms of additional protection for the colony. In the framework of the Antarctic Treaty system (ATS), it pointed out different ways to provide additional protection such as the designation of Specially Protected Species (SPS), the creation of Antarctic Specially Protected Areas (ASPA), and the regulation of visitors through the establishment of Site Guidelines. In highlighting its belief that there were sufficient elements to propose the protection of the colony through the designation of an ASPA, Argentina noted that the actual designation was a process that could take several years. Until it was determined if it was necessary to implement this protection mechanism or another more restrictive measure, according to a preventive approach, Argentina presented a series of specific guidelines for behaviour on the ground for the Snow Hill Island emperor penguin colony that could be adopted and applied immediately. Argentina recommended that the CEP: evaluate the relevance of providing additional protection to the Snow Hill Island emperor penguin colony; consider the behavioural guidelines provided in the Annex to WP 44, until the need to develop more restrictive mechanisms of protection is evaluated; and provide assistance in

the identification of alternative mechanisms of protection that had not been considered in WP 44.

(220) SCAR drew the Committee's attention to the recently published work of Robin Cristofari and others, entitled "Full Circumpolar Migration Ensures Unity in the Emperor Penguin", published in the journal *Nature Communications* in 2016. This work suggested that emperor penguins were a single demographic unit, which implied that local actions related to emperor penguins could be influenced by processes occurring in distant regions of the continent. The United Kingdom noted its intention to present evidence to CEP XXI in relation to emperor penguin colony variation in the Peninsula region which it hoped would add to this analysis.

(221) The Committee thanked Argentina for the paper and agreed on the importance of evaluating the relevance of providing additional protection to the Snow Hill Island emperor penguin colony. The Committee agreed to recommend the application of the *Guidelines for Behaviour Near the Snow Hill Island Emperor Penguin Colony*, presented in WP 44, as an interim measure until the need to develop more restrictive mechanisms of protection was evaluated.

(222) The Committee agreed to support Argentina to undertake further work to develop protection mechanisms for the colony, and encouraged other interested Members and Observers to contribute to that work. The Committee encouraged Members to continue scientific work on emperor penguins in order to monitor population trends in the colonies. The Committee also welcomed IAATO's advice that it would circulate the behavioural guidelines among its Members and provide feedback to the CEP regarding the application of those guidelines. The Committee welcomed SCAR's advice regarding the recent relevant research that could be taken into consideration when Argentina and the Committee were further considering these matters. The Committee looked forward to receiving an update from Argentina at a future meeting.

CEP advice to the ATCM on protection mechanisms for the Snow Hill Island emperor penguin colony

(223) The Committee agreed to advise the ATCM that it had welcomed WP 44 and had agreed to recommend the application of the *Guidelines for Behaviour Near the Snow Hill Island Emperor Penguin Colony* as an interim measure

until the need to develop more restrictive mechanisms of protection was evaluated.

(224) Spain presented IP 20 *The role of monitoring, education and EIA in the prevention of vegetation trampling within ASPA No. 140, Site C: Caliente Hill*, prepared jointly with the United Kingdom. The paper summarised how the extremely rare plant communities located on the geothermally heated ground within Site C: Caliente Hill of ASPA 140 Parts of Deception Island had been subject to cumulative trampling impacts. It reported that the co-authors had developed a high precision mapping system and had mapped each community, and would send this information to all tourist operators and scientists active in the region. The co-authors encouraged other Parties active in the area to educate their scientists and logistical support personnel entering the area on the vulnerability of the plant communities, and to incorporate measures to mitigate potential trampling impact in the environmental impact assessment for the proposed field research.

(225) Germany drew the Committee's attention to IP 37 *Bird Monitoring in the Fildes Region* and IP 39 *Study on monitoring penguin colonies in the Antarctic using remote sensing data*, and highlighted that the full reports of each of the research projects were available online at the following links: IP 37 *http://www.umweltbundesamt.de/publikationen/monitoring-the-consequences-of-local-climate-change* and IP 39 *https://www.umweltbundesamt.de/publikationen/monitoring-penguin-colonies-in-the-antarctic-using*.

(226) The following paper was also submitted under this agenda item:

- IP 75 *A report on the development and use of the UAS by the US National Marine Fisheries Service for surveying marine mammals* (United States).

Item 11: Environmental Monitoring and Reporting

(227) The Committee recalled that ATCM XXXIX had requested the CEP to develop a series of "best estimate" trigger levels to assist in guiding monitoring efforts, as outlined in Recommendation 7 of the 2012 CEP Tourism Study. It noted that Recommendation 7 referred to Recommendation 3, which was the subject of ongoing work to develop a methodology to assess the sensitivity of sites used by visitors.

(228) Australia presented IP 83 rev. 1 *Update on work to develop a methodology to assess the sensitivity of sites used by visitors*, jointly prepared with

New Zealand, Norway, the United Kingdom and the United States, and in conjunction with IAATO. This paper provided a further update on work since CEP XIX to develop a methodology to assess the sensitivity of sites used by visitors (Recommendation 3), and on planned next steps. Following discussion of this topic at CEP XIX in 2016, suggestions on the further development of the draft methodology for site sensitivity were received from other Members and Observers. The authors planned to revise the methodology, drawing on these suggestions, and then conduct 'desktop' testing, in preparation for potential field trials. The paper also presented the co-authors' initial views regarding Recommendation 7 of the 2012 CEP Tourism Study on 'best estimate' trigger levels to assist in guiding monitoring efforts. They noted that identification of trigger levels to guide site monitoring and management efforts would appropriately be informed by an analysis of sites' sensitivity to visitation, and so continued work to further develop the site sensitivity methodology would be a relevant next step for advancing both Recommendation 3 and Recommendation 7.

(229) The Committee thanked the authors for the paper and welcomed their ongoing efforts to develop a methodology to assess the sensitivity of sites used by visitors, noting that this work would contribute to advancing both Recommendation 3 and Recommendation 7 from the CEP tourism study.

(230) IAATO advised that it remained willing to contribute to the process if required.

CEP advice to the ATCM on recommendations from the 2012 CEP Tourism Study

(231) The Committee noted that ATCM XXXIX had requested the CEP to develop a series of 'best estimate' trigger levels to assist in guiding monitoring efforts, as outlined in Recommendation 7 of the 2012 CEP Tourism Study. It had considered a report on ongoing work in accordance with Recommendation 3, to develop a methodology for assessing the sensitivity of sites to tourist visitation, and noted that this work would also be relevant to address Recommendation 7.

(232) The WMO presented IP 113 *The Global Cryosphere Watch and CryoNet*. It explained that the Global Cryosphere Watch (GCW), when fully operational, would enable an assessment of the cryosphere and its changes, and provide wide access to cryosphere information. It also reported on the GCW's network of standardised observing stations (CryoNet) and that eight countries'

ATCM XL Final Report

operating stations in Antarctica had committed stations for inclusion in the GCW observing network. The WMO encouraged Members and Observers to consider contributing to the GCW by: considering if any of the observing stations they manage and operate in Antarctica could be proposed as CryoNet sites or stations; and informing GCW if they were aware of existing sources of cryospheric data for Antarctica that could contribute to GCW and be made discoverable through the GCW Data Portal.

(233) The WMO also presented IP 114 *The Polar Space Task Group: Coordinating Space Data in the Antarctic Region*. It outlined the work of the Polar Space Task Group (PSTG), whose mandate included acquisition and distribution of satellite datasets, and support of the development of products for cryospheric and polar scientific research and applications. These products included a large combination of complementary satellite radar altimetry, synthetic aperture radar images, optical images, and gravimetric datasets. Other tools developed to allow ease of access to these datasets were the TU Dresden Antarctic ice sheet gravimetric mass balance time-series plotting tool (*https://data1.geo. tu-dresden.de/ais_gmb/*), and the ENVEO CryoPortal (*http://cryoportal. enveo.at/*). The Group also produced atmospheric and sea ice products.

(234) The Committee reiterated the value of the WMO's climate-related activities in the Antarctic region.

(235) Portugal presented IP 22 *Trace element contamination and availability within the Antarctic Treaty Area*, jointly prepared with Chile, Germany, the Russian Federation and the United Kingdom. This paper built on earlier reports of trace elements in soil and seawater samples collected from Fildes Peninsula and within ASPA 150 Ardley Island, and reported that contamination originated from specific anthropogenic sources and may have a negative effect on native biota. The proponents encouraged Members to share their monitoring data to help inform future monitoring research and policy development, and consider the implementation of appropriate contamination controls and remediation methods.

(236) SCAR presented IP 68 *Update on activities of the Southern Ocean Observing System (SOOS)*, which highlighted future efforts, summarised activities and identified key challenges facing SOOS. It noted that the SOOS Working Group on Censusing Animal Populations from Space (CAPS) aimed to develop a cost-effective remote sensing-based method for monitoring animal populations from space, of relevance to the Committee's discussion on these matters. It also reported that in 2018 there would be a SOOS-sponsored international conference "Marine Ecosystem Assessment for the Southern

Ocean (MEASO)" which would aim to assess the status and trend of habitats, key species and ecosystems in the Southern Ocean. It highlighted that SOOS was completely aligned with the objectives of the Committee and was vital to understanding the Southern Ocean and its conservation.

(237) WMO highlighted the significant value of SOOS and emphasised the importance of ensuring its continuing funding. It also acknowledged Australia and Sweden for their continuing support.

(238) The Committee reiterated the value of the work being undertaken by SOOS to facilitate the collection and delivery of observations on dynamics and change in Southern Ocean systems.

(239) New Zealand presented IP 76 *Supporting the analysis of environments and impacts: A tool to enable broader-scale environmental management.* It provided an update on a New Zealand research project to develop a tool to assist in the planning, permitting, and implementation of Antarctic activities while limiting adverse impacts on the Antarctic environment. New Zealand highlighted that it would be a user-friendly tool and invited Members to continue their involvement in the development of this tool.

(240) The Committee thanked New Zealand for the paper, welcomed the continuing development of the tool and looked forward to further reports on its development tool.

(241) SCAR presented IP 81 *Report of Oceanites, Inc.*, which described the activities of Oceanites, Inc. since ATCM XXXIX, including: results from the latest, 23rd consecutive field season of the Antarctic Site Inventory; recent scientific papers; update on Oceanites' Mapping Application for Penguin Populations and Projected Dynamics and Oceanites' climate challenge analyses and penguin conservation efforts; and the inaugural *State Of Antarctic Penguins* report.

(242) The United Kingdom recalled that it had worked with Oceanities for many years and that it continued to support its activities.

(243) IAATO reported that its vessels had supported the work of Oceanities since its inception, providing logistical assistance and data collection, and that its operators looked forward to continuing this support.

(244) The following papers were also submitted under this agenda item:

- IP 8 *Field Project Reviews: Fulfilling Environmental Impact Assessment (EIA) Monitoring Obligations* (United States).

- IP 34 *Workshop on Environmental Assessment of the McMurdo Dry Valleys: Witness to the Past and Guide to the Future* (United States).

- IP 79 *Environmental monitoring of the reconstruction work of the Brazilian Antarctic Station (2015/16 and 2016/17)* (Brazil).

- SP 9 *Update on the current state of recommendations of the 2012 CEP Tourism Study* (ATS).

- BP 8 *Using virtual reality technology for low-impact monitoring and communication of protected and historic sites in Antarctica* (New Zealand).

Item 12: Inspection Reports

(245) Chile introduced WP 43 *General Recommendations from the Joint Inspections Undertaken by Argentina and Chile under Article VII of the Antarctic Treaty and Article 14 of the Environmental Protocol*, and referred to IP 126 *Report of the Joint Inspections' Program undertaken by Argentina and Chile under Article VII of the Antarctic Treaty and Article 14 of the Environmental Protocol*, both jointly prepared with Argentina. The co-authors noted general comments and recommendations related to joint inspections undertaken under Article VII of the Antarctic Treaty and Article 14 of the Environment Protocol. These were based on experiences during the Argentine-Chilean joint inspections undertaken between 20 January and 24 February 2017, which involved Johann Gregor Mendel Station of the Czech Republic and Rothera Station of the United Kingdom. Argentina and Chile noted that both stations were compliant with the Environment Protocol, and highlighted the advances in energy efficiency, the number of useful guidelines and training at the stations, and the importance of waste management processes, including for historic waste. Argentina and Chile also warmly thanked the Czech Republic and the United Kingdom for their cooperation and hospitality during the inspections, and noted how inspections represented a valuable learning tool for both the inspecting and inspected Parties.

(246) The Czech Republic thanked Argentina and Chile for their joint inspection of Johann Gregor Mendel Station, and welcomed their constructive recommendations, which provided useful input to improve the operation of the station. It further thanked Argentina and Chile for acknowledging the high percentage of renewable energy used at the station.

(247) The United Kingdom thanked Argentina and Chile for their joint inspection of Rothera Station. It acknowledged the benefits of reducing reliance on fossil fuels. It also outlined the parameters being monitored within the nearby ASPA 129 Rothera Point, Adelaide Island, noting that these had included: monitoring skua numbers and breeding success; monitoring soil pollution; looking for non-native species; and examining the metal content of lichens. The United Kingdom noted that future initial environmental evaluations (IEEs) for modernisation of the wharf and the station would be made available on the British Antarctic Survey (BAS) website and on the EIA database.

(248) The Committee thanked Chile and Argentina for the report on inspections undertaken during 2017. It welcomed the positive findings of the inspection team regarding the high degree of compliance with the Environment Protocol, and also regarding renewable energy use, waste management, and the availability of up-to-date environmental protocols at the inspected stations. Noting that the ATCM would also be considering the inspection report, the Committee expressed its support for the general recommendations presented in WP 43.

(249) A number of general points were raised during the discussion including: the value of having up-to-date information in the EIES; the value of previous inspection reports as a resource for planning inspections; the benefits associated with the cooperative conduct of inspections; and the value of receiving reports back from inspected Parties regarding actions taken in response to recommendations arising from inspections. In that light, the Committee welcomed the reports submitted by Poland (BP 7) and the Czech Republic (BP 14).

(250) Australia presented IP 30 *Australian Antarctic Treaty and Environmental Protocol inspections: December 2016.* It reported on an inspection of the Amundsen-Scott South Pole Station, operated by the United States, and Antarctic Specially Managed Area (ASMA) No. 5 Amundsen-Scott South Pole Station, conducted by Australian observers in December 2016. It drew the attention of the CEP to the inspection team's conclusion that ASMA No. 5 was operating effectively and achieving the management objectives for which it was designated, and that Amundsen-Scott South Pole Station was operating in compliance with the provisions and objectives of the Protocol on Environmental Protection. The United States thanked Australia for its inspection.

(251) The Committee welcomed the inspection team's positive findings that ASMA 5 was effective in achieving the management objectives for which it was designated, and that Amundsen-Scott South Pole Station was operating in compliance the Environment Protocol.

(252) The following papers were also submitted under this agenda item:

- BP 7 *Measures taken on the recommendations by Inspection team at Arctowski Polish Antarctic Station in 2016/2017* (Poland).
- BP 14 *Follow-up to the Recommendations of the Inspection Teams at the Eco-Nelson Facility* (the Czech Republic).

Item 13: General Matters

(253) China introduced WP 36 *Green Expedition in the Antarctic*, jointly prepared with Australia, Chile, France, Germany, India, Republic of Korea, New Zealand, Norway, United Kingdom, and the United States. The paper introduced the "Green Expedition" concept, which referred to the promotion of environmentally friendly activities in the Antarctic by those planning and undertaking activities, and explained that this would involve minimising impacts on the environment by every means. This would include implementing the methods and guidance detailed in current Resolutions and CEP/ATCM discussions, and any new methods developed as a result of recent advances in modern management and technology. The paper contained a proposed Resolution, encouraging Parties to plan and conduct their activities in Antarctica in an efficient and sustainable way.

(254) The Committee thanked China and the co-authors of this paper. The co-authors highlighted China's leadership on this initiative. The Committee supported the "Green Expedition" concept, as outlined in WP 36, to promote the environmentally friendly planning and conduct of all activities in Antarctica. Some Members provided additional examples of initiatives they had taken consistent with the "Green Expedition" concept.

(255) Argentina noted that procedures and conduct guidelines also contributed to the environmentally friendly conduct of activities.

CEP advice to the ATCM on Green Expeditions

(256) The CEP agreed to forward a draft Resolution to the ATCM for adoption, encouraging and promoting the concept of "Green Expeditions".

(257) Portugal presented IP 24 *Future Challenges in Southern Ocean Ecology Research: another outcome of the 1ˢᵗ SCAR Horizon Scan*, jointly prepared with Belgium, Brazil, France, Germany, the Netherlands, SCAR, the United Kingdom, and the United States. The paper reported on an output of the SCAR Antarctic and Southern Ocean Science Horizon Scan. It noted that the work presented reflected contributions from many Antarctic scientists and policy makers. It focused on high-interest research areas related specifically to Southern Ocean life and ecology that, although not all retained as the top priorities among the addressed scientific domains, were of considerable relevance to the biology and ecology of the Southern Ocean. It highlighted that Southern Ocean ecological research would require long-term commitment by Parties to conduct international and interdisciplinary research, aided by the development of technology (in cooperation with organisations such as COMNAP and SCAR). It further noted that education and outreach (in cooperation with organisations such as the Association for Polar Early Career Scientists and Polar Educators International) and coordinated funding strategies for the various stakeholders would be essential to successfully address the challenges in Antarctic research.

(258) The Committee thanked the co-authors for presenting this work. It noted the consistency between science needs identified by the Committee in documents such as the CCRWP, as outlined in WP 34, and the research areas identified in this paper.

(259) Ecuador presented IP 110 *Plan de contingencias y riesgos durante la XXI Campaña Antártica Ecuatoriana (2016-2017)*, which described contingency and emergency plans for the Ecuadorian station Campaña Antártica Ecuatoriana. It noted that the plans address issues related to human safety, security of infrastructure, and environmental protection.

Item 14: Election Officers

(260) The Committee elected Dr Kevin Hughes from the United Kingdom as Vice-chair for a two-year term and congratulated him on his appointment to the role.

(261) The Committee warmly thanked and congratulated Dr Polly Penhale from the United States for her excellent work and significant contributions throughout her four-year term as Vice-chair.

Item 15: Preparation for the Next Meeting

(262) The Committee adopted the Preliminary Agenda for CEP XXI (Appendix 5).

Item 16: Adoption of the Report

(263) The Committee adopted its Report.

Item 17: Closing of the Meeting

(264) The Chair closed the Meeting on Friday, 26 May 2017.

Appendix 1

CEP Five-year Work Plan 2017

Issue / Environmental Pressure: Introduction of non-native species	
Priority: 1	
Actions: 1. Continue developing practical guidelines & resources for all Antarctic operators. 2. Implement related actions identified in the Climate Change Response Work Programme. 3. Consider the spatially explicit, activity-differentiated risk assessments to mitigate the risks posed by terrestrial non-native species. 4. Develop a surveillance strategy for areas at high risk of non-native species establishment. 5. Give additional attention to the risks posed by intra-Antarctic transfer of propagules.	
Intersessional period 2017/18	• Initiate work to develop a non-native species response strategy, including appropriate responses to diseases of wildlife • To help the Committee in assessing the effectiveness of the Manual, request a report from COMNAP on the implementation of quarantine and biosecurity measures by its members • United Kingdom to lead discussion with interested Members and Observers, on the further development of a non-mandatory non-native species response protocol
CEP XXI 2018	• Discuss the intersessional work concerning the development of a response strategy for inclusion in the Non-native Species Manual, and the implementation of quarantine and biosecurity measures by COMNAP members. Review IMO report on biofouling guidelines • Consider report on intersessional discussion on non-native species response protocol and its inclusion in the Non-native Species Manual • SCAR to present information on existing mechanism to assist with the identification of non-native species
Intersessional period 2018/19	• Ask SCAR to compile a list of available biodiversity information sources and databases to help Parties establish which native species are present at Antarctic sites and thereby assist with identifying the scale and scope of current and future introductions • Develop generally applicable monitoring guidelines. More detailed or site-specific monitoring may be required for particular locations • Request a report from Parties and Observers on the application of biosecurity guidelines by their members
CEP XXII 2019	• Discuss the intersessional work concerning the development of monitoring guidelines for inclusion in the NNS Manual. Consider the reports from Parties and Observers on the application of biosecurity guidelines by their members
Intersessional period 2019/20	• Initiate work to assess the risk of marine non-native species introductions
CEP XXIII 2020	• Discuss the intersessional work concerning the risks of marine non-native species

Intersessional period 2020/21	• Develop specific guidelines to reduce non-native species release with wastewater discharge • Review the progress and contents of the CEP Non-native Species Manual
CEP XXIV 2021	• CEP to consider if intersessional work is required to review/update the Non-native Species Manual
Intersessional period 2021/22	• As appropriate, intersessional work to review the Non-native Species Manual
CEP XXV 2022	• CEP to consider report of ICG, if established, and consider adoption of revised Non-native Species Manual by the ATCM through a resolution

Issue / Environmental Pressure: Tourism and NGO activities	
Priority: 1	
Actions: 1. Provide advice to ATCM as requested. 2. Advance recommendations from ship-borne tourism ATME.	
Intersessional period 2017/18	• Further develop methodology for site sensitivity assessment and to consider trigger levels (recommendations 3 and 7 of the tourism study)
CEP XXI 2018	
Intersessional period 2018/19	
CEP XXII 2019	
Intersessional period 2019/20	
CEP XXIII 2020	
Intersessional period 2020/21	
CEP XXIV 2021	

Issue / Environmental Pressure: Climate Change Implications for the Environment	
Priority: 1	
Actions: 1. Consider implications of climate change for management of Antarctic environment. 2. Advance recommendations from climate change ATME. 3. Implement the Climate Change response work programme.	
Intersessional period 2017/18	• Pending ATCM approval, subsidiary group conducts work in accordance with agreed work plan
CEP XXI 2018	• Standing agenda item • Consider advice on how WMO activities map to CCRWP • Pending ATCM approval, consider subsidiary group report • SCAR provides update to ACCE report, with input as appropriate from WMO and ICED, SOOS
Intersessional period 2018/19	• Pending ATCM approval, subsidiary group conducts work in accordance with agreed work plan
CEP XXII 2019	• Standing agenda item • Pending ATCM approval, consider subsidiary group report • SCAR provides update to ACCE report, with input as appropriate from WMO and ICED, SOOS
Intersessional period 2019/20	

CEP XXIII 2020	• Standing agenda item • SCAR provides update to ACCE report, with input as appropriate from WMO and ICED, SOOS • Consider review of subsidiary group • Review implementation of actions arising from 2016 joint CEP/SC-CAMLR workshop • Plan for 5-yearly joint SC-CAMLR/CEP workshop during 2021/22 intersessional period
Intersessional period 2020/21	
CEP XXIV 2021	• As Finalise plans for joint SC-CAMLR/CEP workshop during 2021/22 intersessional period
Intersessional period 2021/22	• Regular 5-yearly joint SC-CAMLR CEP workshop

Issue / Environmental Pressure: Processing new and revised protected / managed area management plans	
Priority: 1	
Actions: 1. Refine the process for reviewing new and revised management plans. 2. Update existing guidelines. 3. Advance recommendations from climate change ATME. 4. Develop guidelines to ASMAs preparation.	
Intersessional period 2017/18	• SGMP conducts work as per agreed work plan • Norway and interested Members prepare paper on guidance for delisting ASPAs
CEP XXI 2018	• Consider SGMP report • Consider paper by Norway and interested Members
Intersessional period 2018/19	
CEP XXII 2019	
Intersessional period 2019/20	
CEP XXIII 2020	
Intersessional period 2020/21	
CEP XXIV 2021	

Issue / Environmental Pressure: Operation of the CEP and Strategic Planning	
Priority: 1	
Actions: 1. Keep the 5 year plan up to date based on changing circumstances and ATCM requirements. 2. Identify opportunities for improving the effectiveness of the CEP. 3. Consider long-term objectives for Antarctica (50-100 years time). 4. Consider opportunities for enhancing the working relationship between the CEP and the ATCM.	
Intersessional period 2017/18	• CEP Chair to consult with Secretariat and interested Members to develop options for obtaining and managing funding to assist the work of the CEP
CEP XXI 2018	• CEP to consider report by CEP Chair • CEP to review list of science needs presented in ATCM XL/WP 34
Intersessional period 2018/19	
CEP XXII 2019	
Intersessional period 2019/20	

CEP XXIII 2020	
Intersessional period 2020/21	
CEP XXIV 2021	

Issue / Environmental Pressure: Repair or Remediation of Environmental Damage	
Priority: 2	
Actions:	

1. Respond to further request from the ATCM related to repair and remediation, as appropriate.
2. Monitor progress on the establishment of Antarctic-wide inventory of sites of past activity.
3. Consider guidelines for repair and remediation.
4. Members develop practical guidelines and supporting resources for inclusion in the Clean-up Manual.
5. Continue developing bioremediation and repair practices for inclusion in the Clean-up Manual.

Intersessional period 2017/18	• ICG to review the Clean-Up Manual
CEP XXI 2018	• Consider ICG report on review of the Clean-Up Manual
Intersessional period 2018/19	
CEP XXII 2019	
Intersessional period 2019/20	
CEP XXIII 2020	
Intersessional period 2020/21	
CEP XXIV 2021	

Issue / Environmental Pressure: Monitoring and state of the environment reporting	
Priority: 2	
Actions:	

1. Identify key environmental indicators and tools.
2. Establish a process for reporting to the ATCM.
3. SCAR to support information to COMNAP and CEP.

Intersessional period 2017/18	• SCAR to consult with COMNAP and interested Members on review of *SCAR's Environmental Code of Conduct for Terrestrial Scientific Field Research in Antarctica* • ICG to consider guidance for environmental aspects of UAV / RPAS
CEP XXI 2018	• CEP to consider report from SCAR on intersessional review of Code of Conduct • Consider report of ICG on UAV / RPAS
Intersessional period 2018/19	
CEP XXII 2019	• Consider *SCAR's Code of Conduct for the Use of Animals for Scientific Purposes in Antarctica*
Intersessional period 2019/20	
CEP XXIII 2020	
Intersessional period 2020/21	
CEP XXIV 2021	• Consider monitoring report by UK on ASPA 107

Issue / Environmental Pressure: Marine spatial protection and management	
Priority: 2	

Actions:
1. Cooperation between the CEP and SC-CAMLR on common interest issues.
2. Cooperate with CCAMLR on Southern Ocean bioregionalisation and other common interests and agreed principles.
3. Identify and apply processes for spatial marine protection.
4. Advance recommendations from climate change ATME.
5. Consider connectivity between land and ocean, and complementary actions that could be taken by Parties with respect to MPAs.

Intersessional period 2017/18	
CEP XXI 2018	
Intersessional period 2018/19	
CEP XXII 2019	
Intersessional period 2019/20	
CEP XXIII 2020	
Intersessional period 2020/21	
CEP XXIV 2021	

Issue / Environmental Pressure: Site specific guidelines for tourist-visited sites	
Priority: 2	

Actions:
1. Periodically review the list of sites subject to site guidelines and consider whether development of guidelines should be needed for additional sites.
2. Provide advice to ATCM as required.
3. Review the format of the site guidelines.

Intersessional period 2017/18	
CEP XXI 2018	• Standing agenda item; Parties to report on their reviews of site guidelines
Intersessional period 2018/19	
CEP XXII 2019	• Standing agenda item; Parties to report on their reviews of site guidelines
Intersessional period 2019/20	
CEP XXIII 2020	• Standing agenda item; Parties to report on their reviews of site guidelines
Intersessional period 2020/21	
CEP XXIV 2021	

Issue / Environmental Pressure: Overview of the protected areas system		
Priority: 2		
Actions:		
1. Apply the Environmental Domains Analysis (EDA) and Antarctic Conservation Biogeographic Regions (ACBR) to enhance the protected areas system. 2. Advance recommendations from climate change ATME. 3. Maintain and develop Protected Area database. 4. Assess the extent to which Antarctic IBAs are or should be represented within the series of ASPAs.		
Intersessional period 2017/18	•	United Kingdom to lead discussion with interested Members and Observers, on Antarctic Specially Protected Areas and Important Bird Areas
CEP XXI 2018	• • •	Plan for a joint SCAR/CEP workshop on Antarctic biogeography, including to: identify practical management applications of biogeographic tools and future research needs Provide a status report to the ATCM on the status of the Antarctic Protected Areas network Consider report of intersessional work on Antarctic Specially Protected Areas and Important Bird Areas
Intersessional period 2018/19	•	Joint SCAR/CEP workshop on Antarctic biogeography
CEP XXII 2019	•	Consider report from joint SCAR/CEP workshop on Antarctic biogeography
Intersessional period 2019/20		
CEP XXIII 2020		
Intersessional period 2020/21		
CEP XXIV 2021		

Issue / Environmental Pressure: Outreach and education		
Priority: 2		
Actions:		
1. Review current examples and identify opportunities for greater education and outreach. 2. Encourage Members to exchange information regarding their experiences in this area. 3. Establish a strategy and guidelines for exchanging information between Members on Education and Outreach for long term perspective.		
Intersessional period 2017/18	•	Celebrate the 20th Anniversary of the CEP
CEP XXI 2018	•	Bulgaria to draw to the Committee's attention any outcomes from the ICG on Education and Outreach of direct relevance to the work of the CEP
Intersessional period 2018/19		
CEP XXII 2019		
Intersessional period 2019/20		
CEP XXIII 2020		
Intersessional period 2020/21		
CEP XXIV 2021		

Issue / Environmental Pressure: Implementing and improving the EIA provisions of Annex I		
Priority: 2		
Actions: 1. Refine the process for considering CEEs and advising the ATCM accordingly. 2. Develop guidelines for assessing cumulative impacts. 3. Review EIA guidelines and consider wider policy and other issues. 4. Consider application of strategic environmental assessment in Antarctica. 5. Advance recommendations from climate change ATME.		
Intersessional period 2017/18	•	Establish ICG to review draft CEEs as required
	•	Parties, Experts and Observers work to progress and coordinate information that will assist development of guidance on identifying and assessing cumulative impacts
	•	Consider potential changes required to EIA database to improve its utility
CEP XXI 2018	•	Discuss changes to the EIA database with a view to giving proposals to the Secretariat
	•	Consideration of ICG reports on draft CEE, as required
Intersessional period 2018/19	•	Establish ICG to review draft CEEs as required
	•	Parties, Experts and Observers work to progress and coordinate information that will assist development of guidance on identifying and assessing cumulative impacts
CEP XXII 2019	•	Consideration of ICG reports on draft CEE, as required
Intersessional period 2019/20	•	Establish ICG to review draft CEEs as required
	•	Parties, Experts and Observers work to progress and coordinate information that will assist development of guidance on identifying and assessing cumulative impacts
CEP XXIII 2020	•	Ask SCAR to provide guidance on how to do an environmental baseline condition survey, and consider their advice in due course
	•	Consideration of ICG reports on draft CEE, as required
Intersessional period 2020/21	•	Establish ICG to review draft CEEs as required
	•	Parties, Experts and Observers work to progress and coordinate information that will assist development of guidance on identifying and assessing cumulative impacts
CEP XXIV 2021	•	Encourage parties to provide feedback on the utility of the revised set of *Guidelines for Environmental Impact Assessment in Antarctica* in the preparation of EIAs
	•	Consideration of the options for preparing guidance on identifying and assessing cumulative impacts
	•	Consideration of ICG reports on draft CEE, as required

Issue / Environmental Pressure: Designation and management of Historic Sites and Monuments		
Priority: 2		
Actions:		
1. Maintain the list and consider new proposals as they arise. 2. Consider strategic issues as necessary, including issues relating to designation of HSM versus clean-up provisions of the Protocol. 3. Review the presentation of the HSM list with the aim to improve information availability.		
Intersessional period 2017/18	•	ICG on development of guidance relating to designation of HSM
CEP XXI 2018	•	Consider ICG report
Intersessional period 2018/19		
CEP XXII 2019		
Intersessional period 2019/20		
CEP XXIII 2020		
Intersessional period 2020/21		
CEP XXIV 2021		

Issue / Environmental Pressure: Biodiversity knowledge		
Priority: 3		
Actions:		
1. Maintain awareness of threats to existing biodiversity. 2. Advance recommendations from climate change ATME. 3. CEP to consider further scientific advice on wildlife disturbance.		
Intersessional period 2017/18		
CEP XXI 2018	•	Discussion of SCAR update on underwater noise
Intersessional period 2018/19		
CEP XXII 2019		
Intersessional period 2019/20		
CEP XXIII 2020		
Intersessional period 2020/21		
CEP XXIV 2021		

Issue / Environmental Pressure: Protection of outstanding geological values	
Priority: 3	
Actions:	
1. Consider further mechanisms for protection of outstanding geological values.	
Intersessional period 2017/18	
CEP XXI 2018	• Consider advice from SCAR
Intersessional period 2018/19	
CEP XXII 2019	
Intersessional period 2019/20	
CEP XXIII 2020	
Intersessional period 2020/21	
CEP XXIV 2021	

Appendix 2

Subsidiary Group on Climate Change Response – Framework

Background

In 2008 the CEP included the issue of climate change on its agenda, and in 2009 SCAR published its Antarctic Climate Change and the Environment Report. In 2010 the ATCM held an Antarctic Treaty Meeting of Experts (ATME) on climate change and implications for Antarctic management and governance, which made 30 recommendations for the ATCM and CEP to consider, including that:

the CEP consider developing a climate change response work programme, and that such a work programme should attempt to incorporate, *inter alia*:

- The need to continue to afford a high priority to the management of non-native species;

- A classification of existing protected areas according to climate change vulnerability;

- The need for more sophisticated and coordinated ecosystem monitoring, including the need for increased collaboration between CEP and SC-CAMLR;

- A review of existing management tools to assess their continuing suitability in a climate change context (eg, EIA guidelines [particularly with regard to planned long-term activities], Specially Protected Species guidelines, the guide to the preparation of management plans).

The CEP established an ICG to develop a climate change response work programme (CCRWP), and in Resolution 4 (2015), the ATCM welcomed the CCRWP, encouraged the CEP implement it as a matter of priority, provide annual progress reports to the ATCM, and keep the CCRWP under regular review. Implementing the CCRWP is a priority 1 item on the CEP Five-Year Work Plan.

Subsidiary Body of the CEP

The Committee may establish, with the approval of the ATCM, subsidiary bodies, as appropriate. Such subsidiary bodies shall operate on the basis of the Rules of Procedure of the Committee as applicable (Rule 10). CEP XX agreed to recommend to the ATCM the establishment of a Subsidiary Group on Climate Change Response (SGCCR) to support the implementation of the CCRWP.

SGCCR Terms of Reference

CEP XX adopted the following terms of reference to guide the Subsidiary Group's work:

Facilitate the efficient and timely implementation of the CCRWP by:

- Facilitating the coordination and communication of the CCRWP between Members, Observers and Experts, highlighting actions identified for the coming year(s) and requesting relevant updates on planned activities;
- Drafting proposed annual updates of the CCRWP, including management, research or monitoring actions;
- Drafting annual progress reports on the implementation of the CCRWP for the CEP to draw on in their updates to the ATCM.

The CEP may amend the ToR of the SGCCR at any time.

Translation

The CEP have agreed that key texts, for example, texts for discussion and or draft annual updates of the CCRWP be translated, on a case by case basis. Noting that the SGCCR will generally conduct its business remotely, the CEP considers that translation of key texts will meet the requirements of Rule 21.

Membership

Membership of the SGCCR is open to all Members, Observers and Experts. It is desirable that SCAR and WMO representatives are members of the group. Members are encouraged to participate in the SGCCR for more than a year, to support continuity in membership and to maintain knowledge.

The Committee has agreed that broad participation in the group is important, and the SGCCR should maintain a minimum of four CEP Member participants. The convenor will have oversight of maintaining the membership of the SGCCR.

Convener

Convenors of the SGCCR may be a CEP Vice Chair or CEP Member, elected under the same conditions as set out for Vice Chairs in Rule 15 of the Rules of Procedure, as applicable. Convenors may, but are not required to, provide technical contribution to the SGCCR's activities.

Review

CEP XX noted its intention to review the effectiveness of the SGCCR after 3 years.

Appendix 3

Procedures for intersessional CEP consideration of draft CEEs

1. The agenda of each CEP meeting shall include an item relating to the consideration of draft CEEs forwarded to the CEP in accordance with Paragraph 4 of Article 3 of Annex I to the Protocol.*

2. The CEP shall, under this agenda item, consider any draft CEE and provide advice to the ATCM on such drafts in accordance with Article 12 and Annex I of the Protocol.*

3. Proponents are encouraged to circulate draft CEEs to the Committee as soon as practicable and, in accordance with Paragraph 4 of Article 3 of Annex I to the Protocol, shall do so at least 120 days before the next Antarctic Treaty Consultative Meeting.

4. At the same time a draft CEE is circulated to Members via diplomatic channels, the proponent shall notify the CEP Chair, preferably by e-mail, that a draft CEE has been circulated.**

5. The proponent should post the draft CEE on a web site in the original language(s). A link to that web site will also be established on the CEP web site. If the proponent does not have a web site on which it is able to post the draft CEE, an electronic version should be forwarded to the CEP Chair who will post it on the CEP web site.**

   [The Secretariat shall also translate each draft CEE into all other official languages and post these versions to the CEP web site as soon as practicable.]

6. The CEP Chair shall immediately notify the CEP contact points of the availability of each draft CEE, and provide details of the web site at which such documents can be accessed.**

7. The Chair shall suggest a convenor for an open-ended intersessional contact group to consider the draft CEE. The convenor should preferably not be from the proponent Party.**

8. The Chair shall allow a period of 15 days for Members to object or offer comments, suggestions or proposals concerning:

   i.   the proposed convenor.

   ii.   Additional terms of reference beyond the following generic issues:

   - the extent to which the CEE conforms to the requirements of Article 3 of Annex I of the Environment Protocol;

- whether the CEE: i) has identified all the environmental impacts of the proposed activity; and ii) suggests appropriate methods of mitigating (reducing or avoiding) those impacts;
- whether the conclusions of the draft CEE are adequately supported by the information contained within the document; and
- the clarity, format and presentation of the draft CEE.**

9. If the Chair does not receive a reply within 15 days it will be considered that the Members agree with the proposed convenor and the generic terms of reference. If the Chair receives comments on i) or ii) listed above within the 15 day limit the Chair shall, as appropriate, circulate a revised suggestion for one or both items. A further 15 day limit applies for Members to respond.**

10. All correspondence shall be available to all representatives via the CEP Discussion Forum.*

11. The right of a Party to raise an issue on a draft CEE at the CEP or ATCM is not affected by its action in relation to the establishment –or non-establishment– of an open-ended intersessional contact group.**

12. The outcome of the contact group's deliberations, indicating areas of agreement and areas where differing views are expressed, shall be reported in a Working Paper submitted by the convenor to the next CEP meeting.**

---

* Copied or modified from "Guidelines for CEP Consideration of Draft CEEs" (Annex 4 to CEP II Final Report, 1999).

** Copied or modified from "Operational procedures for establishing intersessional contact groups for consideration of draft CEEs" (Annex 3 to CEP III Final Report, 2000).

Appendix 4

Guidelines: A prior assessment process for the designation of ASPA and ASMAs

The CEP noted the benefits of a prior assessment process for potential new ASMAs and ASPAs, including: (i) engaging all Parties in the process of designating new sites; (ii) recognising that all ASPAs and ASMAs are internationally designated; (iii) aiding Members in preparing management plans by allowing for feedback and comments from other Members earlier in the process; and (iv) facilitating consideration of the further systematic development of the protected areas system in accordance with Article 3 of Annex V to the Protocol, and with consideration of climate change implications. Proponent(s) of potential new ASPAs or ASMAs are therefore encouraged to engage the Committee in a prior assessment discussion.

Consequently, the following Guidelines were adopted at CEP XVIII Final Report (Appendix 3).

1. The proponent should submit information about planned ASMAs and ASPAs at the first possible CEP meeting after they have identified an area as a potential new ASPA or ASMA irrespective of whether a decision to start working on a management plan has been taken or not. It would be useful if the proponent submitted this information at the latest one year before intending to submit a management plan to the CEP for consideration.

2. The information submitted to the CEP should include:

    *   The proposed location of the ASMA/ASPA.

    *   The initial rationale behind the plans for proposing the designation, including specifying the legal basis for the designation found in Annex V; how it improves the representativeness of the protected areas network, and how it fits within the ACBR planning tool.

    *   Other relevant information relating to the development of a management plan that the proponent country has available at the time of submission to the CEP meeting.

3. The proponent country is encouraged to facilitate further discussions and questions on the preliminary plans through e.g. informal discussions/exchanges on the CEP forum or directly with Member countries.

ASPA prior assessment template

To assist proponents provide the information detailed in the Guidelines (above) for potential ASPAs, a non-mandatory template has been developed for voluntary use and is available at Appendix A: *Antarctic Specially Protected Area prior assessment template*.

Appendix A

Antarctic Specially Protected Area prior assessment template[*]

Proponents should only complete those sections of the template that they consider relevant to the assessment they have completed.

1	Name of potential Antarctic Specially Protected Area (ASPA):			
2	Proponent(s) of potential ASPA:			
3	Location and approximate co-ordinates of potential ASPA:			
4	Is the potential ASPA within an existing Antarctic Specially Managed Area (ASMA)?			
5	Approximate size of potential ASPA:			
6	Main physical components contained within the potential ASPA (e.g. ice-free ground, lakes, ocean, ice shelf, permanent ice):			
7	Description of the initial rational for area protection for the potential ASPA:			
8	Indication of the values to be protected within the potential ASPA, in accordance with Annex V Article 3(1):			
	Value	*Primary value*	*Secondary value*	*Not applicable*
	Environmental values			
	Scientific values			
	Historic values			
	Aesthetic values			
	Wilderness values			
	Combination of values			
	Ongoing or planned scientific activities			
9	Further description of values to be protected			
10	The following characteristics are contained within the potential ASPA:			(Yes/No)
(a)	areas kept inviolate from human interference so that future comparisons may be possible with localities that have been affected by human activities			
(b)	representative examples of major terrestrial, including glacial and aquatic, ecosystems and marine ecosystems			
(c)	areas with important or unusual assemblages of species, including major colonies of breeding native birds or mammals			

(d)	the type locality or only known habitat of any species	
(e)	areas of particular interest to ongoing or planned scientific research	
(f)	examples of outstanding geological, glaciological or geomorphological features	
(g)	areas of outstanding aesthetic and wilderness value	
(h)	sites or monuments of recognised historic value	
(i)	such other areas as may be appropriate to protect environmental, scientific, historic, aesthetic or wilderness values, any combination of those values, or ongoing or planned scientific research	
11	Consideration as to whether the ASPA be protected primarily for conservation or scientific research purposes:	
12	Description of how the quality of the areas merits ASPA designation (e.g. representativeness, diversity, distinctiveness, ecological importance, degree of interference, science and monitoring uses):	
13	Assessment of the risk posed to the area due to human activities and impacts, natural processes, natural variability and viability, non-Antarctic threats, urgency and scientific uncertainty:	

Designation of the protected area within a systematic environmental-geographical framework:		
14	The area lies within the following Environmental Domains Analysis region(s) (Resolution 3 [2008]):	
15	The area lies within the following Antarctic Conservation Biogeographic Region (Resolution 6 [2012]):	
16	The area contains the following Antarctic Important Bird Areas (Resolution 5 [2015]):	
17	Short description of how the potential ASPA has been considered to improve the representativeness of the protected areas network:	
18	Other relevant information from the assessment process:	
19	Any relevant supporting documentation	

* In this context it is relevant to point to the *"Guidelines for implementation of the Framework for Protected Areas set forth in Article 3 of Annex V of the Environmental Protocol"* (held under Resolution 1 [2000]), which includes guidance for such assessment processes.

N.B. For ASPAs with a substantial marine component, prior approval must be obtained from CCAMLR (Annex V, Article 6 [2]).

Appendix 5

Preliminary Agenda for CEP XXI (2018)

1. Opening of the Meeting
2. Adoption of the Agenda
3. Strategic Discussions on the Future Work of the CEP
4. Operation of the CEP
5. Cooperation with other Organisations
6. Repair and Remediation of Environment Damage
7. Climate Change Implications for the Environment
   a. Strategic Approach
   b. Implementation and Review of the Climate Change Response Work Programme
8. Environmental Impact Assessment (EIA)
   a. Draft Comprehensive Environmental Evaluations
   b. Other EIA Matters
9. Area Protection and Management Plans
   a. Management Plans
   b. Historic Sites and Monuments
   c. Site Guidelines
   d. Marine Spatial Protection and Management
   e. Other Annex V Matters
10. Conservation of Antarctic Flora and Fauna
    a. Quarantine and Non-native Species
    b. Specially Protected Species
    c. Other Annex II Matters
11. Environmental Monitoring and Reporting
12. Inspection Reports
13. General Matters
14. Election of Officers
15. Preparation for Next Meeting
16. Adoption of the Report
17. Closing of the Meeting

3. Appendices

Preliminary Agenda for ATCM XLI, Working Groups and Allocation of Items

Plenary

1. Opening of the Meeting

2. Election of Officers and Creation of Working Groups

3. Adoption of the Agenda, Allocation of Items to Working Groups and Consideration of the Multi-year Strategic Work Plan

4. Operation of the Antarctic Treaty System: Reports by Parties, Observers and Experts

5. Report of the Committee on Environmental Protection

Working Group 1: *(Policy, Legal, Institutional)*

6. Operation of the Antarctic Treaty System: General matters

7. Operation of the Antarctic Treaty System: Matters related to the Secretariat

8. Liability

9. Biological Prospecting in Antarctica

10. Exchange of Information

11. Education Issues

12. Multi-year Strategic Work Plan

Working Group 2: *(Science, Operations, Tourism)*

13. Safety and Operations in Antarctica

14. Inspections under the Antarctic Treaty and Environmental Protocol

15. Science issues, future science challenges, scientific cooperation and facilitation

16. Implications of Climate Change for Management of Antarctic Treaty Area

17. Tourism and Non-governmental Activities in the Antarctic Treaty Area, including Competent Authorities Issues

Plenary

18. Preparation for the XLII Meeting

19. Any other Business

20. Adoption of the Final Report

21. Close of the Meeting

Host country communique

The 40th Antarctic Treaty Consultative Meeting (ATCM XL) was held in Beijing, China, from 23 May to 1 June 2017. The meeting was chaired by His Excellency Mr. Liu Zhenmin, Vice Minister of the Ministry of Foreign Affairs of the People's Republic of China. The 20th Meeting of the Committee for Environmental Protection (CEP) was held from 22 to 26 May 2017 and was chaired by Mr. Ewan McIvor (Australia). The meetings were co-organized by the Ministry of Foreign Affairs of China and the State Oceanic Administration of China.

Over 400 participants from the Antarctic Treaty Parties, observers and invited experts from international organizations attended the annual Meeting. His Excellency Mr. Zhang Gaoli, Vice Premier of the State Council of the People's Republic of China, officially opened the ATCM XL. His Excellency Mr. Yang Jiechi, State Councilor of the State Council of the People's Republic of China, met with all delegates.

Discussions in the ATCM focused on the following issues: operation of the Antarctic Treaty System, liability, biological prospecting in Antarctica, exchange of information, education issues, multi-year strategic work plan, safety and operations in Antarctica, inspections under the Antarctic Treaty and the Environment Protocol, science issues, scientific cooperation and facilitation, future Antarctic science challenges, implications of climate change for management of Antarctic Treaty area, tourism and non-governmental activities in the Antarctic Treaty area.

The following topics were discussed in the CEP: operation and the future work of the CEP, cooperation with other organizations, repair and remediation of environment damage, climate change implications for the environment, environmental impact assessment, area protection and management plans, conservation of Antarctic flora and fauna, environmental monitoring and reporting, and inspection reports.

Mr. Albert Lluberas Bonaba from Uruguay was elected as the next Executive Secretary of the Antarctic Treaty Secretariat, for the term 2017-2021. Parties extended their congratulations to Mr. Albert Lluberas Bonaba and appreciation for the excellent performance of Dr. Manfred Reinke, the current Executive Secretary, over the past eight years.

A Special Meeting titled "Our Antarctica: Protection and Utilization", which was initiated by China as the Host Country, took place on 23 May 2017 after the opening of the ATCM XL. Although the meeting was not part of the formal ATCM agenda, all delegates of the ATCM and CEP were invited to attend. His Excellency Mr. Liu Zhenmin chaired the meeting. After the keynote speech of His Excellency Mr. Zhang Yesui, First Vice Foreign Minister of China, eight other speakers, including governmental representatives and scientists from Russia, Poland, Argentina, the United States, China, the United Kingdom,

Chile and Australia, were invited by China to share their views on issues related to the protection and utilization of Antarctica. To reflect the presentations of the speakers, China submitted a Chair's summary in the form of Information Paper under the Agenda Item 6 of the ATCM.

Parties expressed their gratitude to the Chinese government for hosting the ATCM XL and their appreciation for the excellent facilities provided for the meeting.

The next ATCM will be hosted by Ecuador in 2018.

PART II

Measures, Decisions and Resolutions

1. Measures

Antarctic Specially Protected Area No. 109
(Moe Island, South Orkney Islands):
Revised Management Plan

The Representatives,

Recalling Articles 3, 5 and 6 of Annex V to the Protocol on Environmental Protection to the Antarctic Treaty ("the Protocol") providing for the designation of Antarctic Specially Protected Areas ("ASPA") and approval of Management Plans for those Areas;

Recalling

- Recommendation IV-13 (1966), which designated Moe Island, South Orkney Islands as Specially Protected Area ("SPA") No. 13 and annexed a map of the Area;

- Recommendation XVI-6 (1991), which annexed a revised description of SPA 13 and a Management Plan for the Area;

- Measure 1 (1995), which annexed a revised description and a revised Management Plan for SPA 13;

- Decision 1 (2002), which renamed and renumbered SPA 13 as ASPA 109;

- Measures 1 (2007) and 1 (2012), which adopted revised Management Plans for ASPA 109;

Recalling that Recommendation IV-13 (1966) was designated as no longer current by Decision 1 (2011), that Resolution 9 (1995) was designated as no longer current by Resolution 1 (2008), that Recommendation XVI-6 (1991) did not become effective and was withdrawn by Decision (D) 2017 and Measure 1 (1995) did not become effective and was withdrawn by Measure 3 (2012);

Noting that the Committee for Environmental Protection has endorsed a revised Management Plan for ASPA 109;

Desiring to replace the existing Management Plan for ASPA 109 with the revised Management Plan;

Recommend to their Governments the following Measure for approval in accordance with paragraph 1 of Article 6 of Annex V to the Protocol:

That:

1. the revised Management Plan for Antarctic Specially Protected Area No. 109 (Moe Island, South Orkney Islands), which is annexed to this Measure, be approved; and

2. the Management Plan for Antarctic Specially Protected Area No. 109 annexed to Measure 1 (2012) be revoked.

Antarctic Specially Protected Area No. 110
(Lynch Island, South Orkney Islands): Revised Management Plan

The Representatives,

Recalling Articles 3, 5 and 6 of Annex V to the Protocol on Environmental Protection to the Antarctic Treaty ("the Protocol") providing for the designation of Antarctic Specially Protected Areas ("ASPA") and approval of Management Plans for those Areas;

Recalling

- Recommendation IV-14 (1966), which designated Lynch Island, South Orkney Islands as Specially Protected Area ("SPA") No 14 and annexed a map of the Area;

- Recommendation XVI-6 (1991), which annexed a Management Plan for the Area;

- Measure 1 (2000), which annexed a revised Management Plan for SPA 14;

- Decision 1 (2002), which renamed and renumbered SPA 14 as ASPA 110;

- Measure 2 (2012), which adopted a revised Management Plan for ASPA 110;

Recalling that Recommendation XVI-6 (1991) and Measure 1 (2000) did not become effective and were withdrawn by Decision (D) 2017;

Noting that the Committee for Environmental Protection has endorsed a revised Management Plan for ASPA 110;

Desiring to replace the existing Management Plan for ASPA 110 with the revised Management Plan;

Recommend to their Governments the following Measure for approval in accordance with paragraph 1 of Article 6 of Annex V to the Protocol:

That:

1. the revised Management Plan for Antarctic Specially Protected Area No. 110 (Lynch Island, South Orkney Islands), which is annexed to this Measure, be approved; and

2. the Management Plan for Antarctic Specially Protected Area No. 110 annexed to Measure 2 (2012) be revoked.

Antarctic Specially Protected Area No. 111
(Southern Powell Island and adjacent islands, South Orkney Islands): Revised Management Plan

The Representatives,

Recalling Articles 3, 5 and 6 of Annex V to the Protocol on Environmental Protection to the Antarctic Treaty ("the Protocol") providing for the designation of Antarctic Specially Protected Areas ("ASPA") and approval of Management Plans for those Areas;

Recalling

- Recommendation IV-15 (1966), which designated Southern Powell Island and adjacent islands, South Orkney Islands as Specially Protected Area ("SPA") No. 15 and annexed a map of the Area;

- Recommendation XVI-6 (1991), which annexed a Management Plan for SPA 15;

- Measure 1 (1995), which annexed a modified description and a revised Management Plan for SPA 15;

- Decision 1 (2002), which renamed and renumbered SPA 15 as ASPA 111;

- Measure 3 (2012), which adopted a revised Management Plan for ASPA 111;

Recalling that Recommendation XVI-6 (1991) did not become effective and was withdrawn by Decision (D) (2017) and Measure 1 (1995) did not become effective and was withdrawn by Measure 3 (2012);

Noting that the Committee for Environmental Protection has endorsed a revised Management Plan for ASPA 111;

Desiring to replace the existing Management Plan for ASPA 111 with the revised Management Plan;

Recommend to their Governments the following Measure for approval in accordance with paragraph 1 of Article 6 of Annex V to the Protocol:

That:

1. the revised Management Plan for Antarctic Specially Protected Area No. 111 (Southern Powell Island and adjacent islands, South Orkney Islands), which is annexed to this Measure, be approved; and

2. the Management Plan for Antarctic Specially Protected Area No. 111 annexed to Measure 3 (2012) be revoked.

Antarctic Specially Protected Area No. 115
(Lagotellerie Island, Marguerite Bay, Graham Land): Revised Management Plan

The Representatives,

Recalling Articles 3, 5 and 6 of Annex V to the Protocol on Environmental Protection to the Antarctic Treaty ("the Protocol") providing for the designation of Antarctic Specially Protected Areas ("ASPA") and approval of Management Plans for those Areas;

Recalling

- Recommendation XIII-11 (1985), which designated Lagotellerie Island, Marguerite Bay, Graham Land as Specially Protected Area ("SPA") No. 19 and annexed a map of the Area;

- Recommendation XVI-6 (1991), which annexed a Management Plan for the Area;

- Measure 1 (2000), which annexed a revised Management Plan for SPA 19;

- Decision 1 (2002), which renamed and renumbered SPA 19 as ASPA 115;

- Measure 5 (2012), which adopted a revised Management Plan for ASPA 15;

Recalling that Recommendation XVI-6 (1991) and Measure 1 (2000) did not become effective and were withdrawn by Decision (D) 2017;

Noting that the Committee for Environmental Protection has endorsed a revised Management Plan for ASPA 115;

Desiring to replace the existing Management Plan for ASPA 115 with the revised Management Plan;

Recommend to their Governments the following Measure for approval in accordance with paragraph 1 of Article 6 of Annex V to the Protocol:

That:

1. the revised Management Plan for Antarctic Specially Protected Area No. 115 (Lagotellerie Island, Marguerite Bay, Graham Land), which is annexed to this Measure, be approved; and

2. the Management Plan for Antarctic Specially Protected Area No. 115 annexed to Measure 5 (2012) be revoked.

Antarctic Specially Protected Area No. 129
(Rothera Point, Adelaide Island):
Revised Management Plan

The Representatives,

Recalling Articles 3, 5 and 6 of Annex V to the Protocol on Environmental Protection to the Antarctic Treaty ("the Protocol") providing for the designation of Antarctic Specially Protected Areas ("ASPA") and approval of Management Plans for those Areas;

Recalling

- Recommendation XIII-8 (1985), which designated Rothera Point, Adelaide Island as Site of Special Scientific Interest ("SSSI") No. 9 and annexed a Management Plan for the Site;

- Resolution 7 (1995), which extended the expiry date of SSSI 9;

- Measure 1 (1996), which annexed a revised description and a revised Management Plan for SSSI 9;

- Decision 1 (2002), which renamed and renumbered SSSI 9 as ASPA 129;

- Measure 1 (2007), which adopted a revised Management Plan for ASPA 129 and revised its boundaries;

- Measure 6 (2012), which adopted a revised Management Plan for ASPA 129;

Recalling that Resolution 7 (1995) was designated as no longer current by Decision 1 (2011) and that Measure 1 (1996) did not become effective and was withdrawn by Measure 10 (2008);

Noting that the Committee for Environmental Protection has endorsed a revised Management Plan for ASPA 129;

Desiring to replace the existing Management Plan for ASPA 129 with the revised Management Plan;

Recommend to their Governments the following Measure for approval in accordance with paragraph 1 of Article 6 of Annex V to the Protocol:

That:

1. the revised Management Plan for Antarctic Specially Protected Area No. 129 (Rothera Point, Adelaide Island), which is annexed to this Measure, be approved; and

2. the Management Plan for Antarctic Specially Protected Area No. 129 annexed to Measure 6 (2012) be revoked.

Measure 6 (2017)

Antarctic Specially Protected Area No. 140
(Parts of Deception Island, South Shetland Islands): Revised Management Plan

The Representatives,

Recalling Articles 3, 5 and 6 of Annex V to the Protocol on Environmental Protection to the Antarctic Treaty ("the Protocol") providing for the designation of Antarctic Specially Protected Areas ("ASPA") and approval of Management Plans for those Areas;

Recalling

- Recommendation XIII-8 (1985), which designated Shores of Port Foster, Deception Island, South Shetland Islands as Site of Special Scientific Interest ("SSSI") No. 21 and annexed a Management Plan for the Site;

- Resolution 7 (1995) and Measure 2 (2000), which extended the expiry date for SSSI 21;

- Decision 1 (2002), which renamed and renumbered SSSI 21 as ASPA 140;

- Measures 3 (2005) and 8 (2012), which adopted revised Management Plans for ASPA 140;

Recalling that Resolution 7 (1995) was designated as no longer current by Decision 1 (2011) and that Measure 2 (2000) did not become effective and was withdrawn by Measure 5 (2009);

Noting that the Committee for Environmental Protection has endorsed a revised Management Plan for ASPA 140;

Desiring to replace the existing Management Plan for ASPA 140 with the revised Management Plan;

Recommend to their Governments the following Measure for approval in accordance with paragraph 1 of Article 6 of Annex V to the Protocol:

That:

1. the revised Management Plan for Antarctic Specially Protected Area No. 140 (Parts of Deception Island, South Shetland Islands), which is annexed to this Measure, be approved; and

2. the Management Plan for Antarctic Specially Protected Area No. 140 annexed to Measure 8 (2012) be revoked.

Antarctic Specially Protected Area No. 165
(Edmonson Point, Wood Bay, Ross Sea): Revised Management Plan

The Representatives,

Recalling Articles 3, 5 and 6 of Annex V to the Protocol on Environmental Protection to the Antarctic Treaty providing for the designation of Antarctic Specially Protected Areas ("ASPA") and approval of Management Plans for those Areas;

Recalling Measure 1 (2006), which designated Edmonson Point, Wood Bay, Ross Sea as ASPA 165 and annexed a Management Plan for the Area;

Recalling Measure 8 (2011), which adopted a revised Management Plan for ASPA 165;

Noting that the Committee for Environmental Protection has endorsed a revised Management Plan for ASPA 165;

Desiring to replace the existing Management Plan for ASPA 165 with the revised Management Plan;

Recommend to their Governments the following Measure for approval in accordance with paragraph 1 of Article 6 of Annex V to the Protocol on Environmental Protection to the Antarctic Treaty:

That:

1. the revised Management Plan for Antarctic Specially Protected Area No. 165 (Edmonson Point, Wood Bay, Ross Sea), which is annexed to this Measure, be approved; and

2. the Management Plan for Antarctic Specially Protected Area No. 165 annexed to Measure 8 (2011) be revoked.

Antarctic Specially Managed Area No. 5
(Amundsen-Scott South Pole Station, South Pole): Revised Management Plan

The Representatives,

Recalling Articles 4, 5 and 6 of Annex V to the Protocol on Environmental Protection to the Antarctic Treaty ("the Protocol"), providing for the designation of Antarctic Specially Managed Areas ("ASMA") and the approval of Management Plans for those Areas;

Recalling Measure 2 (2007), which designated Amundsen-Scott South Pole Station, South Pole as Antarctic Specially Managed Area No. 5;

Noting that the Committee for Environmental Protection has endorsed a revised Management Plan for ASMA 5;

Desiring to replace the existing Management Plan for ASMA 5 with the revised Management Plan;

Recommend to their Governments the following Measure for approval in accordance with Paragraph 1 of Article 6 of Annex V to the Protocol:

That:

1. the revised Management Plan for Antarctic Specially Managed Area No. 5 (Amundsen-Scott South Pole Station, South Pole), which is annexed to this Measure, be approved; and

2. the Management Plan for Antarctic Specially Managed Area No. 5 annexed to Measure 2 (2007) be revoked.

2. Decisions

Subsidiary Group of the Committee for Environmental Protection on Climate Change Response (SGCCR)

The Representatives,

Recalling Rule 10 of the Revised Rules of Procedure for the Committee for Environmental Protection annexed to Decision 2 (2011), which provides that the Committee for Environmental Protection ("CEP") "may establish, with the approval of the Antarctic Treaty Consultative Meeting, subsidiary bodies, as appropriate" and that such subsidiary bodies are to operate on the basis of the Rules of Procedure of the CEP as applicable;

Recalling Resolution 4 (2015), which encouraged the CEP to begin implementing the Climate Change Response Work Programme ("CCRWP") as a matter of priority;

Noting that the CEP at its twentieth meeting requested the Antarctic Treaty Consultative Meeting to approve the establishment of a Subsidiary Group on Climate Change Response ("SGCCR") to support the implementation of the CCRWP (see paragraph 79 of the Report of the Twentieth Meeting of the Committee for Environmental Protection (CEP XX) ("CEP XX Report");

Noting that the framework for the SGCCR, including terms of reference, is outlined in Appendix 2 to the CEP XX Report;

Decide to approve the establishment by the Committee for Environmental Protection ("CEP") of the Subsidiary Group on Climate Change Response as a subsidiary body of the CEP, in accordance with Rule 10 of the Revised Rules of Procedure for the Committee for Environmental Protection annexed to Decision 2 (2011).

Guidelines on the Procedure to be Followed with Respect to Consultative Party Status

The Representatives,

Recognising the need for an updated procedure of consultation and evaluation in the event that another State, having acceded to the Antarctic Treaty, should notify the depositary Government that it considers it is entitled to appoint representatives to participate in Antarctic Treaty Consultative Meetings ("ATCM");

Recalling the obligation under Article X of the Antarctic Treaty "to exert appropriate efforts, consistent with the Charter of the United Nations, to the end that no one engages in any activity in Antarctica contrary to the principles or purposes" of the Antarctic Treaty;

Recognising that a Contracting Party which has become a Party to the Antarctic Treaty by accession shall be entitled to appoint representatives to participate in ATCM under paragraph 2 of Article IX of the Antarctic Treaty "during such time as that Contracting Party demonstrates its interest in Antarctica by conducting substantial scientific research activity there, such as the establishment of a scientific station or the despatch of a scientific expedition";

Recalling the obligation under paragraph 4 of Article 22 of the Protocol on Environmental Protection to the Antarctic Treaty ("the Protocol") not to act upon a notification regarding the entitlement of a Contracting Party to the Antarctic Treaty to appoint representatives to participate in ATCM unless the Contracting Party has first ratified, accepted, approved or acceded to the Protocol;

Emphasising the importance of Contracting Parties to the Antarctic Treaty that are seeking Consultative Party status approving all Annexes to the Protocol that have become effective;

Taking into account that Decision 4 (2005), adopted at ATCM XXVIII, and the Guidelines on Notification with respect to Consultative Status, adopted at ATCM XIV, need to be updated;

Decide:

1. A Contracting Party which considers itself entitled to appoint representatives in accordance with paragraph 2 of Article IX of the Antarctic Treaty shall notify the depositary Government for the Antarctic Treaty of this view and shall provide information concerning its activities in the Antarctic, no later than 210 days prior to the Antarctic Treaty Consultative Meeting ("ATCM") at which the request for recognition of Consultative Party status is to be considered, in particular as recommended by the ATCM in the present Decision and its Annex. The depositary Government shall forthwith communicate for evaluation the foregoing notification and information to all other Consultative Parties.

2. Consultative Parties, in exercising the obligation placed on them by Article X of the Antarctic Treaty, shall examine the information about its activities provided by the Contracting Party, may conduct any appropriate enquiries (including the exercising of their right of inspection in accordance with Article VII of the Antarctic Treaty) and may, through the depositary Government, urge the Contracting Party to make a declaration of intent to approve the Recommendations and Measures adopted by the ATCM and subsequently approved by all the Contracting Parties whose representatives were entitled to participate in those meetings. Consultative Parties may, through the depositary Government, invite the Contracting Party to consider approval of the other Recommendations and Measures.

3. The Government which is to host the next ATCM shall, in the context of its preparation of the provisional agenda for the ATCM in accordance with the Rules of Procedure of the ATCM, include an appropriate item in the provisional agenda for consideration of the notification.

4. The ATCM shall decide, on the basis of all information available to it, whether the Contracting Party in question is to be accorded Consultative Party status consistent with paragraph 2 of Article IX of the Antarctic Treaty and paragraph 4 of Article 22 of the Protocol on Environmental Protection to the Antarctic Treaty. A Decision of the ATCM to accord Consultative Party status shall be notified by the host Government to the Contracting Party.

5. The *Guidelines on the procedure to be followed with respect to Consultative Party status* are annexed to this Decision.

6. The *Guidelines on Notification with respect to Consultative Status* adopted at ATCM XIV and Decision 4 (2005) are superseded by this Decision and its Annex.

Guidelines on the Procedure to be Followed with Respect to Consultative Party Status

The following Guidelines on notification and procedure with respect to Consultative Party status are to be followed by a Contracting Party to the Antarctic Treaty that considers it is entitled to appoint representatives to the Antarctic Treaty Consultative Meetings ("ATCM") and by the Consultative Parties with respect to the procedure and evaluation of the request by the ATCM:

a. The Contracting Party requesting Consultative Party status (CPrCS) should inform the Consultative Parties of its intention to request recognition of Consultative Party status as early as possible prior to the ATCM at which the request is to be considered.

b. The CPrCS should formally notify the depositary Government and provide the necessary dossier of information no later than 210 days before the ATCM at which its request is to be considered.

c. The dossier of information should be provided through the depositary Government by the CPrCS in at least one of the four official languages of the ATCM, with an executive summary to be translated into the four Treaty languages by the translation services of the Secretariat of the Antarctic Treaty as soon as received.

d. The CPrCS is reminded that a Contracting Party which has become a Party to the Antarctic Treaty by accession shall be entitled to appoint representatives to participate in ATCM under paragraph 2 of Article IX of the Antarctic Treaty "during such time as that Contracting Party demonstrates its interest in Antarctica by conducting substantial scientific research activity there, such as the establishment of a scientific station or the despatch of a scientific expedition", and that these examples are non-exhaustive.

e. The CPrCS information dossier should include a description of all scientific programmes and activities performed in or on Antarctica during the last ten years. This may include:

  • a list of publications related to Antarctica, including both articles in peer-reviewed scientific journals as well as papers to international bodies;

  • a list of publications with co-authors from different countries;

  • details of citations of relevant papers that scored well in a science citation index;

  • details of data contributed by the CPrCS with emphasis on data cited in publications that score well in a science citation index and on data contributed to Antarctic scientific programmes and databases;

  • creation of data sets that are accessible to the scientific community; and/or

  • examples of research prizes or formal recognition of accomplishments.

f. The CPrCS should also include all information that points to sustained contributions to science. This may include:

- ongoing and planned scientific programmes in Antarctica, including involvement in international Antarctic research groups, programmes and organisations;

- details and status of the necessary environmental impact assessments in respect of intended activities in Antarctica;

- details of its research facilities and logistics resources existing or planned to support its Antarctic research activities;

- ratio of science to logistics personnel in summer and winter;

- long-term scientific objectives and research plans; and/or

- the nomination of a competent national authority, according to Article 1 of Annex II of Protocol on Environmental Protection to the Antarctic Treaty ("the Protocol").

g. The CPrCS should give a description of all the planning, management and execution of its scientific programmes and logistical support activities in Antarctica, in compliance with the Antarctic Treaty and the Protocol. This may include:

- how Antarctic affairs are managed within its government's structures;

- legislation necessary to ensure compliance with ATCM binding arrangements by the appropriate national institutions;

- identification of all other governmental and non-governmental institutions involved; and/or

- investments dedicated to both Antarctic scientific programmes and logistical support activities.

h. The CPrCS should provide details about its ability and willingness to promote international cooperation in accordance with Article III of the Antarctic Treaty. This may include information on:

- cooperative arrangements or agreements that the Party may have in place with other Antarctic nations to further its Antarctic science programmes;

- number of scientists from other countries involved in the Antarctic projects (in the field or in laboratories);

- number of the CPrCS's scientists participating in an expedition in the field organised by another Party;

- list of joint international projects in which the CPrCS is partner; and/or

- arrangements made in order to facilitate inspections by any observers designated in accordance with Article VII of the Antarctic Treaty and Article 14 of the Protocol, of its own sites or vessels, or of any logistical support provided.

i.   The CPrCS should note the obligation for Consultative Parties, under Article 22(4) of the Protocol, not to act upon a notification regarding the recognition of Consultative Party status unless the Contracting Party has first ratified, accepted, approved, or acceded to the Protocol, as well as approved all Annexes to the Protocol which have become effective.

j.   The CPrCS should make a declaration of intent to approve the Recommendations and Measures adopted at ATCM and subsequently approved by all the Consultative Parties.

k.   Where a scientific expedition is the sole or primary justification for a request for Consultative Party status, the CPrCS should provide information regarding the degree to which the expedition is self-managed and under its responsibility, using its own assets, those of a service provider, or those of an existing Consultative Party, but organised, financed and headed by the CPrCS.

l.   The CPrCS should note that having its relevant authority become a full member of the Council of Managers of National Antarctic Programs ("COMNAP") will be considered a positive indicator of engagement in Antarctic operational matters in support of science, while having its relevant scientific body being a full member of Scientific Committee on Antarctic Research ("SCAR") and having participated in SCAR related scientific activities will be considered an important indicator of involvement in Antarctic science.

m.   The CPrCS should upload all relevant data to the Electronic Information Exchange System ("EIES") of the Antarctic Treaty Secretariat, including to the "Scientific Information" section.

n.   The CPrCS is encouraged to seek assistance, as appropriate, from other Consultative Parties during the process to achieve Consultative Party status.

Measures Withdrawn

The Representatives,

Recalling Decision 3 (2002), Decision 1 (2007), Decision 1 (2011), Decision 1 (2012), Decision 1 (2014) and Decision 2 (2015), which established lists of measures* that were designated as spent or no longer current;

Having reviewed a number of measures identified by the Secretariat of the Antarctic Treaty as having the status of "not yet effective";

Recognising that the measures listed in the Annex to this Decision are spent or have been overtaken by subsequent measures adopted by the Parties on the same subject-matter;

Decide:

1. that the measures listed in the Annex to this Decision are withdrawn; and

2. to request the Secretariat of the Antarctic Treaty to post the text of the measures that appear in the Annex to this Decision on its website in a way that makes clear that these measures did not enter into effect and have been withdrawn.

---

* Measures previously adopted under Article IX of the Antarctic Treaty were described as Recommendations up to ATCM XIX (1995) and were divided into Measures, Decisions and Resolutions by Decision 1 (1995).

Measures withdrawn

Recommendation XV-2 (1989)

Recommendation XV-16 (1989)

Recommendation XVI-6 (1991)

Recommendation XVII-1 (1992)

Recommendation XVII-4 (1992)

Measure 1 (2000)

Procedure for Appointing Antarctic Treaty Consultative Meeting Working Group Chairs

The Representatives,

Recalling that Rule 11 of the Revised Rules of Procedure for the Antarctic Treaty Consultative Meeting annexed to Decision 2 (2015) ("Rules of Procedure") empowers the Antarctic Treaty Consultative Meeting ("ATCM") to establish Working Groups and to appoint Working Group Chairs;

Noting that Rule 11 of the Rules of Procedure is silent as to the practical arrangements for the appointment of Working Group Chairs;

Recalling that at ATCM XXXIX (2016) the Meeting agreed to develop procedures for the appointment of Working Group Chairs;

Decide that Working Group Chairs shall be selected and appointed in accordance with the following procedure:

1. At least 180 days before each Antarctic Treaty Consultative Meeting ("ATCM"), the Secretariat of the Antarctic Treaty ("the Secretariat") will consult with any Working Group Chairs appointed at the previous Meeting regarding their availability to chair a Working Group, if eligible in accordance with Rule 11 of the Revised Rules of Procedure for the Antarctic Treaty Consultative Meeting annexed to Decision 2 (2015) ("the Rules of Procedure").

2. At least 120 days before each ATCM the Secretariat will issue a circular to:

   a. remind Consultative Parties of the provisional arrangements for Working Groups determined at the previous Meeting, in accordance with Rule 11 of the Rules of Procedure, including:

    i. the Working Groups established;

    ii. the Working Group Chairs appointed; and

    iii. the allocation of agenda items to each Working Group;

and

b. advise the Consultative Parties:

    i. of any provisionally appointed Working Group Chair who has advised that they are unavailable to serve in that capacity at or beyond the coming Meeting or who is not eligible to continue to serve as Chair of a particular Working Group beyond the coming Meeting in accordance with Rule 11 of the Rules of Procedure; and

    ii. the number of consecutive Meetings for which other current Working Group Chairs have served as Chair of the same Working Group, and the number of years for which they were appointed;

and

c.   where vacancies are expected to arise, call for Consultative Parties to submit nominations for Working Group Chairs at least 60 days before the ATCM, specifying that each nomination should:

    i. relate to a candidate with a sound working knowledge of the Antarctic Treaty system, the practices of the ATCM and the issues under consideration;

    ii. indicate that the candidate has the support of their Party to serve in the role for at least the next meeting, and possibly up to 4 years, noting the requirement for Working Group Chairs to participate in, and adequately prepare for, annual meetings and be available to lead or coordinate activities during the intersessional period; and

    iii. indicate the area(s) of expertise for which the candidate is being put forward, noting that the coming Meeting may decide to establish new or different Working Groups.

3. Before the ATCM, the Secretariat will issue a further circular summarising the results of any call for nominations.

4. At the ATCM, under the agenda item dealing with election of officers and creation of Working Groups, the Chair of the ATCM will:

    a.   remind Consultative Parties of the ability to establish Working Groups and appoint Working Group Chairs, in accordance with Rule 11 of the Rules of Procedure;

    b.   confirm the Working Group Chairs provisionally appointed at the end of the previous Meeting and their availability to serve in that capacity at the current Meeting;

    c.   in the event that a Working Group Chair provisionally appointed at the end of the previous Meeting is no longer able to serve in that capacity, confirm whether any nominations were received in advance of the Meeting; and

    d.   invite nominations to be made, and in the event that there are two or more nominations for any one position, the procedure set out at paragraph 5(c) to (f) below will apply.

5.   At the ATCM, under the agenda item dealing with organisation of the next Meeting, the Consultative Parties will, as far as practicable, utilise the following procedure to appoint the Chair (and any co-Chair(s) as applicable) for any Working Group to be provisionally established for the subsequent Meeting:

    a.   the Chair will summarise the current situation regarding the availability and eligibility of current Working Group Chairs to serve at the next ATCM and outline the other expressions of interest and nominations received by the Secretariat;

    b.   the Chair will invite expressions of interest or nominations to be made known to them during the Meeting;

    c.   a quorum will be required for a valid election;

    d.   each Consultative Party will be entitled to one vote (in each round of voting, if multiple rounds are required);

    e.   the outcome of the election will be decided by simple majority of Consultative Parties present and voting; and

    f.   where there are more than two candidates for a Working Group Chair position, rounds of voting will be conducted, eliminating the candidate with the least votes in each round.

6.   When appointing Working Group Chairs, where possible:

    a. the terms of the Chairs of different Working Groups will be staggered to help ensure continuity in the experience of the group of Working Group Chairs across ATCM; and

    b. multiple Working Group Chairs will not be representatives from the same Party, and the appointments will provide gender and geographic diversity.

Secretariat Report, Programme and Budget

The Representatives,

Recalling Measure 1 (2003) on the establishment of the Secretariat of the Antarctic Treaty;

Recalling Decision 2 (2012) on the establishment of the open-ended Intersessional Contact Group on Financial Issues to be convened by the host country of the next Antarctic Treaty Consultative Meeting;

Bearing in mind the Financial Regulations for the Secretariat annexed to Decision 4 (2003);

Decide:

1. to approve the audited Financial Report for 2015/16, annexed to this Decision (Annex 1);

2. to take note of the Secretariat Report 2016/17, which includes the Provisional Financial Report for 2016/17, annexed to this Decision (Annex 2);

3. to take note of the Five Year Forward Budget Profile 2017/18-2021/22 and approve the Secretariat Programme 2017/18, including the Budget for 2017/18, annexed to this Decision (Annex 3); and

4. to invite the host country for the next Antarctic Treaty Consultative Meeting ("ATCM") to request that the Executive Secretary open the ATCM forum for the open-ended Intersessional Contact Group on Financial Issues, and provide assistance to it.

Audited Financial Report for 2015/2016

AUDITOR'S REPORT

To: The Secretary

of the Antarctic Treaty Secretariat

Maipú 757, 4th floor

Tax ID (CUIT) 30-70892567-1

Subject: ATCM XXXX - CEP XX Antarctic Treaty Consultative Meeting, 2017 - Pekin, China

1. Report on Financial Statements

We have audited the attached Financial Statements of the Antarctic Treaty Secretariat, which include the Statement of Income and Expenditure, Statement of Financial Position, Statement of Changes in Shareholders' Equity, Cash Flow Statement and Explanatory Notes for the financial year commencing 1st April 2015 and ending 31st March 2016.

2. Management Responsibility for Financial Statements

The Antarctic Treaty Secretariat, established under Argentine Law No. 25.888 of 14th May 2004, is responsible for the preparation and fair presentation of the attached financial statements in accordance with accounting principles based on cash transactions, pursuant to International Accounting Standards and the specific standards for Antarctic Treaty Consultative Meetings. Such responsibility includes the design, implementation and maintenance of internal controls on the preparation and presentation of the Financial Statements, such that they are free of misstatements due to error or fraud; selection and implementation of appropriate accounting policies, and preparation of accounting estimates which are reasonable under the circumstances.

3. Auditor's Responsibility

Our responsibility is to express an opinion on these Financial Statements based on our audit.

The audit was conducted in accordance with International Auditing Standards and the Annex to Decision 3 (2012) of the XXXI Antarctic Treaty Consultative Meeting, which describes the tasks to be carried out by the external audit.

These standards require compliance with ethical requirements, and planning and execution of the audit so as to provide reasonable assurance that the Financial Statements are free of material misstatements.

An audit includes the execution of procedures in order to obtain evidence on the amounts and the exposure reflected in the Financial Statements. The procedures selected depend on the auditor's judgment, including the assessment of the risks of significant errors in the financial statements.

On conducting such assessment of risks, the auditor considers the internal control relevant to the preparation and reasonable presentation of the Financial Statements by the organisation, in order to design suitable procedures that are appropriate to the circumstances.

An audit also includes an assessment of appropriateness, of the accounting principles used, an opinion on whether the accounting estimates made by management are reasonable, as well as an assessment of the general presentation of the Financial Statements.

We believe that the evidence obtained provides a sufficient and appropriate basis for our audit opinion.

4. Opinion

In our opinion, the attached audited Antarctic Treaty Secretariat Financial Statements for the financial year ended 31st March 2016 have been prepared, in all material aspects, in accordance with International Accounting Standards and the specific standards for Antarctic Treaty Consultative Meetings, and pursuant to accounting principles based on cash transactions.

5. Other matters

Disclosures on Note 1 to the financial statements, establishing that the latter have been prepared by the Antarctic Treaty Secretariat pursuant to the provisions established in Financial Regulations, annexed to Decision 4 (2003), which differ, in terms of specific valuation and presentation criteria, from accounting standards applicable and in force for the City of Buenos Aires, Argentine Republic.

6 . Additional Information Required by Law

Pursuant to the analysis described in point 3, we report that the abovementioned Financial Statements arise from accounting records that are not transcribed into books in accordance with Argentine standards in force.

We also report that, according to bookkeeping as at 31 March 2016, the liabilities accrued for the Argentine Single Social Security System in Argentine pesos and pursuant to calculations made by the Secretariat amounted to $124,004.85 (US$ 14,059.51), none of which was due and payable in Argentine pesos as at that date.

It is worth noting that labour relationships are governed by Antarctic Treaty Secretariat Staff Regulations.

City of Buenos Aires, 27th April 2017

Board of Syndics of the Argentine Republic
(Sindicatura General de la Nación, SIGEN).

[signature]
Horacio Canaveri
Certified Accountant (U.M.)

1. Statement of Income and Expenses for all funds for the period 1ˢᵗ April 2015 to 31ˢᵗ March 2016, comparatively with the prior year.

INCOME	31/03/2015	Budget 31/03/2015	31/03/2016
Contributions (Note 10)	1.379.710	1.378.097	1.378.099
Other income (Note 2)	6.162	1.000	13.956
Total Income	1.385.872	1.379.097	1.392.055
EXPENSES			
Salaries and wages	677.760	706.570	692.454
Translation & Interpretation services	294.318	340.000	304.821
Travel and accommodation	104.207	99.000	92.238
Information Technology	33.224	47.815	39.259
Printing, editing and copying	18.910	24.850	23.963
General services	73.382	49.447	53.818
Communications	15.254	20.685	20.827
Office expenses	12.471	26.110	25.772
Administrative expenses	8.582	16.315	7.101
Representation expenses	4.267	4.000	4.154
Other	0	0	0
Financing	7.986	11.393	2.251
Total Expenses	1.250.361	1.346.185	1.266.656
FUND APPROPRIATION			
Staff Termination Fund	30.314	32.912	32.988
Staff Replacement Fund	0	0	0
Working Capital Fund	6.685	0	0
Contingency fund	0	0	0
Total Fund appropriation	36.999	32.912	32.988
Total Expenses & Appropriation	1.287.360	1.379.097	1.299.644
(Deficit) / Surplus for the period	98.512	0	92.412

This statement should be read together with Notes 1 to 10 attached.

2. Statement of Financial Position as at 31st March 2016, comparatively with the prior year

ASSETS	31/03/2015	31/03/2016
Current assets		
Cash and cash equivalents (Note 3)	1.057.170	1.227.598
Contributions owed (Note 9 and 10)	196.163	136.317
Other debtors (Note 4)	39.306	44.805
Other current assets (Note 5)	146.017	65.550
Total current assets	1.438.656	1.474.271
Non-current assets		
Fixed assets (Note 1.3 and 6)	109.434	100.459
Total non-current assets	109.434	100.459
Total Assets	1.548.090	1.574.730
LIABILITIES		
Current liabilities		
Accounts payable (Note 7)	30.461	17.163
Contributions received in advance (Notes 10)	467.986	347.173
Special voluntary fund for specific purposes (Note 1.9)	13.372	14.516
Remuneration and payable contributions (Note 8)	30.163	73.345
Total current liabilities	541.983	452.197
Non-current liabilities		
Staff Termination Fund (Note 1.4)	207.194	240.181
Staff Replacement Fund (Note 1.5)	50.000	50.000
Contingency Fund (Note 1.7)	30.000	30.000
Fixed Asset Replacement Fund (Note 1.8)	43.137	34.163
Total non-current liabilities	330.332	354.344
Total Liabilities	872.314	806.541
NET ASSETS	675.776	768.189

This statement should be read together with Notes 1 to 10 attached.

3. Statement of changes in Net Assets as at 31ˢᵗ March 2015 and 2016

Represented by	Net Assets 31/03/2015	Income	Expenses and Appropriation	Other Income	Net Assets 31/03/2016
General Fund	445.824	1.378.099	(1.299.644)	13.956	538.237
Contributions owed (Note 9)	0	0			0
Working Capital Fund (Note 1.6)	229.952		0		229.952
Net Assets	675.776				768.189

This statement should be read together with Notes 1 to 10 attached.

4. Cash Flow Statement for the period 1ˢᵗ April 2015 as at 31ˢᵗ March 2016, comparatively with the prior year

		31/03/2016	31/03/2015
Variation in cash & cash equivalents			
Cash & cash equivalent at beginning of the year		1.057.170	
Cash & cash equivalent at year end		1.227.598	
Net increase in cash and cash equivalents		170.428	(174.633)
Causes of variations in cash & cash equivalents			
Operating activities			
Contributions received	969.959		
Payment of salaries and wages	(681.184)		
Payment of translation services	(243.109)		
Payment of travel, accommodation, etc.	(69.052)		
Payment of printing, editing and copying	(23.963)		
Payment of general services	(55.625)		
Other payments to providers	(54.523)		
Net cash & cash equivalents from operating activities		(157.497)	(585.302)
Investment activities			
Purchase of fixed assets	(38.362)		
Special voluntary fund	0		
Net cash & cash equivalents from investment activities		(38.362)	(35.719)
Financing activities			
Contributions received in advance	347.173		
Collection pt. 5.6 of Staff Regulations	159.060		
Payment pt. 5.6 of Staff Regulations	(162.397)		
Net lease prepayment	34.050		
Net AFIP reimbursement	(24.132)		
Miscellaneous revenues	13.793		
Net cash & cash equivalents from financing activities		367.546	454.379
Foreign currency activities			
Net loss	(1.260)		
Net cash & cash equivalents from foreign currency activities		(1.260)	(7.991)
Net increase in cash and cash equivalents		170.428	(174.633)

This statement should be read together with Notes 1 to 10 attached.

Notes to the Financial Statements
as at 31st March 2015 and 2016

1. Basis for Preparation of Financial Statements

These financial statements are presented in US dollars, following the guidelines established in Financial Regulations, annexed to Decision 4 (2003). These financial statements have been prepared in accordance with International Financial Reporting Standards (IFRS), as issued by the International Accounting Standards Board (IASB).

1.1. Historical Cost

The accounts are prepared in accordance with the historical cost rule, except where otherwise indicated.

1.2. Office

The Secretariat Offices are provided by the Ministry of Foreign Affairs, International Trade and Cult of the Argentine Republic. Premises are free of rent and common expenses.

1.3. Fixed Assets

All items are valued at historical cost, less accumulated depreciation. Depreciation is calculated on a straight-line basis at annual rates estimated to write off the assets over their expected useful lives. The aggregate residual value of fixed assets does not exceed their use value.

1.4. Executive Staff Termination Fund

Pursuant to Section 10.4 of the Staff Regulations, this fund shall be sufficiently funded to compensate executive staff members at a rate of one month base pay for each year of service.

1.5. Staff Replacement Fund

This fund is used to cover Secretariat executive staff travel expenses to and from the Secretariat.

1.6. Working Capital Fund

Pursuant to Financial Regulations 6.2 (a), the fund shall stand at one-sixth (1/6) of the budget for the current financial year.

1.7. Contingency Fund

Pursuant to Decision 4 (2009), this Fund was created to cover the translation expenses arising from the unexpected increase in the volume of documentation filed with the ATCM for translation purposes.

1.8. Fixed Assets Replacement Fund

Pursuant to IAS, assets with a useful life beyond the current financial year shall be reflected as an asset in the Statement of Financial Position. Up to March 2010, the balancing entry was an adjustment to the General Fund. As from April 2010, the balancing entry shall be reflected as a liability under such heading.

1.9. Special Voluntary Fund for Specific Purposes

Pt (82) of the XXXV ATCM Final Report, to receive voluntary contributions by the parties. The voluntary fund refers to money to pay lease rents and common expenses for the fiscal year.

Notes to the Financial Statements
as at of 31st March 2015 and 2016

		31/03/2015	31/03/2016
2 Other income			
	Earned interest	6.162	13.810
	Discounts obtained	0	146
	Total	6.162	13.956
3 Cash and cash equivalents			
	Cash US Dollars	61	965
	Cash Argentine Pesos	480	63
	BNA special US Dollar account	539.324	611.910
	BNA Argentine Peso account	17.077	34.327
	Investments	500.170	580.334
	Total	1.057.112	1.227.598
4 Other debtors			
	Staff Regulations pt. 5.6	39.306	44.805
5 Other current assets			
	Advance payments	86.992	8.848
	VAT receivable	54.250	51.995
	Other recoverable expenses	4.776	4.706
	Total	146.017	65.550
6 Fixed assets			
	Books & subscriptions	8.667	10.406
	Office equipment	37.234	37.234
	Furniture	45.466	49.818
	IT equipment and software	120.262	135.452
	Total original cost	211.629	232.910
	Accumulated depreciation	(102.195)	(132.451)
	Total	109.434	100.459
7 Accounts payable			
	Trade	8.670	5.022
	Accrued expenses	18.287	11.991
	Other	3.504	150
	Total	30.461	17.163
8 Remuneration and payable contributions			
	Remuneration	9.274	38.774
	Contributions	20.889	34.579
	Total	30.163	73.353

9 Contributions not received

At the end of each year, there are unsettled contributions. This implies that the
General Fund is increased by an amount equal to unsettled contributions. Pursuant to
Financial Regulation 6.(3), "... notify Consultative Parties about any cash surplus
in the General Fund", $136,317 should be deducted for the year ended 31 March 2016.
Such deduction amounted to $196,613 in the previous fiscal year.

Notes to the Financial Statements
as at of 31st March 2015 and 2016

10 Contributions owed, committed, paid and received in advance.

Contributions Parties	Owed 31/03/2015	Committed	Cancelled $	Owed 31/03/2016	Prepaid 31/03/2016
Argentina		60.347	60.347	0	0
Australia	25	60.347	60.347	25	60.347
Belgium	50	40.021	40.021	50	0
Brazil	40.268	40.021	40.053	40.236	0
Bulgaria		33.923	33.923	0	33.923
Czech Republic		40.021	40.021	0	0
Chile		46.119	46.119	0	0
China	25	46.119	46.119	25	0
Ecuador	34.039	33.923	67.962	0	0
Finland		40.021	40.021	0	40.001
France		60.347	60.347	0	0
Germany	11	52.217	52.217	11	0
India	112	46.119	46.156	75	0
Italy		52.217	52.192	25	0
Japan		60.347	60.347	0	0
Korea		40.021	40.021	0	0
Netherlands		46.119	46.119	0	46.119
New Zealand	25	60.347	60.392	-20	60.342
Norway	60	60.347	60.347	60	0
Peru	1.087	33.923	33.848	1.162	0
Poland		40.021	40.021	0	0
Russia		46.119	46.119	0	46.119
South Africa		46.119	46.119	0	0
Spain	25	46.119	46.144	0	0
Sweden	30	46.119	46.149	0	0
Ukraine	80.220	40.021	25.635	94.606	0
UK		60.347	60.347	0	60.322
USA	25	60.347	60.347	25	0
Uruguay	40.160	40.021	80.115	66	0
Total	196.162	1.378.099	1.437.915	136.346	347.173

Dr Manfred Reinke
Executive Secretary

Roberto A. Fennell
Finance Officer

256

Provisional Financial Report for 2016/17

Estimate of Income and Expenditure for all Funds
for the Period 1 April 2016 to 31 March 2017

APPROPRIATION LINES		Audited Statement 2015/16		Budget 2016/17		Prov Statement 2016/17
INCOME						
CONTRIBUTIONS pledged	$	-1,378,099	$	-1,378,097	$	-1,378,097
*) Other Income	$	-12,466	$	-55,207	$	-58,827
Total Income	$	-1,390,565	$	-1,433,304	$	-1,436,924
EXPENDITURE						
SALARIES						
Executive	$	331,679	$	336,376	$	336,376
General Staff	$	329,957	$	336,801	$	329,047
ATCM Support Staff	$	16,398	$	18,092	$	18,810
Trainee	$	1,867	$	9,600	$	2,313
Overtime	$	12,552	$	16,000	$	13,615
	$	692,454	$	716,869	$	700,162
TRANSLATION AND INTERPRETATION						
Translation and Interpretation	$	304,821	$	326,326	$	302,260
TRAVEL						
Travel	$	92,238	$	99,000	$	73,701
INFORMATION TECHNOLOGY						
Hardware	$	13,019	$	11,000	$	8,140
Software	$	2,287	$	9,000	$	2,193
Development	$	14,123	$	21,500	$	21,136
Support	$	7,242	$	9,500	$	8,067
	$	39,259	$	53,000	$	39,536
PRINTING, EDITING & COPYING						
Final report	$	18,273	$	18,386	$	14,435
Compilation	$	0	$	3,412	$	2,373
Site guidelines	$	5,689	$	3,396	$	0
	$	23,963	$	25,194	$	16,809
GENERAL SERVICES						
Legal advice	$	2,008	$	3,500	$	1,126
External audit	$	9,294	$	10,815	$	9,163
*) Rapporteur Services			$	53,207	$	53,207
Cleaning, maintenance & security	$	8,713	$	15,000	$	9,091
Training	$	4,357	$	6,500	$	2,774
Banking	$	5,254	$	6,489	$	6,342
Rental of equipment	$	2,543	$	3,245	$	2,503
	$	32,169	$	98,756	$	84,205
COMMUNICATION						
Telephone	$	7,251	$	7,000	$	5,046
Internet	$	2,956	$	3,000	$	2,533
Web hosting	$	7,975	$	8,500	$	7,288
Postage	$	2,645	$	2,704	$	1,180
	$	20,827	$	21,204	$	16,047

	Audited Statement 2015/16	Budget 2016/17	Prov Statement 2016/17
OFFICE			
Stationery & supplies	$ 4,273	$ 4,650	$ 5,689
Books & subscriptions	$ 3,079	$ 3,245	$ 984
Insurance	$ 3,216	$ 4,200	$ 3,388
Furniture	$ 4,535	$ 4,565	$ 97
Office equipment	$ 21,650	$ 4,326	$ 1,321
Office improvement	$ 10,669	$ 2,704	$ 5,503
	$ 47,422	$ 23,690	$ 16,982
ADMINISTRATIVE			
Office Supplies	$ 2,582	$ 4,867	$ 2,648
Local transport	$ 351	$ 865	$ 377
Miscellaneous	$ 3,036	$ 4,326	$ 2,567
Utilities (Energy)	$ 1,132	$ 11,897	$ 2,994
	$ 7,101	$ 21,955	$ 8,585
REPRESENTATION			
Representation	$ 4,154	$ 4,000	$ 3,646
FINANCING			
Exchange loss	$ -536	$ 11,893	$ 10,691
SUBTOTAL APPROPRIATIONS	$ 1,263,870	$ 1,401,887	$ 1,272,625
ALLOCATION TO FUNDS			
Translation Contingency Fund	$ 0	$ 0	$ 0
Staff Replacement Fund	$ 0	$ 0	$ 0
Staff Termination Fund	$ 32,988	$ 31,417	$ 31,417
Working Capital Fund	$ 0	$ 0	$ 0
	$ 32,988	$ 31,417	$ 31,417
TOTAL APPROPRIATIONS	$ 1,296,858	$ 1,433,304	$ 1,304,041
Unpaid Contributions **	$ 0	$ 0	$ 49,165
BALANCE	$ 93,707	$ 0	$ 83,717

Summary of Funds

Translation Contingency Fund	$ 30,000	$ 30,000	$ 30,000
Staff Replacement Fund	$ 50,000	$ 50,000	$ 50,000
Staff Termination Fund	$ 240,182	$ 271,518	$ 271,599
*** Working Capital Fund	$ 229,952	$ 229,952	$ 229,952

*

Chile reimbursed the costs for the rapporteurs
in the form of a special contribution

** Unpaid contributions as of 31 March 2016

Maximum Required Amount
*** Working Capital Fund (Fin. Reg. 6.2) $ 229,683 $ 229,683 $ 229,683

Secretariat Programme 2017/18

Introduction

This work programme outlines the activities proposed for the Secretariat in the Financial Year 2017/18 (1 April 2017 to 31 March 2018). The main areas of activity of the Secretariat are treated in the first four parts, followed by a section on management and a forecast of the programme for the Financial Year 2018/19.

The Budget for the Financial Year 2017/18, the Forecast Budget for the Financial Year 2018/19, and the accompanying contribution and salary scales are included in the appendices.

The programme and the accompanying budget figures for 2017/18 are based on the Forecast Budget for the Financial Year 2017/18 (Decision 3 (2016), Annex 3, Appendix 1).

The programme focuses on the regular activities, such as the preparation of the ATCM XL and ATCM XLI, the publication of Final Reports, and the various specific tasks assigned to the Secretariat under Measure 1 (2003).

Contents:

1. ATCM/CEP support
2. Information Technology
3. Documentation
4. Public Information
5. Management
6. Forecast Programme for the Financial Year 2018/19 and the Financial Year 2019/20
   - Appendix 1: Provisional Report for the Financial Year 2016/17, Forecast Budget for the Financial Year 2017/18, Budget for the Financial Year 2017/18, Forecast Budget for the Financial Year 2018/19
   - Appendix 2: Contribution Scale for the Financial Year 2018/19
   - Appendix 3: Salary Scale

1. ATCM/CEP Support

ATCM XL

The Secretariat will support the ATCM XL by gathering and collating the documents for the meeting and publishing them in a restricted section of the Secretariat website. The Secretariat will also provide, in a USB flash drive distributed to all delegates, an application that allows offline browsing of all documents and automatic synchronization with the online database for the latest updates. The Delegates section will provide online registration for delegates and a downloadable, up-to-date list of delegates.

The Secretariat will support the functioning of the ATCM through the production of Secretariat Papers, a Manual for Delegates, and summaries of papers for the ATCM, the CEP, and the ATCM Working Groups.

The Secretariat will organise the services for translation and interpretation. It is responsible for pre- and postsessional translation and for the translation services during the ATCM. It maintains contact with the provider of interpretation services, ONCALL.

The Secretariat will organise the note-taking services in cooperation with the secretariat of the host country and is responsible for the compilation and editing of the Reports of the CEP and ATCM for adoption during the final plenary meetings.

ATCM XLI

The Host Country Secretariat of Ecuador and the Secretariat of the Antarctic Treaty will jointly prepare the ATCM XLI, which will take place in Ecuador tentatively in May/June 2018.

Coordination and contact

Aside from maintaining constant contact via email, telephone and other means with the Parties and international institutions of the Antarctic Treaty System, attendance at meetings is an important tool to maintain coordination and communication.

The travelling to be undertaken is as follows:

- COMNAP Annual General Meeting (AGM) XXIX, Brno, Czech Republic, 31 July - 02 August 2017. Attendance to the meeting will provide an opportunity to further strengthen the connections and interaction with COMNAP.
- CCAMLR, Hobart, Australia, 16 - 27 October 2017. The CCAMLR meeting, which takes place roughly halfway between succeeding ATCMs, provides an opportunity for the Secretariat to brief the ATCM Representatives, many of whom attend the CCAMLR meeting, on developments in the Secretariat's work. Liaison with the CCAMLR Secretariat is also important for the Antarctic Treaty Secretariat, as many of its regulations are modelled after those of the CCAMLR Secretariat.
- Coordination Meetings with Ecuador as Host Country of ATCM XLI in tentatively October 2017 and March 2018.

Support of intersessional activities

During recent years both the CEP and the ATCM have produced an important amount of intersessional work, mainly through Intersessional Contact Groups (ICGs). The Secretariat will provide technical support for the online establishment of the ICGs agreed at the ATCM XL and CEP XX, and will produce specific documents if required by the ATCM or the CEP.

The Secretariat will update its website with the measures adopted by the ATCM and with the information produced by the CEP and the ATCM.

Printing

The Secretariat will translate, publish and distribute the Final Report and its Annexes of the ATCM XL in the four Treaty languages pursuant to the Procedures for the Submission, Translation and Distribution of Documents for the ATCM and the CEP. The text of the Final Report will be published on the website of the Secretariat and will be printed in book form. The full text of the Final Report will be available in book form (two volumes) through online retailers and also in electronic book form.

2. Information Technology

Information Exchange and the Electronic Information Exchange System

The Secretariat will continue to assist Parties in posting their information exchange materials, as well as processing information uploaded using the File Upload functionality.

The Secretariat will continue to provide advice to the ongoing ATCM Multi-Year Strategic Plan discussion on reviewing information exchange requirements and the EIES, and will stand ready to develop the changes, improvements and additions that might arise from those discussions.

Contacts Database

The Secretariat plans to release the new version of this database which includes a complete redesign, improved security and the introduction of new technologies which will make its interface more user friendly and improve usability on multiple devices.

Additionally, improved internal procedures for contact and communications management, including development of required software, will be implemented.

Development of the Secretariat website

The website will continue to be improved to make it more concise and easier to use, and to increase the visibility of the most relevant sections and information.

3. Documentation

Documents of the ATCM

The Secretariat will continue its efforts to complete its archive of the Final Reports and other records of the ATCM and other meetings of the Antarctic Treaty System in the four Treaty languages. Assistance from Parties in searching for their files will be essential in order to achieve a complete archive at the Secretariat. The project will continue in the Financial Year 2017/18. A complete and detailed list of missing papers in our database is available to all delegations interested in collaborating.

Glossary

The Secretariat will continue to further develop the Secretariat's glossary of terms and expressions of the ATCM to generate a nomenclature in the four Treaty languages. It will further improve the implementation of the electronically-controlled vocabulary server to manage, publish and share these ATCM ontologies, thesauri, and lists.

Antarctic Treaty database

The database of Recommendations, Measures, Decisions and Resolutions of the ATCM is at present complete in English and nearly complete in Spanish and French, although the Secretariat still lacks various Final Report copies in those languages. In Russian, further Final Reports are lacking.

4. Public Information

The Secretariat and its website will continue to function as a clearinghouse for information on the Parties' activities and relevant developments in Antarctica.

5. Management

Personnel

On 1 April 2017 the Secretariat staff consisted of the following personnel:

Executive staff

Name	Position	Since	Rank	Step	Term
Manfred Reinke	Executive Secretary (ES)	01-09-2009	E1	8	31-08-2017
José María Acero	Assistant Executive Secretary (AES)	01-01-2005	E3	13	31-12-2018

General staff

José Luis Agraz	Information Officer	1-11-2004	G1	6	
Diego Wydler	Information Technology Officer	01-02-2006	G1	6	
Roberto Alan Fennell	Finance Officer (part time)	01-12-2008	G2	6	
Pablo Wainschenker	Editor	01-02-2006	G2	3	

Name	Position	Since	Rank	Step	Term
Violeta Antinarelli	Librarian (part time)	01-04-2007	G3	6	
Anna Balok	Communications Specialist (part time)	01-10-2010	G4	2	
Viviana Collado	Office Manager	15-11-2012	G5	2	
Margarita Tolaba	Cleaning Professional	01-07-2015	G7	2	

ATCM XXXIX decided to select and appoint a new Executive Secretary at ATCM XL in accordance with Decision 4 (2016). The Secretariat received six applications, which were immediately distributed to the Parties. One application was withdrawn by a Party on 12 December 2016. A further application was ATCM XL Final Report withdrawn in April 2017. The Secretariat will support the ATCM in the implementation of the selection procedure adopted.

The Secretariat will invite international trainees from Parties for internships with the Secretariat. It has extended an invitation to Ecuador as host of the ATCM XLI to send one member of its organizational team for an internship in Buenos Aires.

Financial Matters

The Budget for the Financial Year 2017/18 and the Forecast Budget for the Financial Year 2018/19 are shown in Appendix 1.

Salaries

The cost of living continued to rise considerably in Argentina in the year 2016. Due to changes in the methodology of the calculation of cost rises (Consumer price index CPI) by the Argentine National Office of Statistics and Census (INDEC), final statistical data for the year 2016 are not yet available. Publications from other sources (private companies, the CPI publication of the Argentine Congress) estimate an inflation rate of about 40%. Taking into account the devaluation of the Argentine Peso against the US$ of 18.2%, the rise of public salaries in Argentine Pesos amounted to 32.6%, and some effects from the devaluation of the Argentine Peso in 2015, the Executive Secretary proposes to award the General Staff with a six percent increase (6%) to compensate for the rise in the cost of living. There will be no increase to the Executive Staff.

Regulation 5.10 of the Staff Regulations requires the compensation of General Staff members when they are required to work more than 40 hours during one week. Overtime is requested during the ATCM Meetings.

With the termination of his contract the outgoing Executive Secretary Dr Manfred Reinke will be entitled to receive the payment for staff termination under Regulation 10.4 of the ATCM Staff Regulations. At ATCM XXXIII (Punta del Este) 2010, "the ATCM agreed that Regulation 10.4 applied to all departures from service of executive staff, subject to the specific caveats set out in Regulation 10" (Final Report ATCM XXXIII, p. 35, para. 100).

Funds

Working Capital Fund

According to Financial Regulation 6.2 (a), the Working Capital Fund must be maintained at 1/6 of the Secretariat's budget of 229,952 US$ in the upcoming years. The contributions of the Parties form the basis of the calculation of the level of the Working Capital Fund.

Staff Termination Fund

According to Staff Regulation 10.4 the outgoing Executive Secretary will receive 127,438 US$ from the Staff Termination Fund pursuant to Regulation 10.4 of the ATCM Staff Regulations. The Staff Termination Fund will be credited with 29,986 US$ in accordance with Staff Regulation 10.4 (SP 5 Appendix 1: Provisional Statement FY 2016/17, Forecast FY 2017/18, Budget FY 2017/18, Forecast FY 2018/19).

Staff Replacement Fund

50,000 US$ were transferred from the surplus of the General Fund to "Income" to cover the costs for relocation of the outgoing Executive Secretary and the incoming Executive Secretary (SP 5 Appendix 1: Provisional Statement FY 2016/17, Forecast FY 2017/18, Budget FY 2017/18, Forecast FY 2018/19). The Staff Replacement Fund is maintained with 50,000 US$ (Decision 1 [2006], Annex 3, Appendix 1: Budget 2006/7 and Forecast budget 2007/8 and allocation of resources).

General Fund

On 31 Mar 2017, the cash surplus of the General Fund amounted to 621,954 US$. Outstanding contributions amounted to 49,125 US$. 50,000 US$ will be transferred from the General Fund to "Income" in 2017 to cover the costs of relocation for the outgoing and incoming Executive Secretaries, and 25,000 US$ in 2018 for the incoming AES. The amount of the General Fund is expected to be 621,119 US$ on 31 Mar 2018.

Further Details of the Draft Budget for the Financial Year 2017/18

The Chinese government and the Secretariat agreed that the Secretariat would contract the international rapporteurs for ATCM XL and that the Chinese government would reimburse the costs incurred.

The allocation to the appropriation lines follows the proposal from last year. Some smaller adjustments have been implemented according to the foreseen expenses in the Financial Year 2017/2018.

Appendix 1 shows the Budget for the Financial Year 2017/2018. The salary scale is given in Appendix 3.

Contributions for the Financial Year 2018/19

The contributions for the Financial Year 2018/19 will not rise.

Appendix 2 shows the contributions of the Parties for the Financial Year 2018/19.

6. Forecast Programme for the Financial Year 2018/19 and the Financial Year 2019/20

It is expected that most of the ongoing activities of the Secretariat will be continued in the Financial Year 2018/19 and the Financial Year 2019/2020, and therefore, unless the programme undergoes major changes, no change in staff positions is foreseen for the following years.

Appendix 1

Provisional Statement FY 2016/17, Forecast FY 2017/18, Budget FY 2017/18 and Forecast FY 2018/19

APPROPRIATION LINES	Prov Statement 2016/17 *)		Forecast 2017/18		Budget 2017/18		Forecast 2018/19	
INCOME								
CONTRIBUTIONS pledged	$	-1.378.097	$	-1.378.097	$	-1.378.097	$	-1.378.097
**) Voluntary Contributions	$	-53.207						
***) from General Fund					$	-50.000	$	-25.000
****) from Staff Termination Fund					$	-127.438	$	-175.281
Interest Investments	$	-5.620	$	-2.000	$	-3.000	$	-3.000
Total Income	$	-1.436.924	$	-1.380.097	$	-1.558.535	$	-1.581.378
EXPENDITURE								
SALARIES								
Executive	$	336.376	$	326.636	$	326.636	$	313.333
Staff Termination					$	127.438	$	175.281
Staff Replacement					$	50.000	$	25.000
General Staff	$	329.047	$	345.666	$	362.892	$	372.992
ATCM Support Staff	$	18.810	$	18.092	$	21.160	$	21.160
Trainee	$	2.313	$	9.600	$	9.600	$	9.600
Overtime	$	13.615	$	16.000	$	16.000	$	16.000
	$	700.162	$	715.994	$	913.726	$	933.366
TRANSLATION AND INTERPRETATION								
Translation and Interpretation	$	302.260	$	331.518	$	316.388	$	334.967
TRAVEL								
Travel	$	73.701	$	99.000	$	103.000	$	91.000
INFORMATION TECHNOLOGY								
Hardware	$	8.140	$	11.000	$	10.000	$	10.000
Software	$	2.193	$	3.500	$	6.000	$	3.000
Development	$	21.136	$	21.500	$	22.000	$	22.500
Hardware and Software Maintenance	$	1.620	$	2.040	$	2.250	$	2.250
Support	$	6.447	$	10.000	$	7.500	$	7.750
	$	39.536	$	48.040	$	47.750	$	45.500
PRINTING, EDITING & COPYING								
Final report	$	14.435	$	18.937	$	20.000	$	20.100
Compilation	$	2.373	$	3.271	$	2.500	$	2.512
Site guidelines	$	0	$	3.497	$	3.205	$	3.221
	$	16.809	$	25.705	$	25.705	$	25.833
GENERAL SERVICES								
Legal advice	$	1.126	$	3.605	$	3.000	$	3.060
**) Rapporteur Services	$	53.207						
External audit	$	9.163	$	11.139	$	11.139	$	11.362
Cleaning, maintenance & security	$	9.091	$	16.480	$	11.000	$	11.220
Training	$	2.774	$	7.298	$	8.000	$	8.160
Banking	$	6.342	$	6.683	$	9.983	$	10.183
Rental of equipment	$	2.503	$	3.342	$	3.042	$	3.103
	$	84.205	$	48.547	$	46.164	$	47.087
COMMUNICATION								
Telephone	$	5.046	$	7.210	$	7.210	$	7.354
Internet	$	2.533	$	3.000	$	2.500	$	2.550
Web hosting	$	7.288	$	8.500	$	8.500	$	8.670
Postage	$	1.180	$	2.785	$	2.785	$	2.841
	$	16.047	$	21.495	$	20.995	$	21.415

	Prov Statement 2016/17	Forecast 2017/18	Budget 2017/18	Forecast 2018/19
OFFICE				
Stationery & supplies	$ 5.689	$ 4.789	$ 4.789	$ 4.885
Books & subscriptions	$ 984	$ 3.342	$ 3.342	$ 3.409
Insurance	$ 3.388	$ 4.326	$ 4.326	$ 4.413
Furniture	$ 97	$ 1.255	$ 1.255	$ 1.280
Office equipment	$ 1.321	$ 4.455	$ 4.455	$ 4.544
Office improvement	$ 5.503	$ 2.785	$ 2.785	$ 2.841
	$ 11.479	$ 20.952	$ 20.952	$ 21.371
ADMINISTRATIVE				
Office Supplies	$ 2.648	$ 5.013	$ 5.013	$ 5.113
Local transport	$ 377	$ 890	$ 890	$ 908
Miscellaneous	$ 2.567	$ 4.455	$ 4.455	$ 4.544
Utilities (Energy)	$ 2.994	$ 12.253	$ 7.262	$ 7.407
	$ 8.585	$ 22.611	$ 17.620	$ 17.972
REPRESENTATION				
Representation	$ 3.646	$ 4.000	$ 4.000	$ 4.000
FINANCING				
Exchange loss	$ 10.691	$ 12.249	$ 12.249	$ 12.494
SUBTOTAL APPROPRIATIONS	$ 1.272.625	$ 1.350.111	$ 1.528.549	$ 1.555.006
ALLOCATION TO FUNDS				
Translation Contingency Fund	$ 0	$ 0	$ 0	$ 0
Staff Replacement Fund	$ 0	$ 0	$ 0	$ 0
Staff Termination Fund	$ 31.417	$ 29.986	$ 29.986	$ 26.372
Working Capital Fund	$ 0	$ 0	$ 0	$ 0
	$ 31.417	$ 29.986	$ 29.986	$ 26.372
TOTAL APPROPRIATIONS	$ 1.304.041	$ 1.380.097	$ 1.558.535	$ 1.581.379
*****) **Unpaid Contributions**	$ 49.165	$ 0	$ 0	$ 0
BALANCE	$ 83.717	$ 0	$ 0	$ 0

Summary of Funds

Translation Contingency Fund	$ 30.000	$ 30.000	$ 30.000	$ 30.000
Staff Replacement Fund	$ 50.000	$ 50.000	$ 50.000	$ 50.000
Staff Termination Fund	$ 271.599	$ 174.065	$ 174.065	$ 25.156
******) Working Capital Fund	$ 229.952	$ 229.952	$ 229.952	$ 229.952
General Fund (Fin.Reg. 6.3)	$ 621.954	$ 671.119	$ 621.119	$ 596.120

* Provisional Statement
as of 31 Mar 2016

** Rapporteur services contracted by the
Secretariat and reimbursed by the Host
Country of ATCM XXXIX

*** Reduction costs new Executive Secretary
(Staff Regulations 9.6 (b) and 10.6 (b)) for
the Executive Secretaries in 2017 and the
Assistant Executive Secretary in 2018 taken
from the General Fund

**** Staff termination compensation (Staff
Regulation 10.4 and Final Report ATCM
XXXIII para 100) for the Executive Secretary
in 2017 and the Assistant Executive
Secretary in 2018

***** Unpaid contributions
as of 31 March 2017

****** Maximum Required Amount Working Capital Fund (Fin. Reg. 6.2)	$ 229.683	$ 229.683	$ 229.683	$ 229.683

Appendix 2

Contribution Scale FY 2018/19

2018/19	Cat.	Mult.	Variable	Fixed	Total
Argentina	A	3.6	$ 36,587	$ 23,760	$ 60,347
Australia	A	3.6	$ 36,587	$ 23,760	$ 60,347
Belgium	D	1.6	$ 16,261	$ 23,760	$ 40,021
Brazil	D	1.6	$ 16,261	$ 23,760	$ 40,021
Bulgaria	E	1	$ 10,163	$ 23,760	$ 33,923
Chile	C	2.2	$ 22,359	$ 23,760	$ 46,119
China	C	2.2	$ 22,359	$ 23,760	$ 46,119
Czech Republic	D	1.6	$ 16,261	$ 23,760	$ 40,021
Ecuador	E	1	$ 10,163	$ 23,760	$ 33,923
Finland	D	1.6	$ 16,261	$ 23,760	$ 40,021
France	A	3.6	$ 36,587	$ 23,760	$ 60,347
Germany	B	2.8	$ 28,456	$ 23,760	$ 52,216
India	C	2.2	$ 22,359	$ 23,760	$ 46,119
Italy	B	2.8	$ 28,456	$ 23,760	$ 52,216
Japan	A	3.6	$ 36,587	$ 23,760	$ 60,347
Republic of Korea	D	1.6	$ 16,261	$ 23,760	$ 40,021
Netherlands	C	2.2	$ 22,359	$ 23,760	$ 46,119
New Zealand	A	3.6	$ 36,587	$ 23,760	$ 60,347
Norway	A	3.6	$ 36,587	$ 23,760	$ 60,347
Peru	E	1	$ 10,163	$ 23,760	$ 33,923
Poland	D	1.6	$ 16,261	$ 23,760	$ 40,021
Russian Federation	C	2.2	$ 22,359	$ 23,760	$ 46,119
South Africa	C	2.2	$ 22,359	$ 23,760	$ 46,119
Spain	C	2.2	$ 22,359	$ 23,760	$ 46,119
Sweden	C	2.2	$ 22,359	$ 23,760	$ 46,119
Ukraine	D	1.6	$ 16,261	$ 23,760	$ 40,021
United Kingdom	A	3.6	$ 36,587	$ 23,760	$ 60,347
United States	A	3.6	$ 36,587	$ 23,760	$ 60,347
Uruguay	D	1.6	$ 16,261	$ 23,760	$ 40,021

Budget	$ 1,378,097

Appendix 3

Salary Scale FY 2017/18

Schedule A
SALARY SCALE FOR THE EXECUTIVE STAFF
(United States Dollar)

2017/18

Level		I	II	III	IV	V	VI	VII	VIII	IX	X	XI	XII	XIII	XIV	XV
E1	A	$135,302	$137,819	$140,337	$142,855	$145,373	$147,890	$150,407	$152,926							
E1	B	$169,127	$172,274	$175,421	$178,569	$181,716	$184,863	$188,009	$191,158							
E2	A	$113,932	$116,075	$118,218	$120,359	$122,501	$124,642	$126,783	$128,926	$131,069	$133,211	$135,352	$135,595	$137,709		
E2	B	$142,415	$145,093	$147,772	$150,449	$153,126	$155,802	$158,479	$161,158	$163,837	$166,513	$169,190	$169,494	$172,136		
E3	A	$95,007	$97,073	$99,140	$101,207	$103,275	$105,341	$107,408	$109,476	$111,542	$113,608	$115,675	$116,915	$118,154	$120,193	$122,231
E3	B	$118,758	$121,341	$123,925	$126,509	$129,094	$131,676	$134,260	$136,845	$139,427	$142,010	$144,594	$146,143	$147,693	$150,242	$152,788
E4	A	$78,779	$80,693	$82,649	$84,518	$86,435	$88,347	$90,257	$92,174	$94,089	$96,000	$97,915	$98,448	$100,336	$102,223	$104,110
E4	B	$98,474	$100,866	$103,262	$105,648	$108,044	$110,434	$112,822	$115,217	$117,611	$119,999	$122,393	$123,060	$125,419	$127,778	$130,137
E5	A	$65,315	$67,029	$68,739	$70,452	$72,162	$73,873	$75,586	$77,293	$79,007	$80,719	$82,427	$82,981			
E5	B	$81,644	$83,786	$85,924	$88,065	$90,203	$92,342	$94,482	$96,617	$98,759	$100,899	$103,034	$103,726			
E6	A	$51,706	$53,351	$54,994	$56,641	$58,284	$59,928	$61,575	$63,219	$64,862	$65,862	$66,508				
E6	B	$64,632	$66,689	$68,742	$70,801	$72,855	$74,910	$76,969	$79,024	$81,078	$82,328	$83,135				

Note: Row B is the base salary (shown in Row A) with an additional 25% for salary on-costs (retirement fund and insurance premiums, installation and repatriation grants, education allowances etc.) and is the total salary entitlement for executive staff in accordance with regulation 5.

Schedule B
SALARY SCALE FOR THE GENERAL STAFF
(United States Dollar)

Level	I	II	III	IV	V	VI	VII	VIII	IX	X	XI	XII	XIII	XIV	XV
G1	$64,788	$67,810	$70,834	$73,856	$77,006	$80,291									
G2	$53,990	$56,508	$59,028	$61,546	$64,172	$66,909									
G3	$44,990	$47,089	$49,189	$51,288	$53,477	$55,760									
G4	$37,493	$39,242	$40,991	$42,741	$44,564	$46,466									
G5	$30,972	$32,419	$33,863	$35,310	$36,818	$38,391									
G6	$25,388	$26,571	$27,756	$28,941	$30,177	$31,465									
G7	$12,724	$13,317	$13,911	$14,505	$15,124	$15,770									

Appointment of the Executive Secretary

The Representatives,

Recalling Article 3 of Measure 1 (2003) regarding the appointment of an Executive Secretary to head the Secretariat of the Antarctic Treaty;

Recalling Decision 2 (2013), on the re-appointment of Dr. Manfred Reinke as Executive Secretary of the Secretariat of the Antarctic Treaty for a term of four years from 1 September 2013;

Recalling Decision 4 (2016), on the Procedure for Selection and Appointment of the Executive Secretary of the Secretariat of the Antarctic Treaty;

Recalling Regulation 6.1 of the Staff Regulations for the Secretariat of the Antarctic Treaty, annexed to Decision 3 (2003);

Decide:

1. to appoint Mr Albert Lluberas Bonaba as Executive Secretary of the Secretariat of the Antarctic Treaty for a term of four years, pursuant to the terms and conditions set forth in the letter of the Chair of the XL Antarctic Treaty Consultative Meeting annexed to this Decision; and

2. that this appointment shall commence on 1 September 2017.

Letters

Mr. Albert Lluberas Bonaba

Secretary General of the Uruguayan Antarctic Institute

MONTEVIDEO

Uruguay

Dear Mr. Lluberas Bonaba,

Appointment to position of Executive Secretary

As Chair of the XL Antarctic Treaty Consultative Meeting ("ATCM") and in accordance with Decision X (2017) of ATCM XL, I am pleased to offer to you appointment to the position of Executive Secretary of the Secretariat of the Antarctic Treaty ("the Secretariat").

The terms and conditions of your appointment are set out below. If you accept this offer, kindly sign your acceptance on the attached copy of this letter and return it to me.

Terms and Conditions of Appointment

1. By your acceptance of the appointment you shall pledge yourself to discharge your duties faithfully and to conduct yourself solely with the interests of the ATCM in mind. Your acceptance of the position of Executive Secretary includes a written statement of your familiarity with and acceptance of the conditions set out in the attached Staff Regulations for the Secretariat of the Antarctic Treaty, annexed to Decision 3 (2003) ("Staff Regulations") as well as any changes which may be made to the Staff Regulations from time to time. In particular, your acceptance of the position includes a commitment to:

- adhere faithfully to Staff Regulations 2.6 and 2.7 regarding outside employment and business/financial interests respectively;
- carry out responsibilities relating to appointment, direction and supervision of staff under Article 3(2) of Measure 1 (2003) in accordance with Staff Regulation 6.2 as well as the standards of efficiency, competence and integrity set forth in Staff Regulation 2.3 and particularly in a manner that avoids even the appearance of impropriety or nepotism;
- demonstrate the highest standards of ethical conduct by observing all organization regulations and policies and ensuring that all Secretariat decisions and actions are informed by the standards of efficiency, competence and integrity set forth in Staff Regulation 2.3;
- avoid even the appearance of a conflict of interest; and

275

- responsibly oversee resources entrusted to the Secretariat, including through efficient, transparent and effective use of financial resources in accordance with the Financial Regulations for the Secretariat of the Antarctic Treaty, annexed to Decision 4 (2003) ("Financial Regulations").

2. The duties of the Executive Secretary are to appoint, direct and supervise other staff members and to ensure that the Secretariat fulfills the functions identified in Article 2 of Measure 1 (2003).

3. In accordance with Decision X (2017), your appointment shall commence on September 1, 2017.

4. Your term of office shall be for four years and you shall be eligible for reappointment for no more than one further four-year term, subject to the agreement of the ATCM.

5. The appointment is to the executive staff category. Your salary shall be at Level E1B, Step I, as detailed in Schedule A to the Staff Regulations, as amended.

6. The above salary includes the base salary (Level E1A, Step I, Schedule A) with an additional 25% for salary on-costs (retirement fund and insurance premiums, installation and repatriation grants, education allowances, etc.) and is the total salary entitlement in accordance with Staff Regulation 5.1. In addition, you will be entitled to travel allowances and relocation expenses in accordance with Staff Regulation 9.

7. The ATCM may terminate this appointment by prior written notice at least three months in advance in accordance with Staff Regulation 10.3. You may resign at any time upon giving three months written notice or such lesser period as may be approved by the ATCM.

I wish you well in this role.

Yours sincerely,

{signed}

NAME AND TITLE

Chair of the XL Antarctic Treaty Consultative Meeting

I hereby accept the appointment described in this letter subject to the conditions therein specified and state that I am familiar with and accept the conditions set out in the Staff Regulations and any changes which may be made to the Staff Regulations from time to time.

Mr. Albert Lluberas Bonaba

Signature:

Date:

Mrs. Susana Malcorra

Minister of Foreign Affairs and Worship

Argentine Republic

Buenos Aires

Dear Minister Malcorra,

I address you in my capacity as Chair of the XL Antarctic Treaty Consultative Meeting ("ATCM") with reference to Article 21 of the Headquarters Agreement for the Secretariat of the Antarctic Treaty, annexed to Measure 1 (2003), the letter of the Argentine Republic to the Chairman of ATCM XXVI of 16 June 2003, and the notification of the Argentine Republic to the depositary Government of 19 May 2004.

In accordance with the requirements of Article 21, I hereby notify the Government of the Argentine Republic of the appointment by the ATCM XL of Mr. Albert Lluberas Bonaba to the position of Executive Secretary for a term of four years, effective on 1 September 2017.

I avail myself of this opportunity to express the assurances of my highest consideration.

Yours sincerely,

{signed}

NAME AND TITLE

Chair of the XL Antarctic Treaty Consultative Meeting

Multi-year Strategic Work Plan for the Antarctic Treaty Consultative Meeting

The Representatives,

Reaffirming the values, objectives and principles contained in the Antarctic Treaty and its Protocol on Environmental Protection;

Recalling Decision 3 (2012) on the Multi-Year Strategic Work Plan ("the Plan") and its principles;

Bearing in mind that the Plan is complementary to the agenda of the Antarctic Treaty Consultative Meeting ("ATCM") and that the Parties and other ATCM participants are encouraged to contribute as usual to other matters on the ATCM agenda;

Decide:

1. to adopt the Plan annexed to this Decision; and

2. that the Plan annexed to Decision 6 (2016) is no longer current.

ATCM Multi-year Strategic Work Plan

	Priority	ATCM 40 (2017)	Intersessional	ATCM 41 (2018)	Intersessional	ATCM 42 (2019)	ATCM 43 (2020)
1.	Conduct a comprehensive review of existing requirements for information exchange and of the functioning of the Electronic Information Exchange System, and the identification of any additional requirements	• WG1 to review functioning of the EIES	• The ATS to cooperate with COMNAP in ways to reduce duplication and increase compatibility across their databases • The ATS to continue to improve the EIES, including the provision of the website interface in the four Treaty languages	• WG1 to review functioning of the EIES			
2.	Consider coordinated outreach to non-party states whose nationals or assets are active in Antarctica and states that are Antarctic Treaty Parties but not yet to the Protocol	• ATCM to identify and reach out to non-party states whose nationals are active in Antarctica		• ATCM to identify and reach out to non-party states whose nationals are active in Antarctica			
3.	Contribute to nationally and internationally coordinated education and outreach activities from an Antarctic Treaty perspective	• WG1 to consider the report of the ICG on Education and Outreach	• ICG on Education and Outreach	• WG1 to consider the report of the ICG on Education and Outreach			
4.	Share and discuss strategic science priorities in order to identify and pursue opportunities for collaboration as well as capacity building in science, particularly in relation to climate change	• WG2 to collate and compare strategic science priorities with a view to identify cooperation opportunities	• Continue informal intersessional discussions on strategic science priorities	• Consider outcomes of intersessional discussions on strategic science priorities			

	Priority	ATCM 40 (2017)	Intersessional	ATCM 41 (2018)	Intersessional	ATCM 42 (2019)	ATCM 43 (2020)
5.	Enhance effective cooperation between Parties (e.g. joint inspections, joint scientific projects and logistic support) and effective participation in meetings (e.g. consideration of effective working methods in meetings)	• WG2 to consider the report of the ICG on Joint Inspections	• Continue informal consultations on joint inspections	• Consider outcomes of informal consultations on joint inspections			
6.	Strengthening cooperation between the CEP and the ATCM	• ATCM to consider issues raised in CEP report at ATCM 39 and 40 • ATCM to receive advice from CEP that requires follow-up action					
7.	To bring Annex VI in to force and to continue to gather information on repair and remediation of environmental damage and other relevant issues to inform future negotiations on liability	• ATCM to evaluate progress made towards Annex VI becoming effective in accordance with Article IX of the Antarctic Treaty, and what action may be necessary and appropriate to encourage Parties to approve Annex VI in a timely manner	• [The ATS will set up a webpage within the ATS website which will contain the information on national legislation on Annex 6 implementation, voluntarily provided by Parties and accessible to Parties]	• ATCM to evaluate progress made towards Annex VI becoming effective in accordance with Article IX of the Antarctic Treaty, and what action may be necessary and appropriate to encourage Parties to approve Annex VI in a timely manner			• [ATCM to take a decision in 2020 c the establishment of a timeframe for the resumption of negotiations on liability in accordance with Article 16 of the Protocol on Environmental Protection, or sooner if the Parti so decide in light of progress made approving Measur 1 (2005) – see Decision 5 (2015)
8.	Assess the progress of the CEP on its ongoing work to review best practices and to improve existing tools and develop further tools for environmental protection, including environmental impact assessment procedures	• WG1 to consider advice of the CEP and discuss the policy considerations of the review of Environmental Impact Assessment (EIA) Guidelines		• WG1 to further discuss the issues raised in part 8b of the CEP XX Report		• WG1 to consider advice of the CEP and discuss the policy considerations of the review of Environmental Impact Assessment	
8 bis.	Collection and use of biological material in Antarctica			• WG 1 to discuss the collection and use of biological material in Antarctica			

	Priority	ATCM 40 (2017)	Intersessional	ATCM 41 (2018)	Intersessional	ATCM 42 (2019)	ATCM 43 (2020)
9.	Address the recommendations of the Antarctic Treaty Meeting of Experts on Implications of Climate Change for Antarctic Management and Governance (CEP-ICG)	• WG2 to consider recommendations 4-6 • WG2 to consider outcomes of the SC-CCAMLR and CEP workshop	Interested Parties to prepare for discusssions on outstanding recommendations from the ATME on Climate Change Implications (2010)	• Agree how to deal with any outstanding recommendations from the ATME on Climate Change Implications (2010)		Follow up on any decisions regarding handling of any outstanding recommendations from the ATME on Climate Change Implications (2010)	
10.	Discuss implementation of the Climate Changes Response Work Programme (CCRWP)	• WG2 to consider annual update from CEP on implementation of CCRWP		• WG2 to consider annual update from CEP on implementation of CCRW Pimplementation of CCRWP		• WG2 to consider annual update from CEP on implementation of CCRWP implementation of CCRWP	
11.	Modernisation of Antarctic Stations in context of climate change	• WG2 to discuss exchange of information and COMNAP advice		• WG2 to discuss exchange of information and COMNAP advice			
12.	Review and discuss issues related to increased aviation activity in Antarctica, and assess the need for additional action		• Secretariat to write to ICAO to request any information pertinent to aviation in Antarctica and to invite them to attend ATCM XLI • Ask COMNAP and IAATO to provide an overview of aviation activity, and to present at the next ATCM XLI to inform discussion	• ATCM XLI WG2 to have a dedicated discussion on aviation activity, including non-government air traffic and UAVs/RPAs, in Antarctica • ATCM XLI WG2 to consider any views presented on air safety issues by ICAO	• The meeting to seek advice addressing risks and other issues identified during discussions at ATCM XLI		
12 bis.	To take note of the International Code for Ships Operating in Polar Waters; and to continue to strengthen co-operation among Antarctic marine operators; and to take into account developments in the IMO		• Secretariat to write to the IMO to set out the ATCM's priority interest in maritime safety and invite them to present an update, and engage in ATCM XLI	• WG 2 to consider developments at IMO, and discuss further maritime safety issues		• Exchange views on national experiences in authorising vessel activity in Antarctica, following entry into force of the Polar Code	

	Priority	ATCM 40 (2017)	Intersessional	ATCM 41 (2018)	Intersessional	ATCM 42 (2019)	ATCM 43 (2020)
13.	Hydrographic surveying in Antarctica		• IHO, in consultation with ATS and host, prepare to deliver a seminar on the status and the impact of hydrography in Antarctic waters at ATCM 41	• ATCM to have a dedicated seminar on hydrography in Antarctica, with a presentation of IHO			
14.	Review and assess the need for additional actions regarding area management and permanent infrastructure related to tourism, as well as issues related to land based and adventure tourism, and address the recommendations of the CEP Tourism Study	• Consider a report from the Secretariat concerning progress against recommendation 1 of 2012 CEP Tourism Study		• SCAR and IAATO to provide an interim report on progress of the systematic conservation plan for the Antarctic Peninsula • Discuss the options for developing a standardised monitoring methodology for site management • Discuss proposals in respect of the need for additional actions regarding area management • Review progress against recommendations from CEP Tourism Study	• Follow up on any conclusions regarding the CEP Tourism Study		
15.	Develop a strategic approach to environmentally managed tourism and non-governmental activities in Antarctica	• WG2 to consider Secretariat update • Develop a strategic vision for tourism and non-governmental activities in Antarctica	• Continue discussions to prepare for ATCM XLI	• Discuss specific actions to enhance implementation of the 2009 General Principles of Antarctic Tourism			
16.	Visitor site monitoring			• To analyse CEP progress on recommendations 3 and 7 of the CEP Tourism Study			

Note: The ATCM Working Groups mentioned above are not permanent but are established by consensus at the end of each Antarctic Treaty Consultative Meeting.

3. Resolutions

Guidance Material for Antarctic Specially Managed Area (ASMA) Designations

The Representatives,

Noting that Article 4 of Annex V to the Protocol on Environmental Protection to the Antarctic Treaty ("the Protocol") provides for the designation of Antarctic Specially Managed Areas ("ASMA") "to assist in the planning and co-ordination of activities, avoid possible conflicts, improve co-operation between Parties or minimise environmental impacts";

Recalling the requirements under Articles 5 and 6 of Annex V to the Protocol to prepare and review Management Plans for Antarctic Specially Protected Areas and ASMA;

Noting that the Guide to the Preparation of Management Plans for Antarctic Specially Protected Areas (Resolution 2 [2011]) and *Guidelines for Implementation of the Framework for Protected Areas* set forth in Article 3, Annex V of the Environmental Protocol (Resolution 1 [2000]) were developed to assist Parties in their work under Annex V;

Recognising the value of also having guidelines to assist Parties in consideration of potential ASMA and in the development of management plans for these areas;

Noting the work of the Committee for Environmental Protection in developing such guidance;

Recognising that guidance is non-mandatory;

Recommend to their Governments that:

1. the Guidance for Assessing an Area for a Potential Antarctic Specially Managed Area Designation annexed to this Resolution (Annex A) be used

by those who will engage in assessing an area for potential designation as an Antarctic Specially Managed Area ("ASMA"); and

2. the Guide to the Preparation of Management Plans for Antarctic Specially Managed Areas annexed to this Resolution (Annex B) be used by those engaged in the preparation or revision of Management Plans for ASMA.

Guidance for Assessing an Area for a Potential Antarctic Specially Managed Area Designation

Introduction

The aim of this document is to provide any potential proponent(s) with some guidance and support in their process of assessing and determining whether, why and how an area indeed merits a designation as an Antarctic Specially Managed Area (ASMA). The guidance is non-mandatory, but provides points to consider when a Party or Parties begin to consider designating an area as an ASMA.

Article 4 of Annex V to the Environmental Protocol provides that any area, including any marine area, where activities are being conducted or may in the future be conducted, may be designated as an ASMA to assist in the planning and co-ordination of activities, avoid possible conflicts, improve co-operation between Parties or minimize environmental impacts. ASMAs may include areas where activities pose risks of mutual interference or cumulative environmental impacts, and sites or monuments of recognized historic value. ASMAs can include Antarctic Specially Protected Areas (ASPAs) and Historic Sites and Monuments (HSMs) within their area. Article 5 of Annex V provides that any Party, the Scientific Committee for Antarctic Research (SCAR) or the Commission for the Conservation of Antarctic Marine Living Resources (CCAMLR) may propose an area for designation as an ASMA by submitting a proposed management plan to the Antarctic Treaty Consultative Meeting (ATCM). Article 6 of Annex V describes designation procedures, including the need for prior approval of CCAMLR should the ASMA include a marine area.

Articles 5 and 6 of Annex V to the Environmental Protocol make it clear that the process of designating an ASMA is formally initiated through the submission of a proposed Management Plan to the Committee for Environmental Protection (CEP). This document provides guidance for and assistance to proponents with regard to a suggested practical process leading up to the point at which the formal proposal is made through the submission of a proposed Management Plan.

Experience with the development of existing ASMAs has shown that the process to establish an ASMA can be long and involved. In particular, the complexity of an ASMA designation process may increase with the scale of the area, and with the number of activities and/or Parties or other stakeholders involved.

This document focuses on the process for assessing an area for potential ASMA designation. Depending on the circumstances of the area in question, there are other options that can contribute to achieving the objectives for spatial management of an area (e.g. ASPA designation, bilateral agreements between Parties, national procedures or Codes of Conduct).

All ASMA proposals must be considered by the CEP, and ultimately be agreed by the Antarctic Treaty Consultative Parties at an ATCM. An ASMA management plan is the internationally-agreed instrument applicable to all visitors to the Area, and should be given effect by each Party according to the provisions of the Antarctic Treaty and the Protocol, as implemented by National Authorities through domestic legislation. Consequently, each ASMA proposal has relevance for all Parties, not only for those Parties and other operators conducting activities within the area in question.

This document should be regarded as guidance only, to aid in ensuring that all relevant aspects have been considered appropriately and sufficiently in the process for the potential proponents to consider whether to propose an area as an ASMA or not. All areas considered for ASMA designation will have different qualities, past, current or future pressures and management challenges associated with them, and the specific circumstances will need to be taken into account when it comes to the designation process.

In addition to the guidance provided to the proponent(s), it is the long-term aim that this guidance may contribute to a degree of consistency and comparability among assessment processes (while recognizing that each potential ASMA will have its own requirements and dynamics), and ensure that the process is sufficiently documented for future reference.

This document should be used with reference, as appropriate, to the following material:

- Annex V to the Protocol (specifically Article 4, 5 and 6),
- Guidelines: *A prior assessment process for the designation of ASPAs and ASMAs* (Appendix 3 of CEP XVIII Final Report 2015),
- *Guidelines for the implementation of the Framework for Protected Areas* (Resolution 1 [2000]),[*] and
- *Report of the CEP Workshop on Marine and Terrestrial Antarctic Specially Managed Areas* Montevideo, Uruguay, 16-17 June 2011 (IP136 ATCM XXXIV/ CEP XIV, 2011).

Determining the need for ASMA designation

If a Party or Parties operating within an area identify that current or reasonably foreseeable future activities pose risks of mutual interference or cumulative environmental impacts, or there is a need to assist in the planning and coordination of activities or improve cooperation between Parties, they may wish to give consideration to proposing the area for ASMA designation.

Documentation of process

It is important to document the methods used in the development and submission of a management plan for ASMA designation. Documentation could be in the form of results of science or monitoring projects, workshop reports, discussion papers, lists of major meetings held and key outcomes, list of stakeholders consulted, lists of reference material, etc.

The conclusions from the assessment process should be clearly documented and communicated to the stakeholders, regardless of the final outcome of the assessment process.

Stakeholder identification and engagement

As noted above, the decision on whether to designate an area as an ASMA will ultimately be made by the ATCM, and will reflect the consensus view of the Antarctic Treaty Consultative Parties.

Because any decision on whether to designate an ASMA will likely be informed by a range of views, the Party or Parties initiating the assessment process may find it helpful to involve other stakeholders in the process *in order to get a comprehensive overview of all issues that may have bearings on the future management of the area*. The Party or Parties initiating the assessment process could, for example, seek to identify and engage with other Parties, and where appropriate with relevant organisations (e.g. SCAR, COMNAP, IAATO), that might have an interest in the area as a result of their past, current or planned activities. Where appropriate, such engagement might range from information-sharing to active participation in the assessment process.

It should also be noted that it may be necessary to present an ASMA proposal to CCAMLR for consideration, in accordance with Decision 9 (2005), for areas in which there is actual harvesting or potential capability of harvesting of marine living resources which might be affected by site designation; or for which there are provisions specified in a draft management plan which might prevent or restrict CCAMLR related activities.

Working methods

When the potential proponents are considering whether to propose designating an ASMA to achieve the objectives for spatial management of an area, the following methods supporting the assessment process, *inter alia*, could be applied to ensure stakeholder engagement and a comprehensive screening and assessment of issues:

- Initial Documentation: one or more of the Parties should initiate the process by developing a discussion paper (based on an initial scoping, desktop study, or general discussions with others interested in an area), providing background material for the need to assess and consider management options.
- Workshop(s): arrange a meeting or series of meetings in which key elements of the assessment needs are considered. Invite experts and stakeholders.
- Working groups: establish groups charged with assessing various elements identified as relevant for the area in question, to ensure a comprehensive and focused assessment of the various aspects.

- On-site activities: arrange for a workshop/site-visit, including stakeholders if appropriate and possible.
- Web-based discussion forums and other remote means of communication: use such means to post discussion papers and other relevant documents to engage the broader community of stakeholders in the process.

Identify values, activities and management objectives

The management objectives for an area will depend on the values, activities and pressures in the area. The initial proponent(s) will have an idea of the area management objectives when initiating the assessment, however understanding of these matters is likely to evolve through the process of consultation with other stakeholders with activities or interests in the area. Ultimately, it is important to reach a clear picture of the agreed management objectives for an area, to enable the proponent(s), stakeholders and CEP to proceed.

An ASMA can be established to increase cooperation amongst Parties with interests in the area, to minimize negative impacts from activities on specific values of the area, or to minimize conflict between various activities. In considering area management objectives and options, it is necessary to identify the values of an area, and the past, current and future activities. The following guidance may be of help, and the location and extent of values and activities should be mapped to the degree possible.

Note that this stage of the process is similar to considering areas for potential ASPA designation, and so the following closely reflects the guidance in the *Guidelines for implementation of the Framework for Protected Areas set forth in Article 3, Annex V of the Environmental Protocol.*

Values

Consider whether any of the following values of the area are present:

- *Environmental values*: Does the area contain physical, chemical or biological features e.g., glaciers, fresh water lakes, melt pools, rock outcrops, biota that are particularly unique or representative components of the Antarctic environment (e.g. Important Bird Area)?[*]
- *Scientific values*: Does the area contain physical, chemical or biological features of special interest to scientific researchers where the principles and methods of science would be applicable? Note that a forward-looking assessment as well as an assessment of current scientific interest is relevant in this context. Consider also if there are multiple scientific values in the same area, as this may be relevant in considering potential competing scientific interests and cumulative impact from field science activities.
- *Historic and heritage values*: Does the area contain a Historic Site or Monument(s) designated under Annex V, or other features or objects that represent, suggest or

---

[*] Refer to Resolution 5 (2015) on Important Bird Areas in Antarctica for further information.

recall events, experiences, achievements, places or records that are important, significant or unusual in the course of human events and activity in Antarctica?

- *Aesthetic values:* Does the area contain features or attributes e.g., beauty, pleasantness, inspirational qualities, scenic attraction and appeal that contribute to people's appreciation and sense or perception of an area?

- *Wilderness values:* Does the area contain characteristics (e.g., remoteness, few or no people, an absence of human-made objects, traces, sounds and smells, untraveled or infrequently visited terrain) that are particularly unique or representative components of the Antarctic environment?

- *Educational values:* Does the area provide an opportunity for outreach and education to the public with the aim of promoting the Protocol-identified values listed above and fostering an understanding of the importance of Antarctica in the global context?

In considering the values present in the area, make also note of whether the area contains one or more ASPAs, or other areas managed to protect any of the environmental or other values identified.

Activities

Consider whether any of the following activities take place or are planned or may in the future be conducted in the area, and whether these activities take place regularly / continuously / seldom / seasonally, and how the range of activities have changed in recent years. It is important to consider whether ongoing activities have changed over time or are anticipated to change in the future, as this might have different impacts on other activities and/or values in the area:

- *Scientific activities:* Are scientific activities (including monitoring) conducted in the area? What type and at what locations? Do these activities require separation in time or space from other activities that may cause interference (i.e. a 'buffer'), or do they rely on the state of the environmental values in all or part of the area.

- *Station operations and science support activities:* Are there any (scientific) stations or other facilities or equipment in the area? What location? What is the spatial and temporal extent of the normal operations of the station(s)?

- *Transportation:* Are there areas, corridors or sites that are particularly important for transportation activities? Where are these located?

- *Recreational activities:* Are there areas that are used for recreational purposes by National Antarctic Programs? Where and what kind of activities are these?

- *Tourism:* Are there areas that are used for organized tourism purposes or private expeditions? What type of activities? Where are these areas?

- *Harvesting/fishing:* If an area contains a marine component, does harvesting of marine resources currently occur in the area or is there potential for harvesting to occur in the future, and if so where?

- *Environmental management:* Are there any areas where there are ongoing environmental management activities (e.g. ASPAs, Site Guidelines for Visitors, other)?

- *Other activities:* Are there other activities taking place in the area? What types and where?

- *Future activities:* Is it anticipated that expanded or new activities will take place in the area in the reasonably foreseeable future? What types and where? Are other changes to ongoing activities anticipated, such as diminishing, ending, change in timing, etc.?

Interactions between multiple activities/operators, and between activities and the values of the area

Potential pressures / environmental impacts

Consider the environmental and other values of the area in the context of activities taking place in the area by posing the questions below. Note that it is particularly important to involve scientists and operational managers with knowledge of the area, or with relevant expertise, in discussing these issues, especially with regard to the identification of important environmental values.

- Are there environmental values of particular importance within the area that would be harmed by any current or planned activities taken individually or collectively? Specific activities? Level of activity? Frequency/timing of activity?

- Are there more efficient ways that activities could be carried out while reducing impacts?

- Are there areas/environments within the area that can cause safety concerns?

- Are there certain sites or locations within the area that contain values that are more vulnerable to human impact than others?

Consider whether there are knowledge gaps related to the issues identified above that require further investigations and consider initiating relevant studies (including field work to assess and ground truth values, activities, potential conflicts, etc.) to fill these gaps as required.

Consider whether the potential pressures associated with current or reasonably foreseeable activities in the area are likely to require coordination between parties in order to achieve the management goals desired for the area.

Consider whether there are specific coordination initiatives that could be implemented to minimize impacts in the area, such as:

- Sharing of facilities

- Sharing of logistics, such as personnel movement, transport of goods, etc.

- Encouraging and implementing scientific cooperation to maximize scientific output and minimize unnecessary duplication of research

- Sharing of information through management meetings or other communication initiatives
- Application of management zones (e.g. Restricted, Scientific, Visitor, Historic, etc.). Refer to *Guidelines for the application of management zones within ASMAs and ASPAs*
- Other

Potential for co-ordination, co-operation or conflict

To assess ongoing conflict or potential for conflict,[*] and opportunities for planning, co-ordination or co-operation to avoid such conflict or achieve other management objectives, consider the activities in the context of the environment they take place in, and in relation to other activities taking place in the area by addressing the questions detailed below for all identified activities. Note that it is particularly important to provide Parties and other stakeholders with the opportunity to consider these issues, especially with regard to the sensitivities related to the activity they are engaged in.

- Are there activities currently occurring or planned that are incompatible or specific sites within an area where incompatible activities are currently going on?
- Are current or planned activities particularly prone to being affected by disturbance from other activities? Consider whether this is a general sensitivity or time limited sensitivity. Consider sensitivity to all types of disturbance, not only those stemming from ongoing activities in the area.
- Are there aspects of the activity that are dangerous/risky and therefore hinder/limit other types of activities in the same area? Consider whether this is general or time limited.
- Is the activity particularly disruptive to the environment, or for specific values of the environment, either permanently or temporarily?
- Is it possible to envision future potential conflicts (e.g., in introducing new scientific methods, such as UAVs or ROVs or large scale scientific installations or increasing logistic capabilities) that could increase the numbers of people conducting activities within the site?

Consider whether there are steps that may be taken to limit the potential conflicts identified by posing the following questions to the Parties and other stakeholders:

- Can steps be taken to avoid/limit negative impact on your interests in the area?
- Can steps be taken to avoid/limit negative impact on other interests in the area?

Drawing conclusions

When the potential proponent(s) are considering whether to propose designating an ASMA to achieve the objectives for spatial management of an area, they should consider whether this will require the engagement of multiple parties/stakeholder groups.

[*] Conflict is considered the incompatibility of two or more activities taking place in the same area at the same time.

The suite of management options that can contribute to achieving the objectives for spatial management of an area includes, but is not limited to: ASPA designation, bilateral agreements between Parties, national procedures or Codes of Conduct, etc.

Summarize the results of the previous considerations and evaluate whether the management of the area would be improved by designation of the ASMA, with a management plan. Include in the deliberations, if appropriate and possible, the value of an ASMA Management Group to facilitate and coordinate actions to achieve the management objectives.

If the assessment conducted by the potential proponents concludes that an ASMA designation should be considered in accordance with the Protocol, the Party/Parties involved could at this stage make the CEP aware of a possible proposal for an ASMA and seek feedback and views from other members consistent with the CEP's *Guidelines: A prior assessment process for the designation of ASPAs and ASMAs.*

After the potential proponent(s) have undertaken the assessment process described above they may consider it appropriate for a management plan to be developed for the Area A draft management plan should be developed in a manner consistent with the *Guidelines for the preparation of ASMA management plans*, and then submit for wider consideration in accordance with Article 5 and 6 of Annex V of the Protocol.

References and background information

General

- Annex V to the Protocol (specifically Article 4, 5 and 6)
- Guidelines: *A prior assessment process for the designation of ASPAs and ASMAs* (Appendix 3 of CEP XVIII Final Report 2015)
- *Guidelines for the preparation of ASPA management plans* (Resolution 2 [2011])
- *Guidelines for the application of management zones within ASMAs and ASPAs* (WP 10, ATCM XXXIII/CEP XIII, 2010)
- *Guidelines for the implementation of the Framework for Protected Areas* (Resolution 1 [2000])
- *Report of the CEP Workshop on Marine and Terrestrial Antarctic Specially Managed Areas Montevideo*, Uruguay, 16-17 June 2011 (IP136 ATCM XXXIV/ CEP XIV, 2011)

- *Guide to the presentation of Working Papers containing proposals for Antarctic Specially Protected Areas, Antarctic Specially Managed Areas or Historic Sites and Monuments* (Resolution 5 [2011])
- *Checklist to assist in the inspection of Antarctic Specially Protected Areas and Antarctic Specially Managed Areas* (Resolution 4 [2008])

Documents from previous ASMA processes

- Downie, RH. And Smellie, JL. *A management Strategy for Deception Island* (2001)
- Valencia J. and Downie, RH. (eds.). *Workshop on a Management Plan for Deception Island* (2002)
- Report from workshop: *Description of the biological research program in the vicinity of Palmer Station, Antarctica and possible impacts on the program from activities in the area to serve as a basis for development of a provisional research/ management plan for the Palmer area* (1988)
- Report from McMurdo Dry Valley workshops: *Environmental Management of a cold desert ecosystem: The McMurdo Dry Valleys (1995) and McMurdo Dry Valley Lakes: impacts of research activities* (1998)
- Harris C.M. 1998: *Science and environmental management in the McMurdo Dry Valleys Southern Victoria Land, Antarctica*
- Report from McMurdo Dry Valley workshop: *Environmental Assessment of the McMurdo Dry Valleys: Witness to the Past and Guide to the Future* (2016)
- Report from workshop: *'Larsemann Hills: an Antarctic Microcosm* (1997)

Guidelines for the Preparation of ASMA Management Plans

1. Background

1.1 Purpose of the Guide

In 1991 the Antarctic Treaty Consultative Parties (ATCPs) adopted the Protocol on Environmental Protection to the Antarctic Treaty (Environmental Protocol) to ensure comprehensive environmental protection in Antarctica. The Environmental Protocol designates the whole of Antarctica as "a natural reserve devoted to peace and science".

Annex V to the Environmental Protocol, adopted subsequently at ATCM XVI under Recommendation XVI-10, provides a legal framework for the establishment of specially protected and managed areas within the overall "natural reserve". The text of Annex V is available on the ATS website at *http://www.ats.aq/documents/recatt/Att004_e.pdf*.

Annex V specifies that any area in the Antarctic Treaty area, including any marine area, where activities are being conducted or may in the future be conducted, may be designated as an Antarctic Specially Managed Area (ASMA) to assist in the planning and co-ordination of activities, avoid possible conflicts, improve cooperation between Parties or minimise environmental impacts (Article 4.1, Annex V). Antarctic Specially Managed Areas may include areas where activities pose risk of mutual interference or cumulative environmental impacts and may also include sites or monuments of recognized historic value (Article 4.2, Annex V). An Antarctic Specially Managed Area may furthermore contain one or more Antarctic Specially Protected Areas (Article 4.4, Annex V).

The Annex further specifies that any Party to the Antarctic Treaty, the Committee for Environmental Protection (CEP), the Scientific Committee on Antarctic Research (SCAR) or the Commission for the Conservation of Antarctic Marine Living Resources (CCAMLR) may propose an area for designation as an Antarctic Specially Managed Area by submitting a proposed Management Plan to the Antarctic Treaty Consultative Meeting (Article 5.1, Annex V).

This Guide has been developed in order to assist any proponent in the process of proposing an Antarctic Specially Managed Area, with the following aims:

- to assist Parties in their efforts to prepare Management Plans for proposed Antarctic Specially Managed Areas (ASMA) as required by the Environmental Protocol (Article 5, Annex V);

- to provide a framework which enables Management Plans to meet the requirements of the Environmental Protocol; and

- to help achieve clear content, clarity, consistency (with other Management Plans) and effectiveness to expedite their review, adoption and implementation.

It is important to note that this guide is intended as no more than an aide-mémoire to the production of Management Plans for ASMAs. It has no legal status. Anyone intending to prepare a Management Plan should examine the provisions of Annex V to the Environmental Protocol carefully and seek advice from their national authority at an early stage.

1.2 Identifying areas for special management

The designation of an area as a Managed Area provides a framework for planning, co-ordination and management of current or future activities in order to avoid possible conflicts, improve co-operation between Parties or minimize environmental impacts, including cumulative impacts. When seeking to assess whether an area in fact needs special management provisions, it is necessary to assess the interaction among values, activities and pressures in the area. The CEP has adopted specific guidance for assessing an area for a potential Antarctic Specially Managed Area designation that will assist any proponent(s) in the process of such an evaluation.

Ensuring a thorough and in-depth analysis during the assessment process will help the proponent(s) determine whether the management needs of the area are best served through the development of an ASMA Management Plan. Once a decision has been made by the proponent(s), the guidance provided by this document will assist in the process of developing the Management Plan for the Area,

1.3 Relevant guidance material

- Annex V to the Environmental Protocol *(http://www.ats.aq/documents/recatt/ Att004_e.pdf)*
- Guidance for assessing an area for a potential Antarctic Specially Managed Area designation
- Guidelines for the application of management zones within ASMAs and ASPAs[*]
- Guidelines: A prior assessment process for the designation of ASPAs and ASMAs[**]

2. Format of Management Plans for ASMAs

The CEP has highlighted the benefits of promoting consistency among Specially Protected Area Management Plans. Similarly, while the circumstances, activities and pressures may be quite different among different areas being considered for ASMA designation, consistency among Specially Managed Area Management Plans is desirable. Article 5.3 of Annex V specifies matters that each ASMA Management Plan should address, as appropriate. The following sections of this Guide provide guidance in addressing those requirements (summarised in Table 1).

---

[*] WP10. ATCM XXXIII/CEPXIII, 2010, incl. its attachment "Guidelines for the Application of Management Zones within Antarctic Specially Managed Areas and Antarctic Specially Protected Areas".
[**] Appendix 3 to the Final Report of CEP XVIII.

300

Table 1: Overview of suggested ASMA management plan structure

Management Plan section / section of Guide	Article 5 reference
1. Table of Contents	
2. Introduction	
3. Description of values to be protected	3 a
4. Aims and objectives	3 b
5. Management activities	3 c
6. Period of designation	3 d
7. Maps	3 g
8. Description of the Area	3 e (i - iv)
9. Protected Areas and managed zones within the Area	3 f
10. Supporting documentation	3 h
11. Code of conduct and other guidelines	3 j (i-viii)
12. Advance Exchange of Information	3 k

3. Guidance for the content of Management Plans

Since the development of Management Plans for ASMAs is an evolving process, those preparing Management Plans need to be aware of current best practice and are encouraged to consult current and recently revised ASMA Management Plans as useful examples. The current Management Plan for each ASMA can be accessed from the Protected Areas database on the website of the Secretariat of the Antarctic Treaty, at h*ttp://ats.aq/devPH/apa/ep_protected.aspx?lang=e.*

A Management Plan should provide sufficient details about the special features, activities and pressures within the Area and any provisions needed to manage the activities in the Area to ensure that individuals planning activities in the Area are able to do so in a manner consistent with the aims and objectives for the Area. The following sections provide guidance to proponents on the content addressed under each standard Management Plan heading.

3.1 Table of Contents

A Table of Contents provides the reader with a guide to the location of a particular topic within the often long and complex ASMA Management Plan. Table 1 provides a general outline of a Table of Contents, which can be augmented with sub-contents.

3.2 Introduction

An introduction to the Management Plan is not a stated requirement of Article 5 of Annex V, but can provide a useful overview. Information might include a summary of the important features of the Area, a brief history of designation and revisions, the activities that have been and are carried out there and pressures/threats that indicate the need for specific management.

The rationale for designating the area as a Specially Managed Area is important to convey early in the Management Plan. In doing so it will be appropriate to provide a short summary of pressures, threats and coordination requirements.

3.3 Values to be protected

This section should provide an overview and short description of the values that have been identified in the Area and which have been determined to require management provisions to avoid negative impact or to minimize conflict. Such values can for example be:

- Environmental values
- Scientific values
- Historic and heritage values
- Aesthetic values
- Wilderness values
- Educational values

It is important to note that the description of values will be important factors for planning purposes by those contemplating activities within the Area. Consequently, the values should be described specifically, not generally.

3.4 Activities to be managed

This section should provide an overview and short description of the current, planned or reasonably foreseeable activities in the Area which can pose a pressure/threat to identified values or which require coordination to minimize negative impacts or conflict:

- Scientific activities
- Station operations and science support activities
- Transportation
- Recreational activities
- Tourism
- Harvesting/fishing
- Environmental management

3.5 Aims and objectives

This section should establish what is intended to be achieved by the Management Plan and how the Plan will address proper management of the values described above.

For example, the aims of the Plan might highlight an intention to:

- safeguard long-term, current and future scientific research;
- manage potential or actual conflicts among different activities and the values of the area;

- minimize environmental impacts, including cumulative impact;
- assist with the planning and coordination of human activities; and
- encourage communication and cooperation among users of the Area.
- consider climate change implications in the coordination and management of activities

It is important to note that the description of objectives will be important for planning purposes by those managing the Area and those contemplating activities within the Area. Consequently, the objectives of the plan should be described specifically, not generally.

3.6 Management activities

Management activities outlined in this section should relate to the aims of the Management Plan and to the objectives for which the Area was designated.

For example, the Plan might highlight and describe the following management intents:

- establishment of an ASMA Management Group to facilitate and ensure effective communication among those working in or visiting the Area;
- provision of a forum to resolve any actual or potential conflicts in use and to help minimize the duplication of activities;
- dissemination of information on the Area, in particular on the activities occurring and the management measures that apply within the Area;
- maintenance of a record of activities and, where practical, impacts in the Area and the development of strategies to detect and address cumulative impacts;
- review of past, existing, and future activities and evaluation of the effectiveness of management measures, potentially through site visits; and
- data collection to further support, gain further knowledge and detect any ongoing changes to the values of the Area.

It is important to note in the Management Plan that active management may require an environmental impact assessment, which should be undertaken in accordance with the requirements of Annex 1 to the Environmental Protocol.

3.7 Period of designation

Designation of an ASMA is for an indefinite period unless the Management Plan provides otherwise. It is a requirement under Article 6.3 of Annex V that a review of the Management Plan is initiated at least every five years, and updated as necessary.

3.8 Maps

Maps are a critical component of any Management Plan and should be clear and sufficiently detailed. If the area is particularly large a number of maps that vary in scale may be appropriate.

It is essential that the maps clearly indicate the boundary of the Managed Area as described under section 6.1 below.

Photographs/images can usefully be included in the Management Plan in instances where they carry a clear management purpose and where they demonstrate specific points. When photographs and images are included, they should be clear, have sufficiently high resolution, include source information and the location should be identified clearly.

Guidelines for maps [and images] are given in Appendix 1 together with a check-list of features to be considered for inclusion.

3.9 Description of the Area

This section requires an accurate description of the Area and, where appropriate, its surroundings to ensure that those planning to conduct activities in the Area are sufficiently appraised of the special features of the area.

It is important that this section adequately describes features, activities and coordination needs in the Area that requires particular management, thus alerting users of the Management Plan to features of particular interest. This section should preferably not duplicate the description of the values of the Area.

While it is important that the descriptions are accurate and adequate, it is recommended that descriptions be kept short and at an overview level, avoiding too much detail and numerous scientific references. This will ensure that readers' attention stays directed toward the operational provisions of the Management Plan. Information about flora and fauna that is necessary for the implementation of specific management measures should be included in the description. However, further detailed descriptions with citations and/or species lists of fauna and flora can usefully be made available through other means, such as on a dedicated ASMA website, a National Program website or in a separate appendix to the Management Plan.

The section may be divided into multiple subsections, as indicated in the below.

3.9.1 Geographical co-ordinates, boundary markers and natural features

The boundary of the Area should be delineated unambiguously and the important features clearly described, as the boundary delineation will form the basis for the management of activities. The boundary of the Area should be carefully selected and described. It is preferable to describe a boundary that is identifiable at all times of the year. It is best to choose static boundary markers such as exposed rock features or coastlines. Features that might be expected to vary in location throughout the year or during the five-year review period of the Management Plan, such as the edges of snow fields or wildlife colonies, are unlikely to be suitable. In some instances it may be advisable to install boundary markers where natural features are not sufficient.

Consideration should be given to the likely future impacts of climate change when determining or reviewing the boundaries of the Managed Area. In particular, thought should be given to the designation of boundaries using features other than ice-free ground. For example, future climate change induced glacial retreat, ice shelf collapse and lake level change will have an impact on ASMAs whose boundary definitions follow these features.

Geographical co-ordinates included in the boundary description should be as accurate as possible. They should be given as latitude and longitude in degrees, minutes and seconds. If possible, reference should be made to published maps or charts to allow the boundaries of the Area to be delineated on the map.

The importance of GPS for fixing positions cannot be overstated. It is strongly recommended that GPS positioning is used to document accurate locational information on boundaries, and that such information be included in the ASMA Management Plans. Where possible satellite imagery and/or remote sensing techniques may be useful methods to support such information.

The description of the natural features of the Area should include descriptions of, the local topography such as permanent snow/ice fields, the presence of any water bodies (lakes, streams, pools), the presence of islands or other such features in the case of marine Areas and a brief summary of the local geology and geomorphology. An accurate, brief description of the biological features of the Area is also useful including notes on major plant communities; bird and seal colonies and an estimate of numbers of individuals or breeding pairs of birds and marine mammals.

Remote sensing techniques have great potential in providing relevant documentation for ASMA Management Plans. Uses may include mapping (including identification of Area and Zone boundaries) as well as quantification of vegetation, surface water, and potentially disturbed ground. As the technology develops, including the availability of higher resolution and hyperspectral images, the potential for delivery of management-relevant information will increase greatly.

If the Area contains a marine component, the Management Plan may need to be submitted to CCAMLR for consideration – see the section below on "Approval process for ASMA Management Plans".

3.9.2 Structures within the Area

It is necessary to describe and accurately locate all structures within or adjacent to the Area. These include, for example, boundary markers, sign boards, cairns, field huts, depots and research facilities. Where possible, the date the structures were erected and the country using or having used them should be recorded, as well as the details of any HSMs in the Area. If applicable, the timing of the planned removal of any structures should also be noted (e.g. in the case of temporary scientific or other installations).

3.9.3 Other special status areas in the vicinity of the Area

Article 5.3(iv) specifies that ASMA Management Plans should include description for other protected or managed areas in the vicinity. There is no specific radius to be used when describing other protected areas 'in the vicinity', but a distance of approximately 50 km has been used in many plans adopted so far. All such protected areas (i.e. ASPAs, ASMAs, HSMs, CCAS Seal Reserves, CCAMLR CEMP sites etc.) in the vicinity should be given by name and, where appropriate, number. The coordinates and approximate distance and direction from the Area in question should also be provided.

3.10 Protected Areas and managed zones within the Area

Article 4.4 of Annex V notes that an Antarctic Specially Managed Area may contain one or more Antarctic Specially Protected Areas (ASPAs). This section should provide an overview and short description of all ASPAs contained within the boundaries of the ASMA.

It is furthermore relevant to make note of and provide a short description of any sites covered by Site Specific Visitor Guidelines adopted by the ATCM, as well as any listed Historic Site and Monument (HSM) within the Area.

Additionally, a CCAMLR Ecosystem Monitoring Program (CEMP) site may be located within the boundaries of an ASMA. If this is the case, an overview and short description of the CEMP site should be included. If special protection has been afforded to the CEMP sites through CCAMLR, the CEMP Site Management Plan should be referenced and provided a link to through the ASMA Management Plan. The same approach applies if a formally adopted Marine Protected Area (MPA) is located within the boundaries of the Area.

Article 5.3(f) of Annex V allows for the identification of zones within ASPAs and ASMAs "in which activities are to be prohibited, restricted, or managed for the purpose of achieving the aims and objectives..." of the Management Plan.

Clearly demarcated zones help provide clear information to site visitors on where, when and why special management conditions apply. Zones can be useful to communicate the goals and requirements of management in a clear and simple manner.

In order to help achieve greater consistency in the application of the zoning tool in Antarctica, a standard set of commonly used zones that could meet management needs in most situations has been identified and defined (Table 2).

As is the case with all guidelines, there may arise instances where exceptions are both needed and desirable and the use of alternative zones might be appropriate. It is important to keep in mind, however, that Management Plans should aim to use zones that are as simple and consistent as possible across all sites within Antarctica.

If no zones are designated within the Area, this should be specifically stated in the Management Plan.

Table 2: Overview of potential zones that can be utilized within an ASMA

Zone	Specific Zone Objectives
Facilities and Operations Zone	To ensure that science support facilities and related human activities within the Area are contained and managed within designated Areas
Access Zone	To provide guidance for approach and/or landing of aircraft, boats, vehicles or pedestrians accessing the Area and by doing so protect areas with sensitive assemblages of species or scientific equipment etc and / or provide for safety
Historic Zone	To ensure those who enter the Area are aware of the areas or features within that are sites, buildings and / or artefacts of historic importance and to manage them appropriately
Scientific Zone	To ensure those who enter the Area are aware of the areas within that are sites of current or long-term scientific investigation or have sensitive scientific equipment installed
Restricted Zone	To restrict access into a particular part of the Area and/or activities within it for a range of management or scientific reasons, e.g. owing to special scientific or ecological values, because of sensitivity, presence of hazards, or to restrict emissions or constructions at a particular site. Access into Restricted Zones should normally be for compelling reasons that cannot be served elsewhere within the Area
Visitor Zone	To manage visits by commercial tour operators, private expeditions, and National Antarctic Program staff when undertaking recreational activities within the Area in order to ensure that such visits minimize potential impacts

3.11 Supporting documentation

This section should refer to a location where the reader can find further detailed information and documentation regarding the Area, for example, by providing a link to the ASMA website or National Program home page, Protected Area database, referring to an appendix, etc.

3.12 General Code of Conduct and other guidelines

This section should present a general Code of Conduct for the Area. The general Code of Conduct outlines the management framework and constitutes the main instrument for the management of activities in the Area. It should outline the overall management and operational principles for the Area, and should, as appropriate, cover *inter alia* the following issues:

- *Access to and movement within the Area*: This subsection should include descriptions of preferred access routes to the Area by land, sea or air. These should be clearly defined to prevent confusion and to provide suitable alternatives if the preferred route is unavailable. All access routes as well as marine anchorages and helicopter landing areas should be described and clearly marked on the accompanying map of the Area. Overflight restrictions, should there be any, should be described in the text. The subsection should also describe preferred walking and vehicle routes within the Area.

307

- *Activities that may be conducted in the Area*: This should detail what activities are seen as relevant to be undertaken within the Area and the conditions under which such activities are relevant.

- *Field camps*: The conditions under which field camps may be permitted should be stated. It is possible that field camps would only be acceptable in certain parts of the Area. Such campsites should be identified and recorded on the supporting maps.

- *Restrictions on materials and organisms which may be brought into the Area*: This section should set out prohibitions and give guidance on the management of any materials that are to be used or stored in the Area.

- *Collection or removal of material found in the Area*: It may be permissible to remove from the Area materials such as beach litter, dead or pathological fauna or flora or abandoned relics and artefacts from previous activities. What items or samples can be removed should be clearly stated.

- *Waste management*: This section of the plan should specify requirements for the disposal and removal of wastes which are generated within the Area

- *Installation, modification or removal of structures*: It is useful to identify what, if any, structures are relevant to install within the Area. For example, certain scientific research equipment, markers or other structures might be allowed to be installed within the Area.

The Management Plan should, as appropriate, include specific guidelines for activities that might be undertaken within the Area. Such guidelines should, when they are part of the Management Plan, be included as appendices to the Management Plan and could cover issues as identified above and may include guidelines such as:

- Guidelines for scientific research
- Guidelines for facility and operational activities
- Visitor Sites Guidelines
- Hazard avoidance guidelines
- Non-native species guidelines

In instances where specific guidelines are stand-alone documents adopted by the ATCM, it may suffice to refer to and provide link to these guidelines, rather than including them as appendices.

3.13 Advance exchange of information

A key to the successful implementation of the Management Plan is the annual advance exchange of information of planned activities to be conducted within the ASMA. In this section of the plan, reference to the normal exchange of information by means of the annual national reports to the Parties of the Antarctic Treaty and to SCAR and COMNAP is advised. In addition, the Management Plan should establish appropriate communication and information sharing arrangements regarding activities in the area, possibly including notification by National Antarctic Programs on planned scientific activities in the Area and by appropriate national authorities on authorized, planned non-governmental activities in the area, including tourism and harvesting.

3.14 Appendices

It is relevant to make available interlinked and relevant material as appendices to the Management Plan. The specific details will depend on the Area in question, but could include *inter alia:*

* Specific guidelines for activities that might be undertaken within the Area (cf. section 3.12)
* Management Zone Guidelines (cf. section 3.10)
* Further details and documentation about the Area (cf. section 3.9)
* Plant, bird and mammal species recorded within the Area
* Conservation Strategies for HSMs in the Area
* National Program contact details
* Maps and/or images

Rather than including Management Plans for ASPAs, ATCM adopted Visitor Site Guidelines and CEMP Site Management Plans contained within the Area (cf. section 3.10) as appendices to the ASMA Management Plan, it may be more appropriate to simply provide reference to and preferably links for these stand-alone documents.

4. Approval process for ASMA Management Plans

Article 5 of Annex V provides that any Party, the CEP, SCAR or CCAMLR may submit a draft Management Plan for consideration by the ATCM. In practice, draft Management Plans are generally submitted by one or more Parties to the CEP for consideration.

The process by which Management Plans are handled from drafting through to acceptance is summarised by the flow chart in Figure 1. This is based on the requirements of Article 6 of Annex V, *the Guidelines for CEP Consideration of New and Revised Draft ASPA and ASMA Management Plans* (Annex 1 of Appendix 3 to the CEP XI Final Report), and other related guidelines.

The approval process for an ASMA Management Plan has many critical stages, which can take a long time to complete. However, these stages are necessary, as an ASMA Management Plan requires the agreement of all Antarctic Treaty Consultative Parties at an ATCM.

4.1 Preparing the draft Management Plan

In the initial stages of drafting the Management Plan, it is recommended that widespread consultation, both nationally and internationally, is undertaken on the scientific, environmental and operational elements of the Plan as appropriate. This will aid the passage of the Plan through the more formal process at the ATCM.

Proponents of new Areas are strongly encouraged to consider relevant guidelines and references that will assist in assessing, selecting, defining and proposing Areas that might require special management through designation as an ASMA, including:

- *Guidance for assessing an area for a potential Antarctic Specially Managed Area designation*
- *Guidelines: A prior assessment process for the designation of ASPAs and ASMAs**

When considering the designation of a new ASMA, proponents are encouraged to inform the CEP at an early stage (ideally, well before detailing a Management Plan for the Area) so that proposals can be discussed in the context of the protected areas system as a whole. In this context it is relevant to refer to *Guidelines: A prior assessment process for the designation of ASPAs and ASMAs* adopted as guidance by the CEP.**

When revising an existing Management Plan, it may be informative to use the *Checklist to assist in the inspection of Antarctic Specially Protected Areas and Antarctic Specially Managed Areas* (Resolution 4 (2008)) as a tool to identify necessary changes and improvements.

4.2 Submitting the draft Management Plan for consideration

The draft Management Plan should be submitted to the CEP, as an attachment to a Working Paper prepared in accordance with *Guide to the presentation of Working Papers containing proposals for Antarctic Specially Protected Areas, Antarctic Specially Managed Areas or Historic Sites and Monuments* – Resolution 5 (2016).

If the Area contains a marine component that meets the criteria outlined in Decision 9 (2005) - *Marine protected areas and other areas of interest to CCAMLR*, the draft Management Plan should also be submitted to CCAMLR for consideration. The proponents should make arrangements to ensure that any feedback from CCAMLR is available before the proposal is considered by the CEP. Timing is critical because an initial review of the draft Management Plan will be conducted during the CCAMLR Working Group on Ecosystem Monitoring and Management, which are held in June/July prior to CCAMLR annual meetings, which are held in October/November.

---

* Appendix 3 to the Final Report of CEP XVIII (*http://www.ats.aq/documents/cep/cep%20documents/ATCM38_CEPrep_e.pdf*).
** Ibid.

Figure 1. Flow chart showing the approval process for ASMA Management Plans

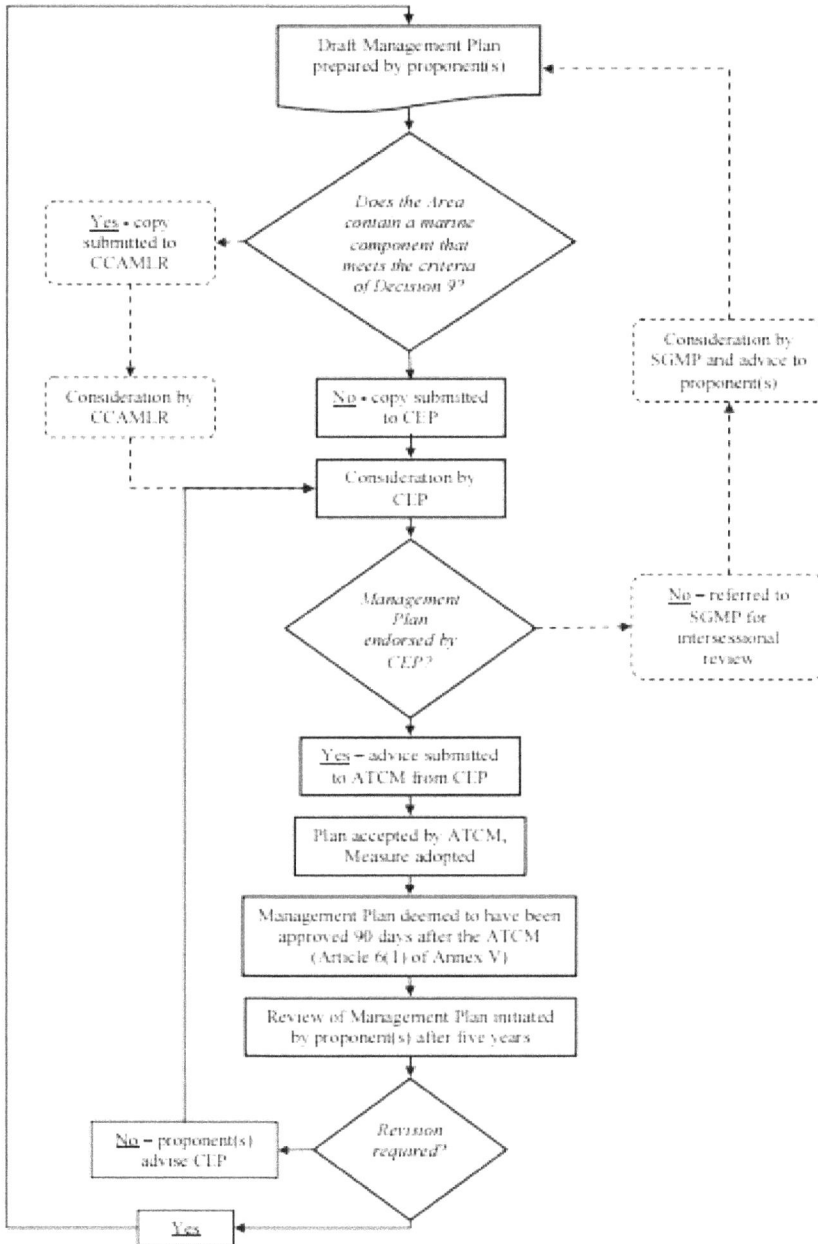

4.3 Consideration by the CEP and ATCM

The CEP will consider the Management Plan, and if appropriate, take into account any comments from CCAMLR. The CEP may refer the Management Plan to the ATCM for consideration and adoption, or to the Subsidiary Group on Management Plans (SGMP) for intersessional review.

In accordance with its terms of reference (see Appendix 1 to the CEP XIII Final Report), the SGMP will consider each draft Management Plan referred to it, advise the proponent(s) on recommended changes, consider any revised version of the Management Plan prepared during the intersessional period, and report to the CEP on its review. The revised Management Plan and the SGMP's report to the CEP would then be considered by the CEP meeting and, if agreed, referred to the ATCM for consideration and adoption.

If the ATCM agrees on the Management Plan, a Measure is adopted in accordance with Article IX.1 of the Antarctic Treaty. Unless the Measure specifies otherwise, the Plan is deemed to have been approved 90 days after the close of the ATCM at which it was adopted, unless one or more of the Consultative Parties notifies the Depository, within that time period, that it wishes an extension of that period or is unable to approve the Measure.

4.4 Review and revision of Management Plans

A review of the Management Plan shall be initiated every five years in accordance with Article 6.3 of Annex V of the Environmental Protocol and updated as required. Updated Management Plans then follow the same course of agreement as before.

When undertaking Management Plan reviews, thought should be given to the need for further or continued management should there be changes in the values to be protected, in the environment, and/ or in the activities to be managed.

Appendix 1

Guidance notes for producing maps for inclusion in Management Plans including checklist of features to be considered for inclusion on maps

Management Plans should include a general location map to show the position of the Area and the location of any other protected areas in the vicinity, and at least one detailed map of the site showing those features essential for meeting the Management plan objectives.

1. Each map should include latitude and longitude as well as having a scale bar. Avoid statements of scale (e.g. 1:50000) because enlargement/reduction renders such statements useless. The map projection, and horizontal and vertical datums used should be indicated.

2. It is important to use up-to-date coastline data including features such as ice shelves, ice tongues and glaciers. Ice recession and advance continues to affect many areas with consequent changes to Area boundaries. If an ice feature is used as a boundary the date of the source from which the data was acquired (e.g. survey or satellite image) should be shown.

3. Maps should show the following features: any specified routes; any restricted zones; boat and/or helicopter landing sites and access points; camp-sites; installations and huts; major animal concentrations and breeding sites; any extensive areas of vegetation and should clearly delineate between ice/snow and ice-free ground. In many instances it is useful to include a geological map of the Area. It is suggested that, in most cases, it is helpful to have contouring at an appropriate interval on all maps of the Area. But contouring should not be too close as to mark other features or symbols on the map.

4. Contours should be included on maps at an interval appropriate to the scale of the map.

5. Be aware when preparing the map that it will be reduced to about 150 x 200 mm size to fit into the ATCM official report. This is of importance in selecting the size of symbols, the closeness of contouring and the use of shading. Reproduction is always monochrome so do not use colours to distinguish features in the original. There may well be other versions of an Area map available but as far as the legal status of the Management Plan is concerned it is the version published with the Final Report of the Antarctic Treaty Consultative Meeting that is the definitive version which will be included in national legislation.

6. If the Area will require evaluation by CCAMLR the location of nearby CEMP sites should be indicated. CCAMLR has requested that the location of bird and

seal colonies and the access routes from the sea should be indicated on a map wherever possible.

7.   Other figures can assist with using the Management Plan in the field:

- For photographs, good contrast prints are essential for adequate reproduction. Screening or digitising of photograph will improve reproduction when the plan is photocopied. If an image such as an aerial photograph or satellite image is used in the map the source and date of acquisition of the image should be stated.
- Some plans have already used 3-dimensional terrain models which again can provide important locational information when approaching an Area, especially by helicopter. Such drawings need careful design if they are not to become confusing when reduced.

A checklist of features to be considered for inclusion on maps

1.   Essential features

1.1   Title

1.2   Latitude and longitude

1.3   Scale bar with numerical scale

1.4   Comprehensive legend

1.5   Adequate and approved place names

1.6   Map projection and spheroid modification

1.7   North arrow

1.8   Contour interval

1.9   If image data are included, date of image collection

2.   Essential topographical features

2.1   Coastline, rock and ice

2.2   Peaks and ridge lines

2.3   Ice margins and other glacial features

2.4   Contours (labelled as necessary) survey points and spot heights

3.   Natural Features

3.1   Lakes, ponds, streams

3.2   Moraines, screes, cliffs, beaches

3.3   Beach areas

3.4   Vegetation

 3.5 Bird and seal colonies

4. Anthropogenic Features

 4.1 Station

 4.2 Field huts, refuges

 4.3 Campsites

 4.4 Roads and vehicle tracks, footpaths features overlap

 4.5 Landing areas for fixed wing aeroplanes and helicopters

 4.6 Wharf, jetties

 4.7 Power supplies, cables

 4.8 Aerials. antennae

 4.9 Fuel storage areas

 4.10 Water reservoirs and pipes

 4.11 Emergency caches

 4.12 Markers, signs

 4.13 Historic sites or artefacts, archaeological sites

 4.14 Scientific installations or sampling areas

 4.15 Site contamination or modification

5. Boundaries

 5.1 Boundary of Area

 5.2 Boundaries of subsidiary zones areas. Boundaries of contained protected area

 5.3 Boundary signs and markers (including cairns)

 5.4 Boat/aircraft approach routes

 5.5 Navigation markers or beacons

 5.6 Survey points and markers

The same approach is obviously required of any inset maps.

At the conclusion of drafting a check should be made on cartographic quality to ensure:

- Balance between the elements.
- Appropriate shading to enhance features but which will not be confusing when photocopied and where degree should reflect importance.
- Correct and appropriate text with no features overlap.
- An appropriate legend using SCAR approved map symbols wherever possible.
- White text appropriately shadowed on all image data.

SCAR's Code of Conduct for the Exploration and Research of Subglacial Aquatic Environments

The Representatives,

Recalling Article 3 of the Protocol on Environmental Protection to the Antarctic Treaty ("the Protocol"), which requires that activities in the Antarctic Treaty area shall be planned and conducted so as to limit adverse impacts on the Antarctic environment and dependent and associated ecosystems;

Recognising that subglacial aquatic environments in Antarctica may support exceptional and potentially unique and diverse microbiological communities and consequently may be of high scientific value;

Recognising also the growing scientific interest in subglacial research;

Acknowledging that these environments may be at risk from impacts associated with research activities, including through the introduction of non-native microbial species or release of contaminants;

Welcoming the development by the Scientific Committee on Antarctic Research ("SCAR") through broad consultation, including with the input of the Council of Managers of National Antarctic Programs ("COMNAP"), of SCAR's Code of Conduct for the Exploration and Research of Subglacial Aquatic Environment that Parties can apply and use, as appropriate, to assist with meeting their obligations under the Protocol;

Recommend that their Governments:

1. endorse the non-mandatory SCAR's Code of Conduct for the Exploration and Research of Subglacial Aquatic Environments ("the Code of Conduct") as representing current best practice for planning and undertaking activities in subglacial aquatic environments in Antarctica; and

2. encourage the consideration of the Code of Conduct during the environmental impact assessment process for activities to be conducted within subglacial aquatic environments and encourage their researchers to be fully conversant with and adhere to the contents of the Code of Conduct in conducting research activities on subglacial aquatic environments.

SCAR's Code of Conduct for the Exploration and Research of Subglacial Aquatic Environments

Background

1. This Scientific Committee on Antarctic Research (SCAR) Code of Conduct (CoC) provides guidance to the scientific community with interests in exploring and conducting research on and in Antarctic subglacial aquatic environments (SAE).

2. The CoC was original prepared by a SCAR Action Group[1] in consultation with SAE specialists from a wide range of disciplines including the Council of Managers of National Antarctic Programs (COMNAP).

3. The CoC was developed in recognition of the value of these environments, the need to exercise environmental stewardship, and the growing scientific interest in subglacial research.

4. The CoC draws on published literature with special attention paid to SCAR Subglacial Antarctic Lake Environments (SALE) Scientific Research Program reports (see *http:// www.sale.scar.org/*) and the U.S. National Academies report on environmental stewardship of SAE.[2]

5. The U.S. National Academies report on environmental stewardship of SAE was presented by the U.S. at ATCM XXXI/CEP XI as IP110.

6. This CoC was submitted as an Information Paper (IP33) by SCAR to CEP XIV in 2011. SCAR coordinated a review of this CoC in 2017 through experts and the broader SCAR community, and the revised version was submitted to CEP XX. It will continue to be updated and refined as new scientific results and environmental impact reports become available from planned SAE exploration campaigns. Research developments in this field are summarized in two edited volumes.[3][4]

Introduction

7. Grounded Antarctic ice is widely recognized as a key constituent of the Earth System driving ocean currents and global climate as well as strongly affecting global sea level.

8. Early models for ice flow from the interior of the continent to the ocean assumed considerable friction between the bottom of ice sheets and the underlying rock.

---

[1] Members of the SCAR Action Group: Warwick Vincent (Chair - CAN), Irina Alekhina (RUS), Peter Doran (USA), Takeshi Naganuma (JPN), Guido di Prisco (ITA), Bryan Storey (NZ), Jemma Wadham (UK), David Walton (UK).

[2] National research Council, "Exploration of Antarctic Subglacial Aquatic Environments; Environmental and Scientific Stewardship", National Academies Press ISBN -13: 978-0-309-10635, 152 pp. (2007).

[3] Siegert, M.J., Kennicutt, M, Bindschadler, R. (eds.). Antarctic Subglacial Aquatic Environments. AGU Geophysical Monograph 192, 246 pp. (2011).

[4] Siegert, M.J., Priscu, J. Alekhina, I., Wadham, J. and Lyons, B. (eds.). Antarctic Subglacial Lake Exploration: first results and future plans. Transactions of the Royal Society of London, A. 374, Issue 2059. (2016).

9. The discovery of subglacial Lake Vostok and subsequently more than 400 other lake-like features beneath the ice has changed our view of subglacial environments.

10. Drilling through ice to bedrock often encounters water at the rock/ice interface and changes in ice surface height over lakes suggest that water is actively flowing beneath the ice.

11. From these and other observations, it has been concluded that in most cases the ice/rock interface will have free water present, water will often collect in lakes within watersheds, and scientific activities that contaminate one area may go on to contaminate subglacial environments downstream.

12. Much scientific attention has been focused on the possibility that subglacial waters will contain active ecosystems including microbial communities that survive and/or thrive in these environments, and research has shown that microbes do exist close to the grounded ice margin and that subglacial lakes can be active microbial ecosystems.[1]

13. To safeguard these unique lakes, and the subglacial aquatic environment as a whole, an internationally agreed CoC is essential.

14. In developing and reviewing this CoC, SCAR built on international discussions at SCAR SALE meetings and on the US National Academies recommendations on environmental stewardship of SAE.

Guiding Principles

15. Responsible stewardship during the exploration of subglacial aquatic environments should proceed in a manner that is consistent with the Protocol on Environmental Protection to the Antarctic Treaty, that minimizes their possible damage and contamination, and that protects their value for future generations, not only in terms of their scientific value but also in terms of conserving and protecting these pristine environments.

16. In accordance with the Protocol on Environmental Protection to the Antarctic Treaty, all proposed activities must undergo environmental impact assessment prior to an activity commencing.

17. Projects aiming to penetrate into subglacial aquatic environments are very likely to require an Initial Environmental Evaluation (IEE), and a subsequent Comprehensive Environmental Evaluation (CEE) may be the appropriate level of assessment given the potential impacts expected from such an activity.

18. Any CEE will ensure that all relevant information is available internationally, that proposals are exposed to a wide range of expert comment and that the scientific community uses best-available practices.

[1] Christner, B.C., Priscu, J.C., Achberger, A.M., Barbante, C., Carter, S.P., Christianson, K., Michaud, A.B., Mikucki, J.A., Mitchell, A.C., Skidmore, M.L.,Vick-Majors, T.J.. A microbial ecosystem beneath the West Antarctic ice sheet. Nature, 512 Issue 7514, pp 310-313 (2014).

19. In accordance with the principle of scientific cooperation found in the Antarctic Treaty, multinational participation in SAE exploration is encouraged.

20. Exploration should take a conservative, stepwise approach in which the data and lessons learned at each step are archived and used to guide future environmental stewardship, scientific investigations and technology development. This information should be freely disseminated in the public domain, including, via national authorities, to the Committee for Environmental Protection.

21. It is recommended that each potential exploration site is evaluated within the context of geophysical datasets and ice-flow modelling that identify lakes and other regions where there is basal melting. This would assist in characterizing the unique character of each site and selecting drilling locations. Additional considerations related to location include water depth, accessibility, connections to non-local subglacial aquatic environments, logistic constraints, cost and potential environmental impacts of the surface camp.

22. Accurate records should be collected, maintained and made freely available, to benefit all future subglacial sampling efforts.

23. Annex V of the Protocol allows areas to be designated as Antarctic Specially Protected Areas (ASPAs), either to manage areas for research purposes or to conserve them as pristine exemplars for future generations. Once sufficient information is available about the characteristics of subglacial lakes, attention should also be given to selecting and designating exemplar subglacial aquatic environments as ASPAs for long-term conservation, in accordance with Article 3 of Annex V to the Protocol.

Drilling and SAE-entry

24. Unless there is site-specific evidence to the contrary, drilling to the base of Antarctic ice sheets should assume that the basal ice is underlain by liquid water, and that this water forms part of a subglacial drainage network requiring a high level of environmental protection. In general, downstream sites, particularly those closest to the sea, can be viewed to have lower environmental risk than upstream sites.

25. Exploration protocols should also assume that the subglacial aquatic environments contain living organisms, and precautions should be adopted to prevent any permanent alteration of the biology (including introduction of non-native species) or habitat properties of these environments.

26. Drilling fluids and equipment that will enter the subglacial aquatic environment should be cleaned to the maximum extent practicable, and records should be maintained of sterility tests (e.g., bacterial counts by fluorescence microscopy at the drilling site). As a provisional guideline for general cleanliness, these objects should not contain more microorganisms than are present in an equivalent volume of the ice that is being drilled through to reach the subglacial environment. This standard should be re-evaluated when new data on subglacial aquatic microbial populations become available.

27. The concentrations of chemical contaminants introduced by drill fluids and sampling equipment should be documented, and clean drilling technologies (e.g. hot water) should be used to the full extent practicable.

28. The total amount of any contaminant added to these aquatic environments should not be expected to change the measurable chemical properties of the environment.

29. Water pressures and partial pressures of gases in lakes should be estimated prior to drilling in order to avoid down flow contamination or destabilisation of gas hydrates, respectively. Preparatory steps should also be taken for potential blow-out situations.

Sampling and instrument deployment

30. Sampling plans and protocols should be optimized to ensure that one type of investigation does not accidentally impact other investigations adversely, that sampling regimes plan for the maximum interdisciplinary use of samples, and that all information is shared to promote greater understanding.

31. Protocols should be designed to minimize disrupting the chemical and physical structure and properties of subglacial aquatic environments during the exploration and sampling of water and sediments.

32. Sampling systems and other instruments lowered into subglacial aquatic environments should be meticulously cleaned to ensure minimal chemical and microbiological contamination, following recommendations under point 26.

33. Certain objects and materials may need to be placed into subglacial aquatic environments for monitoring purposes. This may be to measure the long-term impacts of human activities on the subglacial environment and would be defined in the project's environmental impact assessment, or it may be for scientific purposes, e.g., long term monitoring of geophysical or biogeochemical processes. These additions should follow the microbiological constraints outlined in point 26, and for scientific uses should include an analysis of environmental risks (e.g., likelihood and implications of lack of retrieval) versus scientific benefits outlined in the environmental assessment documents.

Wherever possible, objects and materials put into subglacial aquatic environments should be recovered once the intended objectives have been achieved.

Revised Antarctic Conservation Biogeographic Regions

The Representatives,

Recalling Article 3 of Annex V to the Protocol on Environmental Protection to the Antarctic Treaty which provides for the designation of Antarctic Specially Protected Areas;

Recalling that paragraph 2 of Article 3 of Annex V states that Parties shall seek to identify such areas "within a systematic environmental-geographical framework";

Recalling also that the preamble to Resolution 6 (2012) welcomed "the classification of the ice-free areas of the Antarctic continent and close lying islands within the Antarctic Treaty area into 15 biologically distinct Antarctic Conservation Biogeographic Regions";

Welcoming the advice of the Committee for Environmental Protection that the Antarctic Conservation Biogeographic Regions should be updated to reflect the most recent analyses of the spatial distribution of Antarctic terrestrial biodiversity, including the identification of a 16th biologically distinct region;

Recommend to their Governments that:

1. the revised Antarctic Conservation Biogeographic Regions annexed to this Resolution ("ACBRs Version 2") be used in conjunction with the Environmental Domains Analysis and other tools agreed within the Antarctic Treaty system to support activities relevant to the interests of the Parties, including as a dynamic model for the identification of areas that could be designated as Antarctic Specially Protected Areas within the systematic environmental-geographical framework referred to in paragraph 2 of Article 3 of Annex V to the Protocol on Environmental Protection to the Antarctic Treaty; and

2. the Antarctic Treaty Secretariat post the text of Resolution 6 (2012) on its website in a way that makes clear that it is no longer current.

Antarctic Conservation Biogeographic Regions (Version 2)

The use of quantitative analyses to combine spatially explicit Antarctic terrestrial biodiversity data with other relevant spatial frameworks has identified 16 biologically distinct ice-free regions encompassing the Antarctic continent and close-lying islands within the Antarctic Treaty area (see Table 1). A full description of the methods employed is presented in Terauds *et al.* (2012) and Terauds and Lee (2016). The Antarctic Conservation Biogeographic Regions illustrated in Figure 1 represent the best classification of Antarctic terrestrial biodiversity based on currently available data and spatial layers.

The spatial data layer representing the regions is publicly available for download from the Australian Antarctic Data Centre: *http://dx.doi.org/10.4225/15/5729930925224.*

References

Terauds, A., Chown, S., Morgan, F., Peat, H., Watts, D., Keys, H., Convey, P. & Bergstrom, D. (2012) Conservation biogeography of the Antarctic. *Diversity and Distributions*, 22 May 2012, DOI: 10.1111/j.1472-4642.2012.00925.x.

Terauds, A. & Lee, J.R. (2016) Antarctic biogeography revisited: updating the Antarctic Conservation Biogeographic Regions, *Diversity and Distributions*, 1-5, DOI:10.4225/15/5729930925224.

Table 1 – Descriptions of Antarctic Conservation Biogeographic Regions

Region	Name	Area (km²)
1	North-east Antarctic Peninsula	1215
2	South Orkney Islands	160
3	North-west Antarctic Peninsula	5183
4	Central south Antarctic Peninsula	4962
5	Enderby Land	2188
6	Dronning Maud Land	5523
7	East Antarctica	1109
8	North Victoria Land	9431
9	South Victoria Land	10038
10	Transantarctic Mountains	18480
11	Ellsworth Mountains	2859
12	Marie Byrd Land	1128
13	Adelie Land	178
14	Ellsworth Land	217
15	South Antarctic Peninsula	2875
16	Prince Charles Mountains	5992

Figure 1 – Map of Antarctica showing the 16 Antarctic Conservation Biogeographic Regions

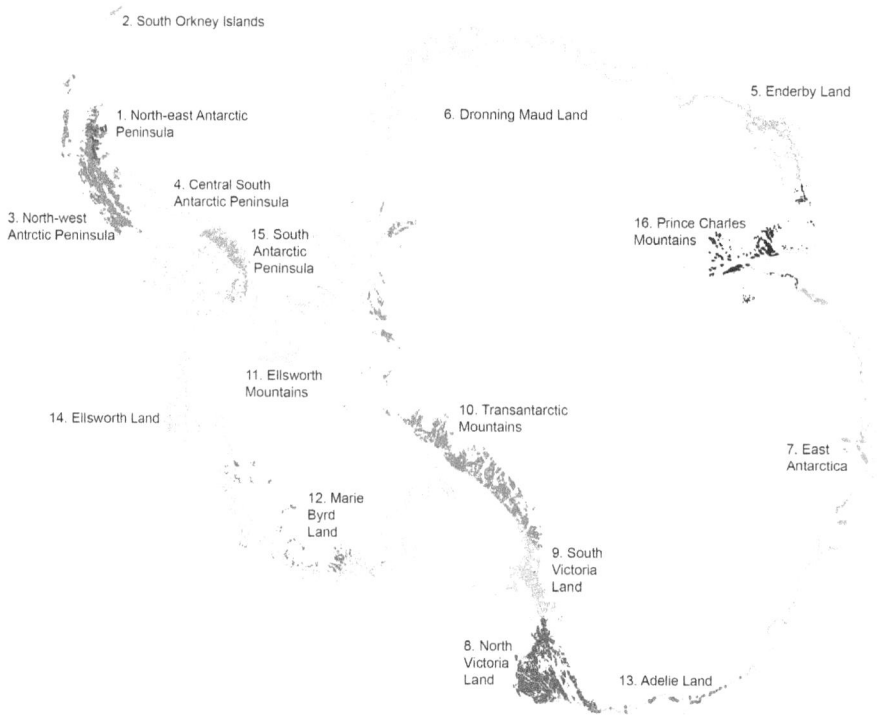

Green Expedition in the Antarctic

The Representatives,

Recalling that the Protocol on Environmental Protection to the Antarctic Treaty ("the Protocol") designates "Antarctica as a natural reserve, devoted to peace and science" and sets out environmental principles which provide guidance for scientific activities, as supported and prioritised both by the Antarctic Treaty and the Protocol;

Recognising that achievements from scientific investigations conducted by the National Antarctic Programmes of the Parties, usually in the name of Antarctic Expedition, contribute greatly to the understanding of Antarctica and its role in global natural processes;

Recognising the legal requirements of, and the benefits that can be gained from, conducting an appropriate Environmental Impact Assessment ("EIA") that highlights how to improve the environmental efficiency of the activity and address cumulative impacts;

Noting that there are growing scientific interests and needs in Antarctica, which may result in additional research and associated logistic supporting activities and also increased pressures on local environments, and that more consideration should be given to the balance between environmental protection and scientific activities;

Recalling that Parties commit to protect the Antarctic environment and dependent and associated ecosystems;

Recognising that the Protocol and its Annexes in force and the effective Measures which are binding tools and some current Resolutions adopted at the Antarctic Treaty Consultative Meeting ("ATCM") by consensus all together contribute to protect the Antarctic environment, and that the Committee for Environmental Protection and the ATCM work continuously to further improve regulation in order to reach the objectives of the Antarctic Treaty and the Protocol;

Acknowledging that environmentally-friendly activities in the Antarctic are much appreciated and encouraged;

Desiring to build the concept of Green Expedition which is based on the ideals of efficiency, harmony and sustainability and aimed at taking all available methods (including those contained in current Resolutions and new ones from the advancement of modern management and technology) to reduce human impact;

Recommend that their Governments:

1. reaffirm their commitment to protect the Antarctic environment and dependent and associated ecosystems and to encourage collaborative efforts to this end;

2. support the concept of Green Expedition by encouraging their National Antarctic Programmes to conduct science in an environmentally-friendly manner in the Antarctic;

3. encourage their National Antarctic Programmes to work more closely with other Parties, including through participation and interaction with organisations such as Scientific Committee for Antarctic Research ("SCAR") and the Council of Managers of National Antarctic Programs ("COMNAP"), to develop more collaborative projects and to promote the sharing of experiences and advanced technology; and

4. produce high-quality Environmental Impact Assessments when new activities are planned that include as far as possible best practices to prevent and minimise environmental impact.

Establishment of the Ross Sea Region Marine Protected Area

The Representatives,

Recalling Resolution 1 (2006) in which the Consultative Parties, conscious that the Convention on the Conservation of Antarctic Marine Living Resources is an integral part of the Antarctic Treaty system, encouraged increased cooperation at the practical level between the Antarctic Treaty Consultative Meeting ("ATCM") and the Commission for the Conservation of Antarctic Marine Living Resources ("CCAMLR");

Recognising the contributions of the ATCM in the designation and implementation of Antarctic Specially Protected Areas and Antarctic Specially Managed Areas, and of CCAMLR in the designation and implementation of marine protected areas to conserve important areas of the Antarctic marine environment;

Noting the agreement reached at the 35th meeting of CCAMLR to establish the Ross Sea Region Marine Protected Area ("RSRMPA"), commencing on 1 December 2017;

Recalling freedom of scientific investigation in Antarctica as enshrined in Article II of the Antarctic Treaty and recognising the importance of scientific research and monitoring to support and evaluate progress in achieving the objectives of the RSRMPA, as well as international collaboration in such research and monitoring;

Noting that CCAMLR Conservation Measure 91-05 provides for the regular review of the RSRMPA;

Noting the importance of collaboration between the ATCM and CCAMLR;

Recommend that their Governments:

1. welcome the establishment of the Ross Sea Region Marine Protected Area ("RSRMPA") as an important contribution towards the conservation of Southern Ocean ecosystems and biodiversity;

2. encourage Antarctic Treaty Parties that are not Members of the Commission for the Conservation of Antarctic Marine Living Resources ("CCAMLR") to familiarise themselves with CCAMLR Conservation Measure 91-05, including the Management Plan and the forthcoming Research and Monitoring Plan for the RSRMPA, and to encourage, as appropriate, compliance with relevant RSRMPA management measures;

3. invite the Committee on Environmental Protection to consider any appropriate actions within the Antarctic Treaty Consultative Meeting's competence to contribute to the achievement of the specific objectives set forth in CCAMLR Conservation Measure 91-05, particularly in the designation and implementation of Antarctic Specially Protected Areas and Antarctic Specially Managed Areas in the Ross Sea region and the management of relevant human activities; and

4. identify opportunities to conduct and support relevant research and monitoring activities that support the objectives and the forthcoming Research and Monitoring Plan of the RSRMPA, in particular through international collaborations.

Guidelines on Contingency Planning, Insurance and Other Matters for Tourist and Other Non-Governmental Activities in the Antarctic Treaty Area

The Representatives,

Welcoming the entry into force of the International Code for Ships Operating in Polar Waters (Polar Code);

Remaining concerned at the potential impacts, including the imposition of additional costs, that tourist or other non-governmental activities may have on national programmes, and the risk to the safety of those involved in search and rescue operations;

Desiring to ensure that tourist or other non-governmental activities undertaken in Antarctica are carried out in a safe and self-sufficient manner;

Desiring further to ensure that the risks associated with tourist or other non-governmental activities are fully identified in advance, and minimised;

Recalling the "Procedures to be Followed by Organisers and Operators", as set out in the Guidance for Visitors to the Antarctic, and the Guidance for Those Organising and Conducting Tourism and Non-governmental Activities in the Antarctic annexed to Recommendation XVIII-1;

Noting Measure 4 (2004) Insurance and Contingency Planning for Tourism and Non-governmental Activities in the Antarctic Treaty Area, and desiring to take certain steps before it enters into effect to promote its objectives in addition to recommending further guidelines to be followed by those organising or conducting activities without the supervision or support in the field of another operator or a national programme;

Recommend that:

1. Parties should require those under their jurisdiction organising or conducting tourist or other non-governmental activities in the Antarctic Treaty area, for which advance notification is required in accordance with paragraph 5 of Article VII of the Antarctic Treaty, to follow the Guidelines annexed to this Resolution; and

2. the Secretariat of the Antarctic Treaty post the text of Resolution 4 (2004) Guidelines on Contingency Planning, Insurance and Other Matters for Tourist and Other Non-governmental Activities in the Antarctic Treaty Area on its website in a way that makes clear that it is no longer current.

Guidelines on Contingency Planning, Insurance and Other Matters for Tourist and Other Non-Governmental Activities in the Antarctic Treaty Area

1. Those organising or conducting tourist or other non-governmental activities in the Antarctic Treaty area should ensure:

   a. that appropriate contingency plans and sufficient arrangements for health and safety, search and rescue ("SAR"), and medical care and evacuation have been drawn-up and are in place prior to the start of the activity. Such plans and arrangements should not be reliant on support from other operators or national programmes without their express written agreement; and

   b. that adequate insurance or other arrangements are in place to cover any costs associated with SAR and medical care and evacuation.

2. Competent authorities may specify the format in which they would prefer to receive information pertaining to paragraph 1a of these guidelines and the equivalent requirement in Measure 4 (2004).

3. Where a competent authority so decides, a ship-based operator may provide a copy of the Polar Water Operational Manual required under the International Code for Ships Operating in Polar Waters (Polar Code), or relevant parts thereof, as part of demonstrating compliance with the maritime components of the requirements referred to in paragraph 2.

4. The following guidelines should also be observed in particular by those organising or conducting activities without the supervision or support in the field of another operator or a national programme:

   a. participants have sufficient and demonstrable experience appropriate for the proposed activity operating in polar, or equivalent, environments. Such experience may include survival training in cold or remote areas, flying, sailing or operating other vehicles in conditions and over distances similar to those being proposed in the activity;

   b. all equipment, including clothing, communication, navigational, emergency and logistic equipment is in sound working order, with sufficient backup spares and suitable for effective operation under Antarctic conditions;

   c. all participants are proficient in the use of such equipment;

   d. all participants are medically, physically and psychologically fit to undertake the activity in Antarctica;

   e. adequate first-aid equipment is available during the activity and that at least one participant is proficient in advanced first-aid.

www.ingramcontent.com/pod-product-compliance
Lightning Source LLC
Chambersburg PA
CBHW051401200326
41520CB00024B/7459